Controversial issues in prisons

Controversial issues in prisons

David Scott and Helen Codd

Open University Press

Open University Press
McGraw-Hill Education
McGraw-Hill House
Shoppenhangers Road
Maidenhead
Berkshire
England
SL6 2QL

email: enquiries@openup.co.uk
world wide web: www.openup.co.uk

and Two Penn Plaza, New York, NY 10121-2289, USA

First published 2010

A catalogue record of this book is available from the British Library

ISBN-13: 978-0-335-22303-9 (pb) 978-0-335-22304-6 (hb)
ISBN-10 0335223036 (pb) 0335223044 (hb)

Library of Congress Cataloging-in-Publication Data
CIP data applied for

Typeset by RefineCatch Limited, Bungay, Suffolk
Printed in the UK by Bell and Bain Ltd, Glasgow

Fictitious names of companies, products, people, characters and/or data that
may be used herein (in case studies or in examples) are not intended to
represent any real individual, company, product or event.

Contents

Foreword

In an ideal world *Controversial Issues in Prisons* would not have been written. In this world, for those individuals who needed to be confined, the function of the prison would be very different as would the relationship between the individual detainee and the process of confinement. Yet it is *precisely* because of this lack of a politically informed, utopian vision surrounding prisons, and the ideological acquiescence to the punitive mentality that underpins, legitimates and drives the institution's existence, that books like this are essential. The abject state of the prison system in England and Wales (and, indeed, globally for many of the nine million individuals who are confined) – psychologically corrosive, culturally toxic, institutionally mendacious, materially desperate – further underlines the need for publications such as *Controversial Issues in Prisons*: books, in other words, that contest and challenge the barren, political philosophy that justifies not only the continuing existence of the prison but also its future expansion. For David Scott and Helen Codd, the institution is rightly identified as a social problem, a harm inducing behemoth that lacerates the lives of that small minority of overwhelmingly poor law breakers who are caught and then packed, parcelled and processed through the criminal justice system.

Controversial Issues in Prisons focuses on eight case studies ranging from prisoners with mental health problems through to the 'collateral damage' inflicted on prisoners' families. The case study chapters are book-ended by two other chapters, the first sets the context for thinking critically about the issues identified by Scott and Codd while the concluding chapter rightly argues for an abolitionist theoretical and political position on prisons and punishment. Individually, each meticulous case study raises profound questions about the state of the prison system and conversely the prison system of the capitalist state. Collectively, the case studies provide a searing indictment, not only of contemporary penal policy and practices, but also of the official discourse that supports and legitimates the institution and a reform industry that endlessly seeks to find the nirvana of penal reform – the chimerical, working prison. As Scott and Codd argue, the endless reforms that have been introduced, which as they rightly recognize have curtailed and constrained the worst excesses of a largely unaccountable system, have ultimately done little to subvert, challenge or undermine the relentless expansion of the system and its concomitant withering impact. This perspective, of course, has a long history in abolitionist literature, in particular, but nonetheless needs to be repeatedly articulated given the still-often uncontested assertion that piecemeal reform is the way forward if we as a society can only find the 'right' strategy. The pain and the anguish that comes through in a number of chapters – self-inflicted deaths, those incarcerated who have mental health problems, women, children and young people, minority ethnic prisoners – directly confronts the often sanctimonious platitudes that inform both official discourse and the reformist agenda.

Scott and Codd are also clear that a radical, transformative programme and agenda is fundamental in order to confront and contest the ideological and material power of the modern prison. They rightly denounce the current system and argue for it to be replaced by a response to the confined based on social justice, human rights and political accountability. This agenda is necessary not only to radically transform the coruscating nature of daily life on the prison wings but also to fundamentally change the wider power structure of contemporary capitalism whose inequalities and iniquities are protected by an often ruthless and parasitic state that will defend the social divisions that lay waste to the lives of individual human beings trapped by, what Mark Fisher has called, 'the remorseless meat grinder of Capital'. This position is often glibly dismissed by many politicians, state servants, media commentators and academics as being too conspiratorial, too theoretically reductive, too excessively idealistic, too instrumental or, most offensively, as being pro-crime and, conversely, deliberately anti-victim. And yet, as the global economic crisis has demonstrated, and as the political crisis surrounding MP's expenses has made apparent, the hypocrisy of the powerful, their egomaniacal lack of self-reflection and, crucially, their unrelenting hostility to any bourgeois law that hinders their ruthless pursuit of wealth, power and privilege, is systemic to neoliberal, capitalist social arrangements. However, despite this, as Scott and Codd make clear, it is the poor and the powerless who are remorselessly pursued and constantly surveilled. It is the endless criminalization of *their* behaviour that remains the focal point of an apparatus of punishment which is embedded within a militarized, authoritarian, disciplinary and violent criminal justice (and state welfare system) which, in turn, is built on a hybridized structure of power involving both state and private agents and agencies engaging in so-called, oxymoronic partnership arrangements.

Michel Foucault once observed that books should be seen as 'instrument[s] . . . in a real struggle'. *Controversial Issues in Prisons* can be seen as part of the tradition that Foucault identified. The book uses the written word to demystify the prison while offering an alternative way of thinking critically about confinement. In doing so, it challenges the puerile definitions of penal reality, and the hypocritical definitions of criminal behaviour, proffered by the powerful, who, despite the contradictions and contingencies within and between their different fractions, continue to exercise power for the benefit of the rapacious few to the detriment and corrosive immiseration of the marginalized majority.

Joe Sim
Liverpool John Moores University

Preface

This book explores some of the most controversial issues in prisons in England and Wales today. It is primarily a book about the people who are sent to prison and what happens to them when inside. The foci of this text therefore revolve around the controversies encompassing prison populations rather than the criminal 'justice' system or penal institutions per se. It is no coincidence that each chapter examines a different dimension of the prison population and that their interrogation highlights some of the most emotive and topical issues concerning imprisonment. We draw upon the sociological imagination to make connections between the personal troubles and vulnerabilities of those incarcerated and wider structural divisions which plague the society we live in. Ultimately we believe that the examination of such penal controversies raises fundamental concerns about the legitimacy of the confinement project and the kind of society in which it is deemed essential.

The focus, context and inspiration for this book has been shaped by three influential penological studies: Mike Fitzgerald and Joe Sim's *British Prisons* (Blackwell, 1979); Barbara Hudson's *Penal Policy and Social Justice* (Macmillan, 1993); and Joe Sim's *Medical Power in Prisons* (Open University Press, 1990). Collectively these three texts identify many of the key themes upon which this book is based – the importance of the insights of penal abolitionism as a means of approaching the current incarceration binge and the structured harms that characterize the prison place; the historical importance and contemporary ascendancy of medical and psychological knowledge in the shaping of penal regimes; the manner in which only certain forms of wrongdoing and harms perpetrated by certain people are policed and penalized in advanced capitalist-patriarchal societies; the importance of highlighting the social backgrounds of the people that the courts send to prison and their general unsuitability for incarceration; the need to contextualize current penal policies within wider determining structural contexts; and that the legitimacy of any responses to human wrongdoing or problematic events must be rooted in the principles of social justice, human rights and democratic accountability.

Prison and punishment in England and Wales, and many places elsewhere, should be understood in the milieu of a society that has deep social divisions and hierarchies of power played out through the structural contexts of neo-liberal forms of capitalism, patriarchies, neo-colonialism and ageism. If we take a metaphor based upon the popular board game Monopoly it seems that the player piece for the Capitalist State, a 'prison truck', only rarely can be seen at the top end of the board in expensive locations such as Mayfair, Park Lane and other exclusive residencies inhabited by the rich and powerful, but undertakes considerable activity through patrolling and soaking up clientele from board spaces representing the cheap end of town, which are disproportionately populated by migrants and people from Black or minority ethnic backgrounds. These people do not regularly collect £200, have no 'get out of jail free' cards on which they can rely when they fall into the hands of the penal authorities, and can end up spending much of their time within the prison place. The acknowledgement then that the underscoring focus of criminal justice agencies is on marginalized, unrespectable and low status lawbreakers is a central assumption of this book. To put it in another, also abstract, way, on a visit to the Natural History Museum in Prague in July 2009 one of us was struck by the representational power of a particular exhibit. After walking through numerous large rooms housing various archaeological and pre-historic remnants visitors could enter a partitioned room. Here people could peruse various interesting exhibits, but when they reached the bottom of the room it became apparent that on the other side of the partition was a life-sized replica of a woolly mammoth. While initially invisible, when viewed it was apparent that it effectively encompassed the whole of the room, dominating the space and perceptions of what had come before.

The 'woolly mammoth' in the room in relation to prison populations is poverty. In this text, as the chapters proceed we perhaps also blinker the reader to a certain extent, leading them down important paths which explore the many different dimensions to the constitution of the prison population. Yet probably the most significant feature of those who are imprisoned is their poverty of resources and life chances. The people we imprison often experience multiple forms of social exclusion and deprivation and have various vulnerabilities which lead to their entrapment within the penal law. Significantly, the poverty of those who make up the prison population of England and Wales is not always acknowledged, but for those prepared to look overwhelming evidence can be found. While our aim is to raise serious concerns regarding the moral legitimacy of the power to punish through highlighting the inherent harms of imprisonment and the focus of the penal law on people with vulnerabilities, it should not go unnoticed that the kinds of harms that are policed and the social backgrounds of those contained within the penal apparatus of the Capitalist State also raise profound questions about its political legitimacy.

The production of an academic book takes a considerable amount of time and writers inevitably accumulate many debts along the way, some of them personal and some of them intellectual. The writing of this book has been no different. Many thanks should go to all of our colleagues at the University of Central Lancashire, especially James Deane, Sue Evans, Billy Frank, Robert Lee, Rachel MacLean, Martin O'Brien, Munira Patel and Ian Turner. Helen Codd would like to thank the Institute of Advanced Legal Studies of the University of London for continued support, and is grateful to Belinda Crothers for her ongoing enthusiasm. For their friendship and intellectual support we would like to thank Anette Ballinger, Andrea Beckmann, Donna Bendelow, Eamonn Carrabine, Eoin Carroll, Roy Coleman, Mary

Corcoran, Karen Corteen, Pamela Davis, Marian Duggan, Peter Francis, Amy Goulding, Maria Kaspersson, Margaret Malloch, Diana Medlicott, Scott Poynting, Mick Ryan, Phil Scraton, Rose Smith, Steve Tombs, Azrini Wahidin, Dave Whyte, Emma Williamson and all our friends in the European Group for the study of Deviance and Social Control. Alana Barton, Barbara Hudson, Alice Mills, John Moore, Chris Pantazis, Rebecca Roberts, Toby Seddon, Joe Sim and Corina Rogerson deserve special mention for their careful reading of full drafts of the manuscript and for their helpful comments and suggestions.

Many thanks are due to our friends and family for their constant encouragement and helpful distractions, especially Ben Scott, Ian Scott, Joan Scott, John Roland Scott, Nick Palmer, Alexandra Palmer, Alan and Jane Codd, Fabrice Andrieux, Elaine and Lin Jenkinson-Bennett, Ralph van Calck, Neil Denham, Fr. Damian Feeney, Eilidh Grant, William 'Harry' Harrison, Rachel Hartland, Kimberly Jones, Vinnie McCalk, Ian Nickson, Susan Ould, Kerry and Michael Parkin, Julie Shaw, Marie Swinfield, Jordana Todd and Richard Wilbraham.

At Open University Press we would like to thank Chris Cudmore, Melanie Havelock, Stephanie Frosch, Katherine Morton and Alison Holt for their patience when the manuscript was delayed and their overall supportive comments in the commissioning and writing of the book. David Scott was the lead author on chapters 1, 2, 5, 6, 7, 8 and 10 and Helen Codd on Chapters 3, 4 and 9 although we take collective responsibility for any inaccuracies that lie within.

Abbreviations

ACCT	Assessment, Care in Custody and Teamwork
ACMD	Advisory Council on the Misuse of Drugs
ADP	Average Daily Population
APF	Action for Prisoners' Families
BME	Black or minority ethnic
CARAT	Counselling, Assessment, Referral, Advice and Throughcare
CBT	cognitive behavioural therapies
CJA	*Criminal Justice Act*
CJIA	*Criminal Justice and Immigration Act*
CJS	Criminal Justice System
CPS	Crown Prosecution Service
CRE	Commission for Racial Equality
CSDD	Cambridge Study in Delinquent Development
DIP	Drug Intervention Programme
DSPD	Dangerous and Severe Personality Disorder
ECtHR	European Court of Human Rights
ECHR	European Convention of Human Rights
GLM	Good Lives Model
HAC	Health Advisory Committee for the Prison Service
HIV	Human Immunodeficiency Virus
HMCIP	Her Majesty's Chief Inspector of Prisons
HRA	*Human Rights Act*
IDTS	Integrated Drug Treatment System
IRC	Immigration Removal Centres
IRR	Institute for Race Relations
MHA	*Mental Health Act*
MHIRT	Mental Health In-Reach Team
NOMS	National Offender Management Service
PBS	points-based system
PDU	problematic drug users
PMS	Prison Medical Service

POPS	Partners of Prisoners
PSO	Prison Service Order
PSU	Professional Standards Unit
QUNO	Quaker United Nations Office
RAPT	Rehabilitation of Addicted Prisoners Trust
RMDT	Random Mandatory Drug Tests
SARN	Structured Assessment of Risk and Need
SASU	Suicide Awareness Support Unit
SID	self-inflicted deaths
SMI	severe mental illness
SOTP	Sex Offender Treatment Programme
SPMG	Suicide Prevention Management Group
VDT	Voluntary Drug Testing
VIR	Viral Infectivity Regulations
VPU	Vulnerable Prisoner Units
VTU	Voluntary Testing Units
WIP	Women In Prison
YJB	Youth Justice Board
YOI	Young Offender Institutions
YOT	Youth Offending Team

1

Thinking about controversial issues in prison

> We face a crisis of punishment – a crisis, however, which presents us with the opportunity to challenge the very foundations of the way we respond to crime.
>
> (The Commission on English Prisons Today 2009: 11)

Since the late 1990s, representing a rather undistinguished level of moral perform-ance, the Prison Service of England and Wales has broken records in terms of average daily prisoner populations; comparative imprisonment rates in Europe; average costs for each prisoner place; levels of physical and mental ill health; families of prisoners left without one or more parent; and the number of people who die in prison. Reliance upon imprisonment is, however, a moral and political *choice*. Increasing the use of the prison, or indeed the deployment of any penal sanctions at all, is something that politicians choose and something which we as members of society implicitly condone. In the last few decades of the twentieth century and the first decade of the twenty-first century this choice appears to have become increasingly attractive.

Revelations by Baroness Vivien Stern (cited in Johnston 2009) put the current emphasis on penalization into perspective. In its time in office since May 1997, the 'New Labour' government has been riding a penal rollercoaster that has gained unprecedented momentum, creating 1036 new offences punishable by imprison-ment. There were 52 new imprisonable offences in 1997, rising to 181 in 2003, 174 in 2005 and 133 in 2007. From 1995 to 2007 the government introduced 66 new pieces of criminal justice legislation, all with new penal sanctions (Carter 2007).[1] What is astonishing is not only the numbers but also the kind of 'crimes' for which prison is increasingly seen as an appropriate response. At the time of writing (October 2009), a person in England can be sentenced to imprisonment for smoking in public; for allowing an unlicensed concert to take place in a church hall; if their child fails to attend school or if their child is in possession of fireworks except in the period leading up to Guy Fawkes night or New Year; or for failing to obtain a passport for a pet donkey (Johnston 2009).[2]

This increasing emphasis on penal law may have gone unnoticed by some as historically penalization has been directed not at the control of all of society, but towards certain identifiable groups. The penal law, disturbingly, is becoming increasingly prominent in the lives of the disadvantaged, poor and vulnerable. Those who are penalized are often confronted with immense social problems and it has long been recognized that prisoners come largely from impoverished social backgrounds.

> For the most part [prisoners] are victims of vicious social surroundings and poverty – a wretched collection of human beings, physically weak, under-nourished, mentally undeveloped, lacking in will power, the outcasts of our civilisation. Let the fact be borne in mind ... that if those whose lot is described have sinned against society, society has in the first place sinned grievously against them.
>
> (Hobhouse and Brockway 1922: 18)

The situation has changed little since the 1920s. From the official data (see Box 1.1) it is clear that the 'unwanted' people filtered into prison through the criminal justice

---

Box 1.1 Social backgrounds of prison populations

1   *Have been in care or have family difficulties:*
    - 27% of prisoners in care as a child (which is **thirteen** times more likely than the general population)
    - Prisoners are **two and a half** times as likely to have had a family member convicted of a criminal offence than general population
2   *Are unemployed or on benefits:*
    - 5% of general population unemployed but 67% of prisoners in the four weeks before imprisonment
    - 13.7% of working age population are in receipt of benefits but 72% immediately before entry to prison
    - 75% of prisoners do not have paid employment to go to on release
3   *Homeless:*
    - one in 14 prisoners are homeless at the time of imprisonment
    - 32% of prisoners not living in permanent accommodation prior to imprisonment
4   *No education:*
    - 80% of prisoners have writing skills, 65% numeracy skills, and 50% reading skills at or below the level of an 11-year-old child
    - 52% of male and 71% of female adult prisoners have no qualifications at all (which is **four** times the rate in the general population)
5   *In poor health:*
    - 80% of prisoners have mental health problems
    - 46% of sentenced adult male prisoners aged 18–49 reported having a long standing illness or disability
    - Prisoners are **fifteen** times as likely to be HIV positive
    - 60–70% of prisoners were using drugs before imprisonment

Source: Social Exclusion Report (2002); Scott (2008a)

system are socially deprived and harmed individuals who do not present a serious danger to society (Scott 2008a). The extent of poverty ingrained in prison populations cannot and must not go unnoticed: indeed the poor, the vulnerable, the ill and the discriminated against are often the *same people*. As Hudson (1993: 152) points out in terms used in the popular Monopoly board game, while some offenders may not collect the 'go to jail card' on their first encounter with the courts, they often embody multiple vulnerabilities and are likely to fall foul of the penal law on numerous occasions. The current intensification of the penalization of poverty has not arisen through a massive increase in recorded 'crime'. Since 1995, for example, there has been a 42 per cent decline in the amount of 'crime' reported to the British Crime Survey while from 1997 to 2007 there was a 55 per cent decline in burglary, a 34 per cent reduction in violent crime and a 52 per cent fall in vehicle thefts (British Crime Survey 2008, cited in The Commission on English Prisons Today 2009: 16).

The factors underscoring the increasing political reliance upon penal sanctions lie beyond the scope of this book (Bell 2010; Scott 2010), but the extent of the penalization of poverty has escalated and led to an unprecedented and exponential growth in prison populations. The recent growth in the Average Daily Population (ADP) of prisoners is staggering. At the end of 1992, for example, the ADP stood at around 40,600 prisoners, which increased to over 77,000 prisoners by 2005. By October 2009 the ADP had surpassed 84,700 prisoners and was still rising. Despite the significant reductions in the volume of 'crime' the number of offenders sentenced in the courts increased from 1,354,294 in 1995 to 1,402,571 in 2006. In addition the average length of prison sentences imposed in the Crown Court increased from 21 months in 1995 to 25 months by 2006. Moreover, 70 per cent of the increase in the prison population between 1995 and 2005 has arisen due to changes in sentencing (Carter 2007: 5–10).

Prison capacity has struggled to keep up with demand and in every one of the years since 1995 the prison system has been overcrowded. Since 1997 the government has provided 20,000 new prison places, increasing overall operational capacity by one third. Yet the insatiable demand continues, with the Ministry of Justice anticipating that the number of prison places required will be as high as 95,800 by June 2015 (Ministry of Justice Statistical Bulletin 2008d). In response Lord Carter (2007) proposed the creation of three new 'Titan' prisons, which would have an unprecedented capacity to hold prisoners. Carter's expansionist recommendations were quickly accepted, and in December 2007 the government revealed that, in addition to the 9500 new prison places it had previously announced, it planned to undertake a new prison building programme that would deliver 10,500 new places by 2014. In April 2009, however, the plan to build 'Titan' jails was abandoned in favour of providing 7500 new places in five 'mini-titan' prisons, each with a capacity to hold 1500 prisoners (Prison Reform Trust 2009). At present England and Wales has an imprisonment rate of 151 per 100,000 of the general population. The creation of the 'mini-titans' is likely to increase the rate of imprisonment to 178 per 100,000 by 2014 (Prison Reform Trust 2009). The significant financial implications of expansionism have not as yet proved a deterrent to further growth. In 2008 each prison place cost on average £39,000 and government expenditure on imprisonment has increased from £2.843billion (bn) in 1995 to £4.325bn by 2007 (Prison Reform Trust 2009).

Indeed by 2008 spending on the criminal justice system as a whole stood at nearly £23bn, an increase of more than £8bn since New Labour first came to power (The Commission on English Prisons Today 2009). Even in times when all the main political parties warn of severe future cut-backs in public services and reduced public spending, penal policy currently remains immune.

Although rising prisoner populations and prison building programmes have played out against a backcloth of chaotic management and considerable uncertainty in the organization of the Prison Service, the core aims of imprisonment remain the same: *protecting victims* and *responsibilizing offenders*. As recently as June 2004 the government created the National Offender Management Service (NOMS) in an attempt to integrate the Probation and Prison Services and improve combined performance. Yet within only five years the future of NOMS has been cast into serious doubt, with the organization widely recognized as an expensive and politically embarrassing failure (Scott 2008a). A further administrative change saw the creation of a new Ministry of Justice, which now runs the penal system. Despite these organizational problems the underscoring rationale of imprisonment remains that of 'making punishment work' through the combined goals of reducing offending and protecting the public. There is, however, little evidence that prisons really do 'work', at least when measured against its official aims (Sim 2009). Forty-seven per cent of adults are reconvicted within one year of release. This figure increases to 60 per cent for ex-prisoners who served sentences of less than 12 months and to as high as 70 per cent for those who have served more than ten prison sentences (Ministry of Justice 2009c).

Flying in the face of hundreds of years of evidence to the contrary, the prison has been conceived as a means to provide an opportunity for offenders to make prudent choices and become responsible citizens (Fitzgerald and Sim 1979; Sim 1994). This transformation is to be achieved through the daily interactions of prison life and the provision of offender treatment programmes. Indeed the number of core offending behaviour programmes rose by 28 per cent from 2004/05 to 2006/07 (Ministry of Justice 2008a), but the justifications upon which such programmes are predicated, remain those of opportunities and responsibilities.

> The overall theme of this package is that of balancing the opportunities we give offenders to turn away from a life of crime with what the community expects of them in return . . . In return for offering opportunities for rehabilitation, whether it is through drug treatment programmes or training for the world of work, the community has a right to expect that as well as serving their sentences, offenders will repay the opportunities presented to them by turning away from crime, by taking the chance to join the law-abiding majority . . . There will be incentives for those who take the chances offered to them, and there will be penalties for those who do not.
>
> (Ministry of Justice 2008a: 3)

To achieve positive change and facilitate prisoner responsibilities the Prison Service has acknowledged that only *decent* prisons can provide the incentives required to foster law-abiding behaviour, and this has been promoted through the 'decency' agenda.

> The decency agenda is intended to run like a golden thread through all aspects of the service's work. Decency means treatment within the law, delivering promised standards, providing fit and proper facilities, giving prompt attention to prisoners' concerns and protecting them from harm. It means providing prisoners with a regime that gives variety and helps them to rehabilitate. It means fair and consistent treatment by staff.
>
> (HM Prison Service 2003a: 29)

'Decency' is a very broad concept encompassing acceptable living conditions, positive relationships, and acknowledgement of institutional racism, officer brutality and high rates of self-inflicted deaths (Scott 2008a). This repackaging of older humanitarian Prison Service obligations under the umbrella concept of decency has, however, largely fallen on deaf ears (Scott 2008a). The commitment to decency has also floundered in the face of massive overcrowding (Carter 2007).[3] The consequences of crowding also include reductions in prisoner activities, fewer work and educational opportunities and total lockdowns on certain days of the week.[4]

The eight 'controversial issues' in this book are focused on the prisoner population. Our intention is not to analyse the workings of the penal system (Cavadino and Dignan 1992), but rather to focus on the people who are processed by it. In the current era of penal expansionism it is very important to raise the visibility of exactly who is imprisoned and problematize the appropriateness of their confinement. In so doing we hope to question the continued value of imprisonment and ultimately offer a plausible political platform for those who wish to reduce radically prison populations.

We argue that even if prison crowding was reduced and indecent prison conditions were vastly improved this would not necessarily lead to greater penal legitimacy. This is not to dispute that it would be much better if people were not sleeping or eating their meals in a lavatory, defecating in front of strangers or spending long and lonely hours in dirty and unhygienic living conditions. Rather the point we wish to make is that even prisons with good living conditions are still rooted in the structured deprivations of the 'prison place' (Medlicott 2001). Our main line of argument is *not* directed primarily at easing prison conditions or reducing prison crowding. Our understanding of, and response to, what we consider to be 'penal controversies' is much more radical.

The remainder of this introduction defines what constitutes a 'controversial issue in prison' and outlines and evaluates four competing interpretive frameworks for understanding penal controversies. We then point to the importance of adopting an alternative normative framework to assess penal legitimacy rooted in the principles of human rights and social justice. The chapter concludes with a brief outline of the contents of the following nine chapters.

The definition of a penal controversy

The criteria for a 'controversial issue' are well documented in education studies (Wellington 1986; Claire and Holden 2007) and the following definition of a 'penal controversy' builds upon these important insights.

a   *Topical and emotive:* A penal controversy must be topical and focused upon penal policy, the actions of offenders or state agents, or the implications of a given event in prison that is considered important by a significant number of people. It is likely that the issue has been recently highlighted in the media, by local grass roots campaigners, or by penal pressure groups, and is generally of considerable public interest and likely to arouse strong emotions.

b   *Competing interpretive frames:* A penal controversy is open to debate, and understandings and meanings are disputed. These contested opinions are likely to be based upon different sets of experiences, interests, values and interpretive frames. There is likely to be a divergence of opinions, the development of specialized knowledge on a given controversy and gatekeepers who guard access to this knowledge.

c   *Questions penal legitimacy:* A penal controversy should be placed in political, historical, policy and socio-economic contexts and may ultimately question the moral and political legitimacy of the penal rationale.

Let us now consider in detail each of these three aspects of a penal controversy.

Topical and emotive

The eight penal controversies included in this book are both topical and emotive and provide excellent examples of recent high profile campaigns by pressure groups and the media. These have also been highly prevalent in recent Prison Service policies and official reports. The case studies are also highly emotive. This is because the categories of prisoners being discussed reflect concerns around the imprisonment of certain populations because of their perceived vulnerabilities.[5] There is extensive debate regarding whether people with mental health problems, women, children and those with a history of suicidal ideation should have more lenient penal regimes to reflect their vulnerabilities or whether they should even be sent to prison in the first instance. There is also considerable debate regarding whether certain offenders, such as people whose drug taking is considered 'problematic' or people who sexually offend, should be dealt with via specialist medical interventions either within the prison or the community. It is sometimes maintained that if the aim of intervention is public protection and to find solutions that 'work' to reduce future harms it would be better to deploy psycho-medical rather than punitive disposals to address such socially harmful conduct. There are also concerns that the prison populations reflect certain structural forms of discrimination, such as a bias against the poor or Black or Minority Ethnic (BME) populations, or that the consequences of imprisonment are so great that it should be avoided for certain groups of people, such as mothers of children. The prisoner populations highlighted in this book reflect such hotly debated and emotionally charged topics.

Competing interpretive frames

There are a number of competing interpretative frames shaping how penal realities are understood. An interpretive frame is a way of conceptualizing and interpreting meanings. Different interpretive frames have different moral and political priorities and different levels of plausibility and acceptance. Further, it is not just what is said that is significant, but who says it; not just what happened but who has the power to determine dominant meanings and understandings of the event (Becker 1963). In other words, not all voices are heard, and not all speakers are viewed with the same levels of credibility. The four interpretive frames referred to most often in subsequent chapters are *common sense*, *legalism*, the *psycho-medical model* and *penal abolitionism*. All four of these frames reflect certain logics, value judgements and conceptions of the legitimacy of pertaining penal practices. The extent to which a given reality in prison is considered controversial, or not, therefore depends somewhat on which interpretive frame is adopted.[6]

'Common sense' is an understanding of the world derived from everyday inter-actions, practices and experiences as well as hearsay, gossip and local and national media coverage. The internal logic of a person's common sense is likely to be incoher-ent, inconsistent, fragmented, and, according to Stuart Hall et al. (1978), dominated by a conservative ideology. Poverty, criminal activity and penalization are perceived as the result of immorality and poor self-discipline. The common sense interpretive frame is closely aligned with the doctrine of less eligibility. Here criminal activity is understood as a free choice that is based upon weighing up the potential benefits and costs of such behaviour and as such it is assumed that if prison is painful, if it really hurts, the cognitive response of the offender will be to restrain from such pleasurable activity in the future. Harsh and punitive regimes will instil moral fibre and discipline into the criminal, thus eradicating the individual deficiencies that caused offending.

Remarkably, despite being widespread, common sense represents merely a form of penological illiteracy (Carlen and Tchaikovsky 1996). Common sense assumptions permeate the prison walls, informing prison officer working personalities and at least some occupational cultures in prisons in England and Wales today (Carrabine 2004; Scott 2006; Sim 2009). Common sense also performs a key part in the institutional-ization of classism, patriarchies, homophobia, ageism and neo-colonialism, and can be used to justify punitive policies rooted in security, discipline, regulation and the denial of prisoners' shared humanity (Sim et al. 1987). One of the key aims of this book is to highlight and challenge such 'bad common sense' and aid penological literacy.

'Legalism' is an interpretive frame which prioritizes legality and guarantees due process, stressing how duties and rights are defined through a rule based system. Laws and formal policies become the key determinants of behaviour, challenges and redress. The aims and justifications of imprisonment focus not on the socio-political and socio-economic functions of the prison but on punishment, retribution and deterrence (Cavadino and Dignan 1992). Legalistic approaches highlight how the role of law provides mechanisms to ensure equality, justice and accountability and in the prison context can be seen in relation to precisely-worded policy documents, rules, regulations and procedures. Legalism, however, has been condemned on the grounds of its reification (abstraction) of problematic events from their individual, social or political contexts (van Swaaningen 1997). While it is tempting to adopt a liberal view of law as a purely positive tool, legalism can also be criticized for being inflexible, insensitive, antagonistic and adversarial rather than cooperative and compassionate. Legalistic approaches conceptualize 'crime' as meaning an action contrary to law and do not question why or how certain activities are criminalized (Hulsman 1986).

Further, legalism alone can provide no assurances that the excesses of the repressive apparatus of the Capitalist State will be controlled, while in this interpretive frame the legitimacy of legal processes are unlikely to be scrutinized in terms of their consistency with the principles of social justice.

The 'psycho-medical model' presents itself as a value free, objective and scientific interpretive frame whose practitioners undertake their duties for humanitarian, altruistic and paternalistic reasons. Under this positivistic logic it is possible, indeed desirable, to identify and classify individuals around the poles on the normal and the pathological.[7] The *abnormal* offender is understood as radically dissimilar from a *normal* person because of their biological or psychological differences. Through identifying and categorizing individual pathologies, the psycho-medical model can diagnose the causes of such abnormalities and promote effective means of curing individualized ailments. In other words it delivers a means of providing classification techniques, categorization, and the normalization of offenders (Foucault 1977). When medicalized conceptions of imprisonment come to dominate, the prison sentence is conceived as a great opportunity for diagnosing social and individual ills and providing a means of cure, treatment and healing. The psycho-medical model, however, can also be utilized to remove the offender from the criminal justice system. Here the offender is understood as suffering from an illness that can only be cured through medical treatments. As such it conceives of social problems through a therapeutic rather than a punitive lens and promotes rehabilitation and treatment rather than punishment and discipline. Modification of the 'pathological' to the 'normal' is to be achieved via the scientific advances of medicine and is done so in the name of individual or *public health*.

It is clear that in recent years there has been a change of emphasis from somatic (biological) to psychological (cognitive-behavioural) interpretive frames. In 2000 £10 million was spent annually on psychological services but by 2006 this figure had increased to £30 million. It was estimated that in 2008 there were over 1000 psychological staff directly employed by public sector prisons in England and Wales (Crighton and Towl 2008). Indeed, in the search for the pathological the prison has performed a crucial role in the development of 'applied' and 'clinical' psycho-medical knowledge (Rose 1985). Psychology needs the prison 'laboratory' to individualize, diagnose and categorize abnormalities. In return psycho-medical knowledge can be used as the basis for individual assessments and to scientifically determine the categorization of problematic individuals. Consequently prison psychiatrists and psychologists have 'discovered' new and complex disorders requiring their expertise, in the process re-classifying people struggling to cope with social problems as inadequates unable to adjust to wider social norms. This 'penal-psychiatric complex' (Seddon 2007: 162) can thus be deployed as an apparently humane way to control the ill-disciplined, biologically and genetically inferior 'other' (Pilgrim and Rogers 1996). Reinforcing individualistic explanations of 'crime', the psycho-medical model de-politicizes experiences and facilitates surveillance (Sim 1990). Significantly though, it is only through such empirical analysis of existing prisoner populations that forensic psychology can claim its scientific status (Rose 1985). This has, however, led to significant epistemological (knowledge) limitations and flawed theory and practice, such as programmes for people who sexually offend.

For its critics the psycho-medical interpretive frame is a social construction representing political and moral human judgements rather than scientific authority (Berridge 1999). Medical judgements are not neutral but rather reflect certain understandings of the real. This model mandates medical intervention, but whether the potentially insidious controls deployed are necessary or rooted in humane benevolence is far from certain. Explanations of individual pathology are however highly attractive to the powerful at an ideological level. In the 'prison place' this means that problems encountered by the prisoner are perceived as individual personality flaws rather than as being produced by the processes of imprisonment (Medlicott 2001). As such, the psycho-medical model ultimately reinforces existing penal structures and realities.

In contrast 'penal abolitionism' provides an anti-positivist interpretive frame that acknowledges the social construction of problematic behaviours, troubles and conflicts and looks to find pragmatic solutions to such difficulties without adopting the punitive rationale (logic of punishment). Rather than providing a solution, the penal law is understood as creating new, rather than dealing with existing, social problems. Prisons are understood as counter-productive and as institutions that create 'crime' rather than resolve social and moral conflicts (Foucault 1977). Penal abolitionists maintain that there are *no radical differences* between criminals and non-criminals and divisions between such categories are largely achieved because similar behaviours are treated differently.[8] The penal law is seen as being disproportionately applied to the poor, underprivileged, the unskilled and the 'unrespectable'. At the heart of this process is the use of separating or 'dividing practices' (Foucault 1977; Seddon 2007). Through the act of dividing the manipulative from the genuine, the deserving from the undeserving, and the 'us' from the 'them', a false dichotomy is established facilitating the differential treatment of people. This means of 'othering' is also linked to the construction of social and psychic distancing of the offender – the greater the distance between offender and victim, the more likely the criminal law will be used, particularly if they are deemed to be unrespectable and low status (Baumgartner 1992).

The insights of penal abolitionism then tap into what has been referred to as the 'sociological imagination' (Mills 1959). This involves an examination of the relationship between the individual and the social through emphasizing the boundaries placed upon everyday interactions, choices, meanings and motivations of wrongdoers and recognition of the political and ideological construction of the real. Crucially it also connects individual biographies with the broader structural relations of a given historic period and examines how penalization operates within a society that is deeply divided around the structural fault lines of 'race', class, gender, sexuality and age (Barton et al. 2006; Scraton 2007).

For penal abolitionists the prison place is understood as a toxic environment and all humans placed in such a degrading and damaging place are vulnerable to its structured harms. For abolitionists, one way to draw attention to the inherent immoral practices of the prison place is through highlighting the everyday problems, troubles and conflicts of prison life and their detrimental impact upon the health of prison populations. These *troubles* are a private matter that occurs within the lived experiences of individual prisoners and affects their immediate relationships and social world. They become, however, a [controversial] *issue* when they are transformed into a public matter and linked to the political and economic structures of a given society (Barton et al. 2006). Individual troubles in prison can be used to make connections between the micro-realities of prison life and a new and plausible 'bigger picture' of the social world.

Questioning penal legitimacy

The claims of penal authorities to legitimacy regarding the eight controversial issues explored in this book are closely tied to the concept of the *healthy* or *health promoting prison*. Health can be understood as being both a presence and an absence. It has a presence in that it entails feeling *more* than just well. It involves the ability and capacity to grow, develop, find fulfilment and be creative. It has an absence in that it is a state of unconsciousness of either health or disease. For Georges Canguilhem (1978: 91) a 'state of health is a state of unawareness where the subject and his body are one. Conversely, the awareness of the body consists in a feeling of limits, threats, obstacles to health'. A place which creates restrictions or awareness of constraints is unlikely to be a place of dynamic and prodigious human development – the signs of good health. While the notion of the prison as a *healthy* place appears then to be a contradiction in terms (Smith 2000), official penal policy has maintained otherwise.

> The official view of the effects of imprisonment upon health, both physical and mental, is that it improves. As long ago as 1894, when conditions were less good, the Prison Commissioners in their annual report claimed that 'residence in prison in England and Wales is favourable to the maintenance of health and strength'. 'Physical strength nearly always improves' a governor declares. 'Any mental weakness generally improves . . .'
>
> (Hobhouse and Brockway 1922: 252)

The argument today, this time by two senior forensic psychologists in the Prison Service, is remarkably similar: 'Prisoners seem to make physical health gains while in custody, with improved diet, reduced alcohol and drug use and better access to health care all playing a part' (Crighton and Towl 2008: 62).

The 1999 thematic review *Suicide is Everyone's Concern* by Her Majesty's Chief Inspector of Prisons (HMCIP) provided the normative criteria for what a healthy prison would entail. Deriving the concept from a commitment to ensure that the Prison Service adhered to the principles promoted by the Woolf Report (1991), importantly the HMCIP (1999: para 7.9) report does not claim that prisons are actually healthy. Rather '[w]e believe the phrase "healthy prison" is useful in helping to demonstrate positive aspects of custody but the term in no way implies that prisons, even those that are very well run, are "healthy" in the full sense of the word'. The HMCIP (1999) subsequently identified four criteria for a healthy prison:

1   *The weakest prison feels safe.* Influenced by Woolf's notion of justice and control, a physically and emotionally safe environment fostering feelings of security and trust should be a priority. This includes a commitment to challenging bullying, victimization and emotional abuse; the fair and transparent administration of

prison rules; tolerable prison conditions; and incentive schemes that encourage responsible behaviour.

2 *All prisoners are treated with respect.* Prisoners are treated as fellow human beings. This includes clean living conditions, access to showers and clean clothes; decent quality of food; prisoners spoken to with courtesy; and healthcare equivalent to services in the community. Such commitments are however predicated on prisoners being provided with opportunities to make responsible 'choices'.

3 *All prisoners are busily occupied, are expected to improve themselves and are given the opportunity to do so.* Prisoners are given the opportunity to make responsible choices that lead to personal development. This includes a commitment to purposeful and constructive activities around employment, exercise and education and helping prisoners improve their basic literacy and numeracy skills.

4 *All prisoners can strengthen links with their families and prepare for release.* This is primarily a commitment to providing offending behaviour programmes and an attempt to reduce the harmful social consequences of imprisonment by trying to provide resettlement programmes that foster family networks, increased employability options and suitable accommodation on release.

Prisons which meet the above criteria are considered to be legitimate institutions. Recently, a more ambitious idea of *health promoting prisons* has been introduced. The health promoting prison looks once again to conceive of the prison as an effective means in reducing reoffending, but this time through tackling health inequalities. Imprisonment is understood as a 'unique chance to tackle some serious health issues' (Prison Health Policy Unit and Prison Health Task Force 2002: 1) among 'a population it would normally be hard to reach'. Like most official statements on this topic, the Prison Service claims that 'the good news is that prison has been shown to be a tremendous opportunity to meet health needs' (p. 1). As prisoners are believed to have 'led chaotic lifestyles prior to prison', the prison is seen as 'their only opportunity for an *ordered approach to assessing and addressing health needs*' (p. 10, original emphasis). Each prison is believed to have the potential to be a healthy setting that can improve spiritual, physical, economic and social health.[9]

Health promoting prisons dovetail with the wider 'making punishment work' agenda. The prison is seen as a key player in reducing reoffending and protecting the public and it also makes a clear connection between health and law abiding behaviour. Through tackling mental and physical ill health, substance usage and social exclusion in the prison setting the government utilizes a psycho-medical interpretive frame to deploy the prison as a public health intervention in the fight against 'crime'. The question to ask though is whether prisons really can be healthy places? Critical sociological literature indicates that they cannot. The prison is a 'total institution' where a significant number of like-situated people are 'cut off from the wider society for an appreciable period of time, [and] together lead an enclosed, formally administered round of life' (Goffman 1963: 11). A new world is created within its walls shaping the interests and meanings for those on the 'inside'.

Extreme physical violence, bullying and intimidation all often occur in prisons, but it would be inaccurate to present a picture where such events are seen to characterize day-to-day life in every prison. It is the dreadful emptiness of prison life that is the real terror. As Diana Medlicott (2001: 101) perceptively states, while prison initially seems 'ordinarily bleak and austere, not extraordinary' where the 'over-riding impression is often one of blankness and emptiness' the 'puzzle . . . is that it is so mundane, and yet so hard to bear'.

The deprivation of liberty will always be painful and there are constant and systemic threats to humanity in the daily practices of imprisonment.[10] At times prisons are places of frantic activity yet, paradoxically, at others they are empty, dull and motionless (Cope 2003). Yet this conscious wasting of life, the enforced passivity and the emptiness of time are all 'sources of acute suffering' (Medlicott 2001: 131). These inherent harms cannot be removed through improving prison conditions – the environment could be very pleasant but the structured pains of the prison place remain unaltered. The negation of the ability to control time and space is something which affects the wellbeing of *everyone*. Recent evidence indicates that prisoners in the UK commonly experience serious physical and mental ill health, with one study estimating that approximately half of all sentenced male prisoners have a significant illness or disability (Bridgwood and Malbon 1994). It seems undoubted that there currently exists a 'disastrous health situation in prisons' (Fuhrer and Nelles 1997: 22).[11] What is required now is recognition and action.

Questions concerning the legitimacy of current penal practices demand the adoption of moral and political normative value judgements that move beyond the current dimensions of healthy prisons. Prisons are places of pain and blame and a controversial issue must be understood within the context of a prison place that is inherently harmful and systematically undermines human dignity. Legitimate responses to wrongdoing must therefore be consistent with the legal and moral touchstone of *human rights*. A controversial issue must also be understood through an awareness of how the application of the penal law is biased towards the poor and, consequently and however subtly, performs a role shoring up a society riddled with social injustice. Legitimate responses to wrongdoing must also then be consistent with the promotion of policies that facilitate *social justice*. It is on this criterion that we assess the following eight controversial issues in prisons.

Overview of chapters

The following chapters share a common structure and look to answer the following key questions:

- How have people conceptualized this penal controversy?
- What does the official data tell us and what are its limitations?
- What is its historical context?
- What are the contemporary policies of the Prison Service?
- Are they legitimate and, if not, what are the alternatives?

In Chapter 2 we consider prisoners with mental health problems, highlighting the increasing dominance and influence of the psycho-medical model. The chapter problematizes current data and definitions of mental health in prison and emphasizes the importance of understanding the phenomena within its social and historical contexts. This chapter also analyses the increasing priority of improving prison healthcare and critically reviews the limitations of current Prison Service policies and practices. Chapter 2 concludes by discussing legitimate non-punitive responses to people with mental health problems. Chapter 3 critically explores the experiences and needs of women in prison from an abolitionist feminist perspective. This chapter outlines current Prison Service data and policy and points to the ongoing dominance of the psycho-medical models of female offending. Chapter 3 concludes with a consideration of the possibility of the selective abolition of imprisonment for women.

Chapter 4 discusses the highly topical and emotive issue of placing children in custodial institutions. Current data, definitions and policies are situated in the historical context of the politicized battle between 'justice' and welfare approaches to children who offend. The chapter critically assesses the detention of children, and, following the lead of abolitionists such as Barry Goldson, argues that this state of affairs amounts to state-sponsored institutional child abuse. In Chapter 5 we examine the inherent racial bias in the penalization process, focusing on the experiences of BME people in custody and foreign national prisoners. This chapter identifies the key issues, policies and data in the prison setting, focusing upon historical and contemporary day-to-day manifestations of racism in penal institutions. Significantly, Chapter 5 explores the importance of conceptualizing current penal policies as an expression of 'state racism', highlighting the illegitimacy of the relationship between the prison and immigration control.

Chapter 6 investigates whether people with suicidal ideation should be excluded from imprisonment. This chapter points to the difficulties of adopting a 'scientific' approach to definitions, data, and policy pertaining to self-inflicted deaths and questions a number of assumptions about how prisoners cope, or not, with the prison place. In Chapter 7 we provide a critical overview of the historic development of the 'Sex Offender Treatment Programme' (SOTP) in prisons in England and Wales. This policy is contextualized through a critical appraisal of the main assumptions and efficacy of cognitive behavioural therapies. Chapter 7 concludes with a consideration of the merits of non-custodial means of responding to sexual abuse. In Chapter 8 we critically reflect upon the main data, definitions and interpretive frameworks concerning illicit drug taking in prison. Debates are located within both historical and contemporary Prison Service policies and Chapter 8 concludes with a consideration of the legitimacy of penalization strategies of certain substance usage. Chapter 9 considers the many difficulties experienced by prisoners' partners and children in maintaining contact and promoting positive family relationships. It problematizes the dominant models of the 'prisoners' family' and explores the diversity of kin relationships. Chapter 9 concludes with an assessment of penal campaigns and the importance of abolitionist perspectives in relation to supporting people who have a family member in custody.

In the concluding chapter of the book we attempt to weave together the critical insights gleaned from considering the above issues and aim to move beyond penal controversies by calling for new forms of dealing with problematic conduct which, if implemented, could lead to a substantial fall in the prison population and cause less harm to troubled and troublesome people and their families.

2

Mental health problems in prison

We all can suffer from mental health problems. Mental ill health largely involves trouble coping with life in general or certain highly stressful situations. Such difficulties often manifest themselves in terms of low self-esteem, self neglect, alienation and social isolation. Although there is no consensus regarding the most appropriate terminology to adopt when referring to mental health, in this chapter we use the phrase 'mental health problems', as this indicates that a problem genuinely exists for the sufferer, and potentially other people, without necessarily privileging a medical explanation (Pilgrim and Rogers 1996). It should be recognized at the outset that mental health problems are undesirable, disabling and potentially frightening for all involved. Yet while sufferers do have *real* problems the application of a negative label such as 'mental illness' is likely to be applied only when sufficient social or psychic distance can be established.

The concepts of 'crime' and 'mental health' are social constructs, and the criminal justice system historically has focused on only a small minority of wrongdoers, primarily the poor and unrespectable. Prison populations therefore tell us not so much about 'crime' but rather the mechanisms of social control and processes of criminalization in a given society at a given time. Though fear and stigma are closely associated with those successfully labelled, the evidence overwhelming suggests that most people with mental health problems do not break the law and those who do are largely petty offenders involved in minor property offences (Laurence 2003). As mental health problems are often linked with homelessness, poverty, drug taking and unemployment, it should be recognized that some sufferers may have broken the law as a means of getting basic human necessities such as food, shelter and warmth. In this sense offending may be a desperate cry for help from someone in need of care and support (Hudson 1993).

Although for some offenders prison acts as a 'stabilizer' (Durcan 2008: 31), the mental wellbeing of the vast majority of prisoners deteriorates. Prolonged passivity leads to isolation and the prison place presents a serious danger to the mental health of those confined. Numerous aspects of the daily prison regime are potentially damaging: crowding; frustrations dealing with the minutiae of everyday life; lack of mental or physical stimulation; the preponderance of negative relationships rooted in fear, anxiety and mistrust; physical, emotional, sexual or financial exploitation; and inadequate care with an over-emphasis on medication (Birmingham 2003; Nurse et al. 2003; HMCIP 2007; Durcan 2008). Sitting alongside these harms are the ever-present structured pains of confinement (Medlicott 2001).

Many, but by no means all, of the people with mental health problems in prison are likely to have had significant difficulties prior to incarceration. Three different ways of responding to offenders with pre-existing mental health problems have at different times dominated penal policy: (1) delivery of appropriate healthcare provision in prison, (2) transfer to mental institutions after sentence and (3) diversion prior to custody. On numerous occasions since the nineteenth century prison authorities have claimed that not only are mental health problems largely imported but that the prison place could be a major opportunity to address them (Home Office 1959; HMCIP 1996). In present day parlance imprisonment is conceived as a health promoting environment.

The credibility of this approach has been questioned and a considerable body of evidence has accumulated suggesting that prison is a highly unsuitable location for people with such vulnerabilities (Hudson 1993; Laing 1999; Seddon 2007). Penal history is also littered with official recognition that the deprivations of daily prison life can either create or exacerbate mental health problems (Butler Committee 1975; Bradley 2009). At various points in time, most recently from the 1970s to 1990s, official emphasis has been placed on hospital transfer[1] or diversion[2] rather than improved prison healthcare. Transfer involves legally handing over a prisoner under the requirements of Mental Health legislation to a hospital, whilst diversion

> is a process whereby people are assessed and their needs identified as early as possible in the offender pathway (including prevention and early intervention), thus informing subsequent decisions about where an individual is best placed to receive treatment, taking into account public safety, safety of the individual and punishment of an offence.
>
> (Bradley 2009: 16)

Significantly, aspirations for the removal of people with mental health problems from the prisons have largely failed with those advocating such a strategy focusing almost exclusively on those who are difficult to manage in prison (Seddon 2007). Painting with very broad brushstrokes, when the prison is justified primarily on the grounds of punishing and disciplining offenders, diversion and transfer are advocated; on the other hand, when prison is conceived as an opportunity to treat *all* offenders, there is a greater investment in healthcare. Mental health policies therefore need to be contextualized within the aims of imprisonment (Seddon 2007; Scott 2007a).

Abolitionists have understood the control of mental health problems as the *essence of confinement* (Foucault 1967; Seddon 2007). From this perspective prisons are not opportunities for promoting health but inherently harmful institutions that are part of a wider historical project to control deviant populations. Prisoners with mental health problems are understood as being systematically failed by welfare services, criminalized and abandoned in stressful environments likely to exacerbate coping difficulties. Locating mental health problems within wider structural contexts, abolitionists call for the end of imprisonment and radical social transformations rooted in the principles of social justice and human rights (Hudson 1993).

This chapter first highlights the importance of thinking critically about mental health problems, including a consideration of the rising influence of the psycho-medical model and its relationship with legalism. The chapter proceeds to problematize current data on mental health problems in prison, and the importance of understanding such findings within both social and historical context. We then move on to consider the history of mental health policy and practices and the insights that can be gleaned by understanding how the control of people with mental health problems is central to the confinement project. The debate continues with an analysis of developments since the 1970s and the increasing priority of improving prison healthcare. The limitations of current policies and practices are then reviewed and the chapter concludes with a consideration of alternative responses to dealing with lawbreakers with mental health problems.

Thinking critically about mental health problems

Mental health is often conceived in a way similar to that of physical health, where a deviation is understood as an 'illness' caused by some kind of psychological malfunction or genetic defect. The medical interpreters, decipherers and labellers of health are either somatically (biologically) trained doctors, psychiatrists or psychologists, described here collectively as representing the psycho-medical model. The authority of the above professions derives from the belief that their practices are caring, compassionate and paternalistic and that not only can they accurately identify maladjusted individuals but can also provide a cure.

Lawbreakers with mental health problems inevitably fall between the realms of legalism and the psycho-medical model. Though competing with legalism for the exercise of penal power, forensic psychiatrists and psychologists rely upon the law for clientele (Bartlett and Sandland 2008). Inevitably legalism and the psycho-medical model have a reciprocal relationship (Rose 1985; McCallum 2001). Indeed for Nikolas Rose (1986: 202) '[p]enality relies upon psychiatry to provide the rationale and the technology for confinement when the law reaches its limits – in offences without motive, the bizarre, the monstrous and the perverse'. This relationship is central to responses to 'Dangerous and Severe Personality Disorder' (DSPD). DSPD is believed to be a permanent and deeply entrenched personality problem rather than a temporary illness that can be cured. People with DSPD are seen as 'psychological vampires' (Bowers 2002: 2) who deserve to be punished as their 'grossly abnormal "inner world"' does not mean they are 'suffering from mental illness' (Keith 2006: 144).

Political debates on DSPD reached fever pitch following the murders of Lin and Megan Russell by Michael Stone in 1996. This case highlighted concerns that sentencing powers for perceived incurable 'dangerous offenders' were inadequate. It was argued that the penal law failed to protect the public as people with DSPD were released while still dangerous but could not be detained in a mental hospital. One early attempt to address this quandary was the introduction of the 'hospital direction' by the *Crime (Sentences) Act* (1997). This hybrid order allowed for an offender to be sent to hospital in the first instance but then transferred back to prison if treatments failed. This compromise, however, did not appease political anxieties.

The concept of DSPD was first introduced in 1999 in a Green Paper entitled *Managing Dangerous People with Severe Personality Disorders*, one of two Green Papers circulated that year exploring the possibility of indefinitely detaining people considered to have DSPD. In this document DSPD referred to 'people who have an identifiable personality disorder to a severe degree, who pose a high risk to other people because of serious anti-social behaviour resulting from their disorder' (Home Office and Department of Health 1999: 9).[3]

Initial attempts to push through a new law failed and after much controversy in early 2006 specific DSPD legislative powers were abandoned. A new *Mental Health Act* (MHA) was enacted in July 2007, replacing the 'treatability test', which had existed for half a century to ensure people were only detained for their own good, with the 'appropriate treatment test'.

> In this Act, reference to appropriate medical treatment, in relation to a person suffering from mental disorder, are references to medical treatment which is appropriate in his case, taking into account the nature and degree of the mental disorder and all other circumstances of his case.[4]
>
> (S 4. ss 3., MHA, 2007)

Rather than wholesale reform, in the end the government opened four new DSPD units with 300 places in total: two highly secure special hospital units (Broadmoor and Rampton) operating under the authority of the MHA (2007), and two prison units (Whitemoor and Frankland), operating under the powers of the *Criminal Justice Act* (CJA) (2003).

Policies on DSPD raise key ethical questions regarding the indefinite detention of individuals who have not broken the law (Scott 2009). Further, DSPD is a politically invented concept plagued with difficulties regarding accuracy and reliability and predicated upon a circular argument: people considered at high risk of causing serious harm are defined as having DSPD, while those deemed to have a severely disordered personality are defined as inherently harmful (Seddon 2007, 2008).[5] Ultimately, the concept is a 'dumping zone for a host of problems which do not necessarily interrelate', and has 'overtones of despair' (Gunn et al. 1978: 38). DSPD is profoundly exclusionary and people so labelled may become social pariahs who find it difficult to get support (Fennell 2002). It also seems a rather convenient diagnosis, placing blame on individual prisoners when treatments fail. Evidence suggests, however, that long term interventions involving patience, tolerance and well informed confrontations can help people with 'DSPD' find alternative less problematic paths and new meanings in life (Prins 2005). Indeed some of the most notorious prisoners have successfully addressed their problematic behaviours (Rickford and Edgar 2005).

Both legalism and the psycho-medical model then are deployed as a means to classify, manage and normalize the mad, bad and sad, with the law setting the perimeters of psycho-medical powers (Foucault 2006). Indeed the psycho-medical model largely informs current legal and policy understandings of 'mentally disordered offenders'. These people are lawbreakers, who may be acutely or chronically mentally ill; those with neuroses, behavioural and/or personality disorders; those with learning difficulties; some who, as a function of alcohol and/or substance abuse, have a mental health problem . . . [I]t also applies to . . . some sex offenders and some abnormally aggressive offenders, who may benefit from psychological treatments.

(NACRO Mental Health Advisory Committee 1995: 4)

Under the psycho-medical model it is possible to use classification systems to identify numerous forms of mental health problems. This cataloguing largely revolves around the categories of psychosis, neurosis, psychopathy and mental impairment (Prins 2005). Although the MHA (1983) had a number of different subcategories of mental disorder, such as mental impairment and psychopathy, the MHA (2007) omits these categories (S.1, ss. 3) providing a much simplified definition of 'mental disorder' as 'any disorder or disability of the mind' (S.1, ss. 2). Significantly the MHA (2007) clearly states that dependence on alcohol and drugs is expressly precluded from inclusion as a mental disorder. This has significant implications for many recent studies which have attempted to measure the extent of mental health problems among prison populations.

Though the psycho-medical model may at first appear plausible, and is certainly appealing to policy makers as it implies low cost individualized solutions, fundamental concerns have been raised about its interventions. These include an *epistemological crisis* concerning the serious limitations of somatic knowledge; the *iatrogenic effects* of treatment; and *ethical dilemmas* around the contradictions between medical 'care' and custody (Pilgrim and Rogers 1996; Coppock and Hopton 2000).

There is only limited evidence to support the claim that there is a biological basis to mental health problems (Conrad and Schneider 1992; Scull 1993). A strong somatic basis is often assumed because practitioners utilize medical interventions, yet though pharmacological treatments have been effective suppressants of the manifestations of some disorders, treatment efficacy is not proof of biological causation (Coppock and Hopton 2000). Indeed, drug treatments have generally not only failed to provide a 'cure' but have proved on occasion to be harmful to recipients (Laurance 2003). Tranquillizers can be addictive and have been linked to problems of Parkinsonism and tardive dyskinesia while 'talking treatments' may have iatrogenic effects such as 'therapeutic regression' (Pilgrim and Rogers 1996). Coppock and Hopton (2000: 177) provide a rather sobering summary of the kinds of treatments currently available:

[A]ll conventional psychotherapy can offer is a new vocabulary for the person to express his/her happiness. Alternatively, medication would merely blunt a person's emotions so they would be less troubled by the misery of their experience, while all cognitive therapy could offer would be [a] redefinition of the problem to make it appear less unpalatable.

Prisoners can become psychologically dependent on medication and prisoners on medication may be bullied by other prisoners for their prescribed drugs (HMCIP 2007; Durcan 2008). In addition drugs themselves may be given out because they are the cheapest and less labour intensive, rather than the most appropriate response

(Mills 2005). There is also an ever present temptation to utilize medical solutions to deal with prisoners whom prison authorities find difficult to control (Carlen 1986; Sim 1990). When consulted prisoners with mental health problems felt they need 'someone to talk to'; therapy and advice about medication; 'something meaningful to do'; support from staff, family and other prisoners; help when facing a 'crisis' and support with future planning (HMCIP 2007: 45; Durcan 2008: 7). Such support, however, is rarely realized.

The use of classificatory systems dividing the 'normal' from the 'pathological', ultimately create a false 'us and them' dichotomy that can be used to manage and control differences and distance the 'other' (Foucault 1977). In reality such obvious divisions do not exist and it is probably more accurate to understand mental health as a continuum. Many sufferers have moments of crisis and remission, often exacerbated by stressful life events, and it is not always easy to identify the dividing lines between mental health problems and mental wellbeing.

For the most extreme critics there are no physical, biological or organic bases to mental health problems at all. The concept of 'mental illness' is simply an excuse to justify morally problematic behaviours and legitimate repressive state powers infringing civil liberties (Szasz 1972). These arguments, however, are counter-intuitive as they deny the reality of mental health problems. As Andrew Scull (1993: 5, original emphasis) argues, it is difficult to accept the 'claim that mental alienation is simply the product of arbitrary social labelling or scapegoating, a social construction *tout court*'. It seems more plausible to accept that mental health problems have a social dimension alongside their physical manifestation (Scheff 1966; Conrad and Schneider 1992). Abolitionists, drawing on labelling theory, identify that whether a person is designated as being 'mentally ill' or not is dependent upon a number of contingencies regarding where an action occurs; the respective power, status, respectability of the audience; and the ease with which an alleged person may be distanced. This perspective also reminds us that the application of such a master status unfairly reduces complex human beings to a one dimensional stereotype (see Table 2.1). Consequently we argue in this chapter that mental health problems in prison must be understood through consideration of historically specific socio-economic, legal, and political intersections (Scull 1993).

Problematizing data on prisoners with mental health problems

Prisoners have been diagnosed as suffering from mental health problems ranging from schizophrenia and personality disorder to depression and insomnia (Singleton et al. 1998). At any given time, it is estimated that up to 5000 people with 'severe and enduring mental illnesses' are in prison (NACRO 2007: 2). Estimates of the numbers of prisoners sufficiently unwell to require immediate admission to a psychiatric hospital range from around 500 to 3500 prisoners (Joint Committee on Human Rights 2004), while Durcan and Knowles (2006) estimate that around 40 per cent of prisoners held on healthcare wings should be held in secure NHS accommodation. Mental health problems are even more prevalent among unsentenced prisoners, with one study highlighting that as many as one third have a problem and 5 per cent are acutely psychotic (Brook 1996).

Table 2.1 Three interpretive frames on offenders with mental health problems

	Disposal	Key principles	Strengths	Weaknesses
Legalism	• Prison • Community punishments • High security hospitals and hybrid hospital/prison orders	• Legality, offender rights and due process • Punishment, retribution and deterrence • Criminalization • Equality • Justice	• Protection of legal rights of people with mental health problems • Controls over psycho-medical powers and professionals • Opportunities for treatment of mental health problems (but within penal system)	• Reification (abstraction) of social problems from actual social contexts • Law not designed to deal with mental health problems: Insensitive, inflexible, adversarial and antagonistic rather than compassionate • Definitions of 'crime' / 'health' not problematized • Excessively punitive: prison may exacerbate health problems and medical care in prisons likely to be inadequate
Psycho-medical model	• High security hospital and hybrid hospital/prison orders • Community Treatment Centres • Diversion • Social services/ NHS	• Expert knowledge and professional discretion • Medical model, illness and public hygiene • Rehabilitation • Humanitarianism, duty of care and compassion for sufferers	• Dealing with offenders with dignity and humanity • Access to therapeutic care and treatment in healthcare setting at the earliest possible opportunity • Not subjected to the detrimental effects of penal sanctions • Emphasis on care and *treatment* not to bolster legal safeguards	• Danger of self-serving professionals pushing expansionism • Psychiatric knowledge is limited: talk of illness may be misplaced and treatments may create more harm than good • Individual pathology with individualized solutions • Loss of legal safeguards, use of indeterminate sentences, and people confined before 'crime'

Abolitionism			
• Social services/ NHS • Abolition of custody for the vulnerable • Alternative means of redress and social solidarity	• Labelling theory and scepticism of psycho-medical model • Continuum of mental health problems • Social justice and legal safeguards • Recognition of service user needs • Understanding of problems within social contexts and psychiatric power	• Non-punitive responses/ social policies to address individual and social troubles • Transformations of socio-economic contexts • Acknowledgement of views and needs of people with mental health problems • Allows possibility of negotiated medical interventions where appropriate	• Psycho-medical knowledge legitimates state coercion and mental health system just as oppressive as penal system • Danger of over-emphasis of social constructionism and denial of mental health problems • Abolitionism is politically marginalized • Requires fundamental social change based on principles of social justice

The Social Exclusion Unit Report (2002, cited in Scott 2008a: 116) also provides some very worrying headline figures:

- 80 per cent of prisoners have mental health problems.

- 72 per cent of male and 70 per cent of female sentenced prisoners suffer from two or more mental health disorders.

- 40 per cent of male and 63 per cent of female sentenced prisoners have a neurotic disorder.

- 7 per cent of males and 14 per cent of female sentenced prisoners have a psychotic disorder.

- 20 per cent of male and 15 per cent of female sentenced prisoners have previously been admitted to a mental hospital.

- 95 per cent of young prisoners aged 15 to 21 suffer from a mental disorder. 80 per cent suffer from at least two.

While this may seem conclusive it is important to recognize the serious limitations of prison data (Gunn et al. 1978; Mills 2005; Brooker et al. 2007; Seddon 2007). The definitional criteria of 'mental health' and the expertise of the researchers can drastically impact upon findings. It is not just *how* something is measured, but *what* is measured and *who* does it that can lead to radically different results. This is evidenced in two major studies: Gunn et al. (1991) and Singleton et al. (1998) (see Table 2.2). The findings of these studies varied enormously regarding the perceived prevalence of personality disorder, with Gunn et al. (1991) estimating that this accounted for around 8 per cent of the prison population, while Singleton et al. (1998) estimated the figure to be between 50 and 78 per cent, depending on gender and sentencing status. Indeed the Singleton study appears to indicate that there has been a major increase in mental health problems in prison since the early 1990s.

Alice Mills (2005) highlights that while Gunn et al. (1991) used clinical interviews undertaken by psychiatrists, Singleton et al. (1998) relied upon lay interviews. The differences in definitions deployed also makes comparisons between the two studies difficult, something readily acknowledged by Singleton et al. (1998: 9) who point out that '[e]stimates from the ONS study of psychiatric morbidity among prisoners will not necessarily be comparable with those obtained from other studies using different concepts and methods or using samples which may not be representative of the prison population'.

Toby Seddon (2007) concludes that it is likely that the ONS survey overestimates the extent of mental health problems in prison as two of the five mental disorders investigated were drug and alcohol dependency, while the category of 'personality disorder' itself is essentially contested.

The validity of prison data has also been questioned by those who argue that mental health problems are significantly underestimated, at least by penal practitioners. Screenings at reception is perceived as one of the key areas for identification but has been criticized because it has often been undertaken by poorly trained officers and nursing staff (Sainsbury Centre 2007). Birmingham et al. (1996) found that

Table 2.2 Two major studies of mental health problems

Main author	Sample	Findings
Gunn (1991)	1769 males, several prisons	38% psychiatric diagnosis 19% substance dependence 8% personality disorders 5% neurosis 2% psychoses
	301 females, several prisons	56% psychiatric diagnosis 29% substance dependence 8% personality disorders 13% neuroses 1% psychoses
Singleton (1998)	1254 sentenced men, several prisons	64% personality disorders 63% alcohol misuse 51% drug dependence 40% neurotic disorders 7% psychoses
	1415 men on remand, several prisons	78% personality disorders 58% hazardous drinking 51% drug dependence 59% neurotic disorders 10% functional psychosis
	676 sentenced women, several prisons	50% personality disorders 39% alcohol misuse 41% drug dependence 64% neurotic disorders 10% psychosis
	218 women on remand, several prisons	50% personality disorders 54% drug dependence 36% hazardous drinking 21% functional psychosis 76% neurotic disorders

Source: Seddon (2007: 76; 128)

75 per cent of mental disorder was not recognized at reception and a recent study also found that the

> prison reception health screenings we observed were all brief, lasting a maximum of five minutes. The mental health element of all these was minimal, and consisted of asking questions about self-harm, service use and substance misuse. At only one prison were any questions asked about current mental health state and even this was limited. Part of the screening process involved a review of medical notes. Yet many prisoners arrived without any notes and others arrived with

partial notes. Even for those who did arrive with notes there was very limited time for this process.

(Durcan 2008: 27)

The prison place itself also has a significant impact upon findings. Many studies assume that mental health difficulties are imported, failing to consider that the pains of imprisonment can distort the prevalence of mental health problems. Anxiety, distress and other forms of neurosis may be a natural reaction to punitive regimes. Mental health may significantly deteriorate, or only start to manifest itself as a problem, in prison (Mills 2005; Seddon 2007; Durcan 2008). Mental health problems and confinement may then go hand in hand. What is clear is that there is an increasing readiness to recognize 'pathological' traits in prisoners who may formerly have been regarded as 'normal' (Seddon 2007). Personal troubles deemed to constitute 'mental illnesses' are not rooted in objective standards, but facile and fluctuating constructions which can expand or contract. The present willingness to utilize such dividing practises should be understood as a historically contingent stretching of the 'elastic' mental health label (Scull 1993). The current expansion dovetails with the increasing influence of the psycho-medical model and a wider shift in penal policy justifying imprisonment as major opportunity for health promotion.

Paradoxically then, there are concerns that mental health problems are significantly over-estimated in 'scientific' studies and under-estimated in day-to-day practices. The lessons to be learnt from the above discussion are that while there are a significant number of people in prison with mental health problems, which may or may not indicate a rising prevalence in the prison place, official prison statistics are notoriously unreliable and we should be constantly aware that such data is socially constructed.

Historical context

Prior to the mid-eighteenth century, people with mental health problems in England were largely treated like slaves: chained, whipped, handcuffed, beaten and starved. Sufferers were in effect 'wild beasts . . . in fetters' subject to 'purges, vomits, bleedings, [and] mysterious coloured powders' (Scull 1993: 67). For administrative penologists the mass confinement of the 'mad' in the nineteenth century arose as a result of the benevolent intentions of humanitarian reformers who aimed to liberate them from unenlightened barbarism (Jones 1993). Yet in reality institutional solutions were more likely to breed dependency and despondency rather than humane 'cures'. Believed medical advances proved false. Treatments were promoted for profit rather than ability to relieve pain. Barbarisms of the past were exaggerated to justify the barbarism of the present. State institutions became merely a way of keeping the odd, troubled and degenerate out of sight and out of mind (Scull 1993).

While there is no mechanical fit between the labour market and state confinement they are conjoined on an ideological level (Scull 1993; Scott 2010). The emergence of a capitalist market system and modern consumerism dramatically increased the importance of being able-bodied while at the same time reduced the capacity of the poor and their families to cope with economic hardship. Consequently unproductive labourers, such as the 'mad', became a major burden on family economic resources (Scull 1993). Apparent medical progress provided an ideological cloak to a process of segregation that in fact was all about the discipline, surveillance and regulation of the poor, idle and deviant. But confinement was to do more than just contain: it became a systematic means of identifying the proper subjects of medical and penal controls, categorizing between able-bodied and economically productive poor who could be recycled back into the labour market from the work-shy, non-able-bodied poor and 'lunatics'. Troubled and troublesome people were divided between those who could be disciplined in prison and those who needed to be siphoned into specialist mental institutions (Scull 1993).

By the late eighteenth century workhouses, houses of correction and madhouses became increasingly significant in response to this profound social change, with the prison becoming a 'natural repository' for the 'mad' (Scull 1993). John Howard in his comprehensive survey of prisons in England in the 1770s stated,

> in some few gaols are confined idiots and lunatics. These serve for sport to idle visitants and assizes, and other times of general resort. Many of the Bridewells are crowded and offensive, because the rooms which were designed for prisoners are occupied by the insane. Where these are not kept separate they disturb and terrify other prisoners. No care is taken of them, although it is probable that by medicines, and proper regimen, some of them might be restored to their senses, and to usefulness in life.
>
> (Howard, 1777 cited in Walker and McCabe 1973: 1)

Being housed 'among the mad' became one of the central pains of imprisonment, but while their presence was considered an injustice, it was not perceived as an injustice for the 'insane', 'but *for others*' (Foucault 1967: 217, emphasis in original). The prison required a relatively docile population if it was to discipline the able-bodied and 'the mad' disrupted this. The first steps towards specialist provision for the criminally insane were made under the *Criminal Lunatics Act* (1800), which eventually led to the creation in 1816 of a new wing at Bethlem (Bedlam) Hospital. Despite such reforms nineteenth-century asylum administrators were generally reluctant to receive prisoners because of concerns about costs and security (Eastman 1993). Consequently transfers to mental institutions removed only small numbers. When HMP Pentonville opened in 1842 it was estimated that 'prisoner lunatics' were ten times over-represented compared to the wider population, and during that decade between five and fifteen prisoners were transferred from Pentonville to asylums every year (Ignatieff 1978).

Medicalization of disruptive prisoners became a more realistic solution and, as such, psycho-medical knowledge became deeply entwined with upholding penal regimes (Sim 1990). The 1840s saw the introduction of a prison rule requiring doctors to 'note prisoners' liability to be affected by mental, as well as physical disorder' (cited in Gunn et al. 1978: 4) and to partially combat the high number of 'lunatics' a hulk ship became the designated prison for the 'weak minded'. This decision was based on the assumption that the seaside air would facilitate a healthier environment, but in reality conditions proved no better than elsewhere (Walker and McCabe 1973).

There was also accumulating evidence of the detrimental impact of convict prisons on prisoner health. Dr William Baly (1852, cited in Gunn et al. 1978: 6), Medical Officer at HMP Milbank, noted that there were significant dangers of the 'increasing risk of insanity that attends the protraction of imprisonment' and that prisoners of 'any considerable degree of imbecility or great dullness of intellect will certainly be rendered actually insane or idiotic by a few months separate confinement'. Policies were subsequently developed for 'mentally infirm' prisoners to be housed together at the 'invalid depot' at HMP Dartmoor, and by 1855 it had at least 100 such convicts in its care (Cummings 1999). In 1863 it was decided that the 'weak minded' were to be concentrated in a new observation centre at HMP Millbank and by 1864 those housed at Dartmoor had been transferred there. Broadmoor Criminal Lunatic Asylum opened in 1863 but its impact was fairly limited. The transfer of convicts in the first ten years of its existence proved problematic as ex-prisoners were difficult to control and attempted to escape. As a result, from 1874 to 1885 the transfer of male convicts to Broadmoor was suspended and 'insane prisoners' were sent to a special wing at HMP Working instead (Cummings 1999).

By the 1880s it was clear that there existed large numbers of 'obviously insane men and women who were being dumped' in prison and released before a place could be found in an asylum (Walker and McCabe 1973: 41). Consequently under the *Criminal Lunatics Act* of 1884 modifications were made in penal regimes for prisoners 'who appear to be from imbecility of mind unfit for the same penal discipline as other prisoners' (Hobhouse and Brockway 1922: 284). In an attempt to tackle the problem in 1889 a Home Office Circular introduced a policy of diversion where magistrates were encouraged to send offenders with suspected mental health problems to asylums under the provisions of the *Lunacy Acts*. In 1897 HMP Parkhurst was officially designated the place for 'weak minded' prisoners and in 1900 special rules initiated the modification of prison rules regarding employment, diet, and breaches of discipline for those with mental health problems (Hobhouse and Brockway 1922). By 1904 it was estimated that 'weak minded' prisoners constituted about 10 per cent of the overall prison intake. The process deployed in the official definition, however, is rather illuminating.

> We quote 10 per cent as a *minimum* estimate, because it is based upon the number of prisoners officially designated as weak-minded only. Now a prisoner is often not thus officially classified until, in addition to, or rather as a result of, mental deficiency, he is found *unmanageable by ordinary penal discipline*, and to require special treatment under the regulation of the feeble minded.
>
> (Goring 1913: 255, emphasis added)

At the start of the century the focus remained on transfer and diversion with, for example, The Commissioners of Prisons and Directors of Convict Prisons (1910, cited in Gunn et al. 1978: 10) arguing that the mentally infirm should be removed if prisons were to properly fulfil their wider function. The *Inebriates Act* (1898) created provisions to commit inebriate (drunken) offenders to two special 'State Reformatories' that were in effect hybrids of the prison and the asylum. By 1921, however, the State Reformatories had been abandoned and their populations reintegrated into the

Table 2.3 History of legislation for prisoners with mental health problems

Strands of legislation	Main implications
Madhouses Act (1774)	Allowed for privately governed madhouses
An Act for Preserving the Health of Prisoners in Gaol and Preventing Gaol Distemper (1774)	Requirements of cleanliness provisions, sick rooms and appointment of experienced surgeon or apothecary (medical officer) in prison
County Asylum Act (1808)	Allowed for creation of state mental asylums (mandatory by 1845)
Criminal Lunatics Act (1800)	Allowed for opening in 1816 of new wing at Bethlem (Bedlam) Hospital for 'criminally insane' and later at the privately run Fisherton House, Salisbury
Criminal Lunatics Act (1860)	Establishment of Broadmoor Asylum for 'criminally insane' in 1863
Criminal Lunatics Act (1884)	Relaxation of prison discipline for prisoners who suffer from 'imbecility of mind'
The Lunacy Act (1890)	Consolidation of previous strands of the legislation (some provisions remaining in force until 1959).
The Inebriates Act (1898)	New State Reformatories (1901–1921) for drunkenness
Mental Deficiency Act (1913)	New legal definitions for the 'mentally deficient' and introduction of specific institutions for their confinement
Mental Deficiency Act (1927)	Change of name from 'moral imbeciles' to 'moral defectives'
Mental Health Act (1959)	Consolidation of previous legislation and introduction of mental health review tribunals
Mental Health Act (1983)	New laws with greater emphasis on patient rights
Mental Health Act (2007)	Changes to legal definition and treatability test

Source: Bartlett and Sandland (2008)

wider prison population. The *Mental Deficiency Act* (1913) also allowed for new state institutions to be established for people coming under the following four grades of the mentally deficiency: idiots, imbeciles, feeble-minded and moral imbeciles (renamed moral defectives by the 1927 *Mental Deficiency Act*). Dr Smalley (cited in Hobhouse and Brockway 1922: 285), estimated, however, that only 30 per cent of 'moral defectives' in prison would come within the scope of the *Mental Deficiency Act* (1913) while the Medical Commissioners (1929, cited in Gunn et al. 1978: 14) estimated provisions only reduced the average daily population by around 200.

Problems within the prison itself still remained:

I was transferred to the landing in a hall used for the mentally deficient. The

landing was known in prison parlance as 'Rotten Row'. This was the most dis-
tressing period of my imprisonment. To walk down the hall and pass several cells
with the doors replaced by iron railings, like a cage at the Zoo, and to see behind
them men whose reason was impaired, perhaps muttering to themselves, or
making grimaces, or walking the cell or lying on the floor shouting and singing,
was more than one's reason could bear without acute depression. Sometimes one
would be awakened at night by the shrieking of a prisoner, and twice there was a
terrible racket owing to a prisoner smashing his windows and utensils; on these
occasions most of the occupants of the landing seemed to join in the din by
shouting and banging their doors and ringing their bells.

(Hobhouse and Brockway 1922: 286)

The 1920s witnessed a transformation in penal policy and a move away from the diversion and transfer of prisoners with mental health problems. The 'mentally disordered
offender' now became 'paradigmatic' for all offenders as the prison was reconceived
as place of treatment and 'cure' (Seddon 2007). The aim was to treat all offenders
within a psycho-medical model. From 1919 to the mid-1930s a special mental health
unit was established under Dr Hamblin-Smith at HMP Birmingham. Importantly
Hamblin-Smith (1934, cited in Seddon 2007) came to the conclusion that prisons
could not be an effective means of delivering psychological treatments because the
punitive ethos and the deliberate structural pains of confinement were anti-
therapeutic. HMP Holloway also devised strategies of intensive observation and
supervision of women prisoners suspected to have mental health problems in the
1920s. Indeed all medical officers were now required to have 'practical knowledge of
insanity', although HMP Parkhurst remained the main depository for 'mentally weak'
prisoners.

Medical surveillance and classification continued to have institutional utility, notably whether prisoners were fit enough to withstand the demands of prison discipline
(Seddon 2007). This 'grey area' facilitated the creation of a new category of offender:
prisoners who were neither 'mad' enough to be sent to a specialist institution but were
not healthy enough to be considered suitable for the normal regimes. These prisoners
became known as the 'non-sane non-insane' (Norwood East 1949 cited in Gunn et al.
1978: 18).[6] The ascendancy of the psycho-medical model in the post war period is
also illustrated in the Home Office publication (1959) *Penal Practice in a Changing
Society* which stated that psychiatry and psychologists were to help prisoners to
'change their general attitudes' and 'adjust themselves to prison life' (cited in Gunn et
al. 1978: 30).[7]

The consolidation of the prison as a place of rehabilitation from the early twentieth century must also be contextualized within a dramatic decline in state asylum
populations and an equally dramatic rise in prison populations. For some commentators this apparent process of 'transcarceration' provides evidence of an increasing
reliance upon the prison as the institutional means of dealing with mental health
problems (Bartlett and Sandland 2008).[8] While there is no 'simple hydraulic relationship' (Hudson 1993: 120) changes in the site of confinement can be linked with a
tilt in emphasis in the ideologies underscoring mechanisms of social control. In a time
of reduced emphasis on welfare, people with mental health problems are seen first

and foremost as lawbreakers rather than people in need (Erickson and Erickson 2008).

When understood in social and historical context it is apparent that the presence of large numbers of people with mental health problems in prisons is not an aberration but an essential part of the confinement project (Seddon 2007). Their constant presence in prison indicates that imprisonment and the asylum share the same historical mission: to identify, classify, contain or transform the unproductive, distasteful and unwanted elements of society (Scull 1993; Harcourt 2006; Seddon 2007). Confinement and the control of mental health problems in capitalist societies are intimately tied. Indeed the 'presence of madmen among prisoners is not the scandalous limit of confinement, but its truth; not abuse but essence' (Foucault 1967: 214).

Contemporary penal policy

By the 1970s the 'rehabilitative ideal' reached at its lowest ebb and was superseded by a more pragmatic approach rooted in humane containment (Scott 2007a). The most influential review of the imprisonment of 'mentally abnormal' offenders following this change in orientation was the Butler Report (1975). In contrast to the optimism of the previous decade, Lord Butler (1975) acknowledged the limitations of healthcare in a penal setting and called for diversion or transfer at the earliest possible opportunity, especially when the risks to the general public were perceived as limited. Recognition that penal custody was not a healing environment, coupled with a commitment to an explicit policy of diversion, was further endorsed by penal administrators in the 1980s. As the decade progressed, however, it became increasingly evident that existing policies were not very effective and on 3 September 1990 the Home Office (1990: para 2) published a new directive stating that 'wherever possible, mentally disordered persons should receive care and treatment from the health and social services'. The Woolf Report (1991) also placed emphasis on the diversion and transfer of prisoners while the government response to that report, *Custody, Care and Justice*, categorically maintained that offenders with 'serious mental disturbances'

> should be diverted to the health or social services when they first come into contact with the criminal justice system. Where it is unavoidable that those requiring in-patient treatment are committed to prison, then they should be transferred to suitable health service facilities as soon as possible.
>
> (Home Office 1991, para 9.9)

The following year the Reed Report (1992) on 'mentally disordered offenders' stated that such lawbreakers should receive care and treatment from health and social services rather than be placed in custody, but by the mid-1990s the winds of penal change had blown again. Interest shifted back towards rehabilitation in a healthy penal environment. One of the key indicators of this was the increased pressure to change prison healthcare delivery.[9] In 1992, the Prison Medical Service changed its name to the Health Care Service for Prisoners and the consultation document, *Patient or Prisoner?*, published by HMCIP in 1996 generated enormous interest when it called for an end to the parallel systems of the prison and national health services.[10]

Although the 1999 report *The Future Organization of Prison Health Care* (HM Prison Service & NHS Executive 1999) ultimately rejected the HMCIP recommendations, it did propose that the NHS become responsible for mental health support.

Changing the Outlook (DoH/HM Prison Service/the National Assembly for Wales 2002), published in December 2001, is the most important recent policy document on mental health problems in prison. This report stated that there are 'too many prisoners in too many prisons who, despite the best efforts of committed prison health care and NHS staff, receive no treatment, or inappropriate treatment for their mental illness' (Ibid: 5). Outlining plans for 300 new mental healthcare professionals, and new care plans for prisoners on release, *Changing the Outlook* was steeped in the language of managerialism, talking of consumers, choice and the importance of 'user involvement'. Personal autonomy was advocated as a means to 'prepare prisoners for the resumption of individual responsibility on release (for example, being able to choose meals)' (Ibid: 16), presumably chosen from a preset Prison Service menu. The renewed emphasis on improved healthcare was intimately tied to the claim that the prison place could provide an opportunity to reduce the risk of reoffending.

> This approach not only benefits individual prisoners, who will receive more effective mental health services, but can also have wider benefits for society in general . . . Untreated mental disorder can be the underlying cause of a significant proportion of offending behaviour, as well as contributing to the social exclusion that is a feature of so many offenders' lives. If we can offer proper, effective treatment while offenders are in prison, we can contribute towards the Government's wider goals of reducing crime and re-offending rates as well as playing a part in tackling social exclusion.[11]
>
> (Ibid: 10)

One of the key aims of *Changing the Outlook* was to introduce Mental Health In-Reach Teams (MHIRT) into prisons. The first teams were operational from July 2001 and by 2008 there were over 360 mental health in-reach workers providing services to people with mental health problems in 102 prisons, dealing with more than 4700 prisoners (Mills 2008). The average caseload for each MHIRT practitioner is 44 clients, which is much higher than the recommended size for a community based worker, which is 10–12 clients (Durcan 2008: 40). MHIRTs are also shackled by prison security, the inherent harms of prison life and the contradictory ideologies of punishment and care. It is estimated for example that there is a 30–35 per cent non-attendance of in-reach appointments, with security and daily routine largely responsible (Durcan and Knowles 2006). In a recent survey by HMCIP (2007: 11) only 19 per cent of the 84 MHIRTs surveyed thought they met the needs of prisoners. The boundaries between primary and secondary mental healthcare are not clear cut and in-reach services appear to concentrate largely on those who are considered a problem to the prison authorities (Durcan and Knowles 2006). MHIRT were initially established to serve people with severe mental illness (SMIs) but teams no longer focus on such people because they are swamped by other cases. Indeed the vast majority of prisoners with SMI are not even identified, with less than a quarter of prisoners with SMI assessed by MHIRTs and only 14 per cent currently on in-reach caseloads (Bradley 2009). The HMCIP (2007) is also concerned at the low level of engagement by MHIRTs for adult BME and foreign national prisoners (for additional information see Box 2.1).

Box 2.1 Evaluations of mental health in-reach team services

Prevalence of disorders
Psychosis (22%)
Major depression (20%)

60% of prisoners on in-reach caseloads did not have a diagnosis of current SMI.
Of the 60% of in-reach clients who had no diagnosis of SMI:

> 41% had personality disorder
> 34% had minor mental illness
> 42% did not currently have either a minor mental illness or personality disorder
> 70% had substance misuse problems
> 62% had a history of prior contact with community mental health services
> 76% had a history of previous contact with mental health services in prison

Delivery of services

Medication	76%
Regular appointment with a mental health professional	58%
Out of cell activity	5%
Therapeutic community	5%
Occupational therapy groups	5%

Source: Shaw et al. (2008, cited in Bradley 2009: 103–4); HMCIP (2007: 43)

While there is evidence that many prisoners feel that mental healthcare professionals do listen to them (Gray et al. 2007), this experience is not universal (HMCIP 2007). Prisoners in the healthcare centre sometimes spend only 3.5 hours a day unlocked rather than the recommended 12 hours a day (Reed and Lyne 2000). Prisoners have also raised concerns that not all staff understand their problems and that they do not have much time with highly trained medical staff (Gray et al. 2007).

> Some staff are OK and are doing their jobs worth 100 per cent, others dismiss anxiety and depression and forms of bullying. Seek help and the situation has to escalate where you have to become a discipline problem, thus the situation can't be resolved as the behaviour shown is then concentrated and not the cause behind it!
>
> (prisoner, cited in HMCIP 2007: 33)

Because prisoners with mild symptoms are often dumped together with much more problematic cases the result is that many prisoners with complex needs are given little or no support (Durcan and Knowles 2006). Consequently there is too much reliance on pharmacological treatments and a lack of access to 'talking therapies' (Sainsbury Centre for Mental Health 2007: 6).

> When I first got sentenced I was really fucked up and mad, I was thinking about killing myself, but they didn't want to know anything about that, they didn't care. I've been put on medication now. Every time I keep putting an application in to see the psychiatrist they increase my dose. I'm like 'No I want to talk' but it's 'Is anything wrong with your medication?' that's all they want to talk about.
>
> (prisoner cited in Farrant 2001: 10)

Legitimacy

Commitment to the 'making punishment work' agenda from the 1990s has seen emphasis placed on improving the management of prison healthcare provision rather than on the goals of diversion and transfer. This focus on reducing offending should be understood through the lens of risk, public protection and the responsibilization of prisoners with mental health problems (Scott 2007a, 2007b). Psycho-medical powers within the institution have had a renaissance, especially as a means of controlling recalcitrant prisoners (Sim 1990). Yet prisons will never be able to provide the same level of care as a hospital and the quest for equivalence remains only a forlorn hope. Indeed the above evidence leads us to question whether we should punish people with mental health problems at all. We believe that policy makers should grasp the nettle and start to initiate moves towards *decarceration*.

A legitimate means of dealing with lawbreakers with mental health problems requires responding to their problematic behaviour without an automatic reliance upon the penal law; a commitment to listening to the wrongdoer and the democratic participation of all parties in a given conflict when deciding the best means of redress (de Haan 1990). It must be acknowledged that psycho-medical treatments can lead to an increase in harm and that people with mental health problems require detailed information about treatment options and help in developing skills, rather than being simply 'drugged up' or left in the hands of psychiatric 'experts' (Laurance 2003). This requires consultative interventions rooted in respect, support and patience (MIND 2007). On the ground there needs to be active engagement with service users; the development of services people actually want to use; recognition of legal rights; and real support around housing, jobs and other initiatives aimed at ending social exclusion.

There are crises in mental health and many people with such problems cope most of the time. Mental health problems are not only *real problems*, but are also social constructions and how the label is applied reflects prevailing social contexts. This means understanding the private troubles of prisoners within wider structural problems, such as poverty, racism and patriarchies. If we are to take the mental health problems of lawbreakers seriously we need to deploy social policies that emphasize social justice and human rights. In truth, state confinement is a major obstacle to the wellbeing of those confined and largely increases mental health problems. Prisons 'are not equipped to provide anything more than "first-aid" care for individuals suffering from severe mental illness' (Gunn et al. 1991: 98).

Imprisonment damages health. Ultimately what are needed are creative solutions that look beyond the confinement project.

Further reading

Bartlett, P. and Sandland, R. (2008) *Mental Health Law: Policy and Practice*. Oxford: Oxford University Press.

Coppock, V. and Hopton, J. (2000) *Critical Perspectives on Mental Health*. London: Routledge.

Laing, J. (1999) *Care or Custody? Mentally Disordered Offenders in the Criminal Justice System*. Oxford: Oxford University Press.

Scull, A. (1993) *The Most Solitary of Afflictions: Madness and Society in Britain, 1700–1900*. London: Yale University Press.

Seddon, T. (2007) *Punishment and Madness: Governing Prisoners with Mental Health Problems*. London: Routledge-Cavendish.

Sim, J. (1990) *Medical Power in Prisons: The Prison Medical Service in England 1774–1989*. Milton Keynes: Open University Press.

Students will find journals such as the *British Journal of Psychiatry, Critical Public Health* and the *International Journal of Law and Psychiatry* useful for up-to-date discussions of key issues. We would also recommend the websites of pressure groups such as Mentality, Mental Health Alliance and Mind alongside those of official bodies such as the Department of Health and Ministry of Justice.

3

Women in prison

Despite the popularity of mainstream television programmes such as *Bad Girls* and *Prisoner Cell Block H* there remains little accurate public knowledge or debate about what happens inside women's prisons, except perhaps for sensationalist accounts of the containment of notorious female prisoners such as the late Myra Hindley or Rosemary West. Although women in prison have appeared in the literature for hundreds of years (Fry 1827; Lombroso and Ferrero 1895; Ward and Kassebaum 1965; Giallombardo 1966) it is only since the 1980s that there has been a sustained and concentrated body of work which has challenged the use and practice of women's imprisonment in the United Kingdom. This literature developed from pioneering feminist research on women, 'crime' and criminology begun by Heidensohn (1968) and Smart (1976) and was augmented by others in the early to mid-1980s (Carlen 1983; Carlen et al. 1985; Dobash et al. 1986: Morris 1987). The focus of this later critical work has been to raise the visibility of women in custody and explore the nature and extent of the inherent harms women face in the prison place.

The deployment of the custodial sanction against women lawbreakers involves situating them within a system conceived by, intended for and dominated by men. Prison is a masculinist penalty and consequently women prisoners present penal authorities with a multiplicity of needs which differs from those of the male populations they were originally intended to contain. It is well documented that women experience the structured pains of imprisonment differently from men, with many penologists concluding that incarceration is much harsher for women than their male counterparts (Carlen 1983). Part of the explanation for this increased infliction of pain derives from the different social expectations and family demands on women, and also that the women lawbreakers that the criminal courts are most likely to imprison have frequently experienced high levels of social exclusion, victimization and abuse.[1] Women in prison are often *women with vulnerabilities* and both official and feminist studies have identified high rates of self-harm, self-inflicted deaths and mental health problems (Carlen and Worrall 2004; Corston 2007a, 2007b). Since the 1980s reports have surfaced of women gouging out eyes, cutting their breasts and repeatedly tying ligatures around their necks (Benn and Tchaikovsky 1987; Scraton 2007) and some young women 'cut up' as a way of coping with the pains of imprisonment, even though self-harm is often viewed and reacted to negatively by prison staff and other prisoners (Hutson and Myers 2006).[2]

Although some women prisoners undoubtedly do have mental health problems (which may or may not have some link to acts of self-harm or self-inflicted deaths), a key concern during the 1980s and 1990s was the tendency in official policy towards medicalizing and psychiatrizing women's behaviour (Sim 1990). Concerns were also aired during this period about levels of psychotropic drug administration and the methods and means by which women were labelled as in need of psychiatric help where men would not have been (Padel and Stevenson 1988). The problem of 'adding women in' to a male-focused system remains a matter of considerable concern, with contemporary critics highlighting problems such as the masculinist foundations and limited applicability of prison based cognitive behavioural therapies (Kendall 2002; Batchelor 2005).

Women offenders are usually held further away from home than men, which can make it difficult for women to maintain contact with their families. For example, in 2007 the average distance adult women in prison were held from their home address was 55 miles, with around 800 women serving their sentences more than 100 miles from home (Prison Reform Trust 2008). Maintaining contact with their children is a key worry of imprisoned mothers. Consequently for many women prisoners the wasting effects of 'prison time' are not just felt with regard to detriments to the self, but also in terms of how this wasting process may negatively impact on the lives of others, especially partners and dependants.

This chapter provides a critical exploration of the experiences and needs of women in prison. In so doing we utilize an abolitionist feminist perspective to examine the extent of the women's population and day-to-day realities of prison life. It outlines the historical and contemporary dominance of psycho-medical explanations of female offending and its implications for Prison Service policies and concludes with a review of the arguments in favour of selective abolition. Interspersed throughout this chapter are case studies documenting three important aspects of contemporary debates on women in custody.

Thinking critically about women in prison

The social control and punishment of women has often been undertaken without recourse to the penal law. Women who deviate from social rules and norms have time and again been controlled via informal mechanisms of regulation, such as the family or the church, and when women have become subject to more formal social controls there has often been a tension between the priorities of legalism and the psycho-medical interpretive frames. The 'pathological' woman lawbreaker has historically been understood as suffering from an 'illness' and, even if the penal law is invoked, assumptions of mental abnormality do not always disappear. The use of psycho-medical powers, and in recent times the inappropriate reliance on over-generous psychiatric or psychological diagnoses, are inextricably linked with women's prison regimes (Sim 1990). While initially appearing munificent and offering a scientific analysis of the lawbreaker's personal troubles, the application of the psycho-medical gaze has more often than not proved insidious.

> In short, the regimes of women prisoners, though subject to the general plethora of prison rules and security regulations, have been routinely fashioned by a mixture of ideologies of womanhood which portray women criminals as masculine, mad, menopausal and maladjusted to their roles in the family and labour market. Consequently, women in prison have not only been physically secured by all the hardware and disciplinary control paraphernalia of the men's establishments, they have, in addition, been psychologically interpolated (if not always constrained) by the triple disciplines of feminisation, domesticisation and medicalisation.
>
> (Carlen and Worrall 2004: 8)

Hutson and Myers (2006) conclude that the experiences of incarcerated female young offenders have changed little in recent decades, and, like Genders and Player (1987), they found that the idea of girls 'being "mad" rather than "bad" ' still prevails. The view that when women offend they are 'mad, sad or bad' has had profound influences on women's custodial institutions. Women and girls are more likely than boys and men to have their offending explained in biological or psychiatric terms, as a 'cry for help' or as a consequence of biological factors such as hormones, pregnancy, birth or menopause. Women and girls are being medicated, or offered medication, at a high level, when they are not 'sick' but suffering from 'normal' difficulties associated with imprisonment (Hutson and Myers 2006). As a result women[3] prisoners today may be offered anti-depressants and sleeping pills as a response to 'normal' levels of stress in the prison setting. The rationale for this over-prescribing could be ostensibly benevolent, 'as an attempt to alleviate some of the negativity of a prison sentence, and soften the experience with medication' (p. 151), or it may be to compensate for the stress of putting young women into a man's world.

The concept of 'double deviance' is of central importance for any critical understanding of women who are incarcerated (Carlen 1983). When women offend, their offending is reacted to not only as a breach of the criminal law but also as a breach of acceptable female gender roles. Women who break the law are thus not only committing criminal offences but are also offending against socially accepted perceptions of femininity. This is particularly visible in the demonization of women who offend against children, as in the case of Myra Hindley. As a consequence, until her death far more media and public vitriol was directed towards her than her co-defendant, Ian Brady. Such women are 'bad', that is, inherently evil. Alongside this goes the concept of women who offend as 'mad'. Here the assumption is that 'crime' is so 'unnatural' for women that their offending must be a sign of 'mental illnesses'. Both of these approaches stress the individual pathologies of female offenders and draw attention away from the gendered and socio-economic contexts of women's lives.

A more recent development in the application of psycho-medical knowledge has been the deployment of cognitive behavioural therapies (CBT), although CBTs have been criticized for pathologizing women's decision-making and ignoring the social and economic challenges which might prompt a woman to act criminally (Kendall 2002). CBTs render women responsible for their own poor decision-making without recognizing that social and economic factors can limit and circum-scribe women's own actual and perceived choices. For example if women have poor educational attainment and have been victims of emotional, physical, sexual or other forms of abuse, as many women in prison have, then, alongside issues of low self-esteem women may not perceive choices as open to them in the same way as other, more privileged, women. Women's offending is seen as the result of *bad choices*. This 'responsibilization' renders women as solely and individually culpable for their own choices, even in a prison setting where women are not allowed to choose when to get up or when and what to eat (Hannah-Moffat 2001).

It is striking when reading the research carried out with women prisoners (as opposed to 'on' them) how limited 'malestream' penological approaches are. Women prisoners have found their own explanations and understandings disqualified and excluded and it is only since the early 1990s that there has been any awareness of women prisoners' own voices 'breaking the silence' and speaking out. Even now, professionals such as doctors, psychiatrists and psychologists are deemed by policy makers to 'know about' and 'understand' women who offend to a greater extent than women themselves (Sim 1990).

Feminist research has placed women's imprisonment in the context of society as a patriarchal construct and analysed the role of prison in enforcing patriarchal expect-ations about appropriate femininities (see Box 3.1). Women who do not conform to a particular expectation of womanhood, that is of the woman as passive and conformist, can find themselves subjected to the gendered controls of the prison (Carlen 1983; Watterson 1996; Owen 1998; Bosworth 1999; Kruttschnitt and Gartner 2005). Since the early 1980s it has been recognized in the feminist literature that policies pertaining to female prisoners infantilize and look to reinforce dependency. In her classic study *Women's Imprisonment*, Pat Carlen (1983) detailed how prison regimes can under-mine confidence, instil feelings of helplessness and render women passive, although there is evidence that at least some women can and do resist (Bosworth 1999). Carlen

---

Box 3.1 Feminist agenda

Feminist writers on women in prison have emphasized:

1   POWER: women's 'crimes' are 'crimes' of the powerless
2   HARM: women who are in prison generally undertake only minor and petty offences
3   GENDER: women lawbreakers have different social backgrounds and experiences shaped by social constructions of femininity and womanhood
4   JURISPRUDENCE: importance of being womanwise and developing a feminist conception of justice
5   PRAXIS: combining research with campaigning and activism for penal change and/or abolition

Source: Carlen and Worrall (2004)

(1983) highlighted the importance of domesticity, something which still underpins women's imprisonment today, with women being encouraged to display appropriate female characteristics, achievements and interests. At the time she was writing these training programmes focused primarily on perceived 'appropriate' jobs and skills for women, such as sewing and hairdressing. Women were not being equipped with skills which would enable them to 'make it' in the workplace or succeed in running their own business after release. For Carlen (1983) women in custody can be analysed through a series of denials: denial that they are 'real' women; denial that they are adults; and denial that they can be responsible human beings. Alongside this, women's prisons are somehow not seen as 'real' prisons (Carlen 1983).

Carlen (1983) also identified a further ongoing theme, which is that women in prison are under higher levels of surveillance, regulation and control than men (Sim 1990). Women prisoners experience extremely high levels of discipline, being chastised for minor infractions which would not only be tolerated but would be viewed as normal in a men's establishment (Carlen et al. 1985). The evidence indicates that this is still the case. In 2001 women were charged with offences against discipline at a rate of 224 offences per 100 women compared with 160 per 100 men (Butler and Kousoulou 2006). It has always been the view of the Prison Service that women prisoners were more hysterical, potentially volatile and uncontrollable than male prisoners, and thus high levels of disciplinary regulation were required. In contrast Alexandra Mandaraka-Sheppard (1986) argued that women acted aggressively and unpredictably because of the high levels of control: women felt so suppressed by the disciplinary governance of even minor matters, that they 'acted out'. This has also been linked to self-harming, where women act in order to 'feel something'.

Case Study 3.1 Women in prison

The penal pressure group 'Women In Prison' (WIP) was formed by ex-prisoner Chris Tchaikovsky in October 1983. The organization comprises of mainly women prisoners and ex-prisoners. Like other members of the radical penal lobby, WIP has looked to use the contradictory nature of the law to defend the rights of women in prison. Its manifesto in 1983 called for specific reforms of women's prisons and prisons generally. WIP has developed campaigns to challenge the unmediated power of the Capitalist State in prison and demanded penal accountability, the acknowledgement and protection of rights and ultimately the abolition of prisons for women. In a concerted effort to put women onto the penal agenda, WIP has both drawn attention to the plight of women and worked towards concrete improvements in their everyday circumstances. WIP is the only women-centred and women-run organization that provides specialist services to women offenders both in prison and in the community throughout England. They began in London and now have bases in London and Halifax. They provide important services for women offenders and have also worked with academic researchers and the media to raise visibility of the realities of imprisonment for women.

The feminist penological research of the 1980s refocused the debate by viewing women's imprisonment though a gendered lens. Since then, other writers have developed supplementary critiques focusing on difference, considering women imprisoned for differing offences and/or diversity between women. Thus research has emerged on 'Black' and 'Asian' women in prison; mothers in prison; female young offenders; older women; and women as paramilitary prisoners. It is thus, thankfully, no longer possible to use the word 'prisoner' and then simply discuss men (Bosworth 1999; Hannah-Moffat 2001; Wahidin 2004; Corcoran 2006; Codd 2008).

For women who are often already abused and vulnerable, prison perpetuates this and does little to empower women to change their lives. Mary Bosworth (1999), however, documented the strategies used by imprisoned women to reassert agency and to resist the regime, appropriating issues of biological femininity in order to achieve their own ends. For example, during the struggle for better quality toilet paper the women in her study adopted several different arguments for why the designated rough and ineffective paper should be replaced. First, they simply demanded ordinary paper, but this was unsuccessful and in response the women attempted to steal softer paper from the staff toilets. They then attempted a group demonstration by means of blocking the sewerage system but insufficient women agreed to participate. Finally, through arguments based on the suitability of the paper for women with periods or haemorrhoids and formal means such as complaints forms, complaints to personal officers and going to the governor, the women won. Similar arguments about biological issues and feminine hygiene were used to challenge the dominance of starchy food, especially chips, in their diet. Bosworth (1999) also highlights personal appearance as a site of corporeal-focused strategies of resistance. This raises interesting questions as to whether the women were simply situating themselves rigidly within a position of weakness by relying on these ideals of femininity, or whether they were able to influence and shape the meaning of 'femininity' themselves (Bosworth 1999). Where women were mothers too, they utilized this identity to maintain their own self-value.

> The women's positive image of themselves are undermined by institutional constraints which encourage them to exhibit traditional, passive, feminine behaviour at the same time as their identities and responsibilities as mothers, wives, girlfriends and sisters are denied. Women in prison – and in the community – are expected to conform to a particular ideal of feminine behaviour, which is predicated upon a silencing of their desire for autonomy and agency. In order to survive the pains of imprisonment, women must redefine the meaning of femininity and so break through its limitations.
>
> (Bosworth 1999: 6)

Thus the women were not passive victims and rarely endorsed or practised the passive feminine behaviour encouraged by the institution, resisting and challenging the stereotypes which were being forced on them. Identity was under constant negotiation, although of course ultimate power remained vested in the prison.

One of the most significant recent contributions to thinking critically about women's imprisonment is *Punishment in Disguise* (Hannah-Moffat 2001). In this text Kelly Hannah-Moffat (2001) analysed attempts in Canada to implement radical reforms in women's prisons, finding that the feminist language of empowerment, woman-centred corrections and healing were co-opted by the penal apparatus of the Capitalist State to create what she calls 'a feminized technology of penal governance' (p. 189). Despite apparently committing to reform, the security priorities of the prison never really changed. Women themselves were rendered responsible for their own empowerment. The use of imprisonment was never challenged and 'to some extent the feminizing of women's prison regimes legitimates the incarceration of women' (p. 197). The accountability of the Capitalist State was reduced and ultimately removed by the discourses of responsibilization which constructed women prisoners as responsible for their own rehabilitation and reduction in 'riskiness'.

These strategies *denied* the power relationship between the prison and prisoners, the coercive nature of the prison, oppression and the removal of freedom. As Hannah-Moffat (2001: 197) puts it 'regardless of the form and content of a women-centred regime, it is still in many respects about punishment, security and discipline'. Thus the rhetoric of women-centred corrections simply led to a repackaging of punishment incorporating therapeutic discourses and an alleged emphasis on healing and an ethic of care. The darker side of the institutionalization of women's concerns is the unanticipated redefining of women's issues to make them compatible with the existing institutional arrangements of incarceration. Various terms used in the correctional narratives such as empowerment or healing serve to make the activity of punishing less visible and open to scrutiny. Such analysis has clear implications in the United Kingdom, for example as a template to consider the reforms proposed by the recent women-centred Corston Report (2007a).

Feminist qualitative research has involved reflexive working, with researchers and activists coming together with imprisoned women themselves (Carlen et al. 1985; Girshick 1999), challenging invisibility and misrepresentation.[4] Biographical and life history research has been especially illuminating, ranging from Carlen's work (Carlen et al. 1985) to the autobiographical accounts of the not-so-usual prison experiences of middle-class, older, white women as exemplified in the Peckham (1985) and Wyner (2003) biographies. This research has stressed that women's prisons are real prisons and are a world away from popular stereotypes.

Case Study 3.2 Women's experiences of prison in their own words

Ruth Wyner (2003: 88) talking about visits and despair in prison:

'I am desperate to see them and ready way before time. At 1.45 pm we get called out from behind our spurs . . . We go in one by one. More waiting. I get my usual feeling of rising anxiety as we sit patiently at our tables, straining to look through the windows to see if our visitors are there. They get frisked too and my special three arrive at last. I stand up to exchange huge hugs with them, which we are allowed to do at the start and the end of the visit. I make my only physical contact of the week last as long as I can.'

'We all had to cope with the waves of sadness that came upon us, often when we least expected it. I imagined that there was a spirit of despair inhabiting the prison and that it moved indiscriminately from inmate to inmate, so you never knew where it was going to descend next. When it was my turn I could feel it knitting my brows, churning my stomach, pulling every part of my body into itself. All I could do was endure, and await its departure. I fought it in the gym and worked furiously in the gardens, but this demon spirit made its own choices about when to move on' (p. 148).

Audrey Peckham (1985: 128) discussing night-time while on remand:

'Most of us slept badly. Everybody in the place had grief and worry to contend with, the innocent and guilty alike. Everybody had a trial to prepare for. Many women had families to worry about. By day, you could sometimes forget what had happened, but with the night came the thinking and the suffering. Whatever our backgrounds, whatever we were charged with, we were there because something had gone seriously wrong with our lives, and guilt about the past and fear of the future haunted us all.'

Josie O'Dwyer (In Carlen et al. 1985: 164) commenting on her experiences of psychiatry:

'No one asks you about the crime. No one asks you about prison. They always asked me about my early life but not about what had happened to me in those institutions, since the age of fourteen. And, personally, I think it was those institutions which were responsible for what happened from then on. I never knew anything *except* institutions. No one took me out and said, "Look, this is the real world, let's go slowly, let's help you." No one mentioned any kind of social problem. It was just me. According to psychiatrists I was either crazy or bad. It was always "What's wrong with Josie?" Not, "What's wrong with prison?" '

Following on, there has been illuminating work on women's experiences after prison, such as that by Mary Eaton (1993), which has explored the different priorities and needs of women as they leave prison. Challenging the assumption that, as for male prisoners, employment is a core goal, feminists have argued instead that when women leave prison they are more concerned with finding stable accommodation and maintaining or rebuilding relationships, especially with their children. A further problem identified by feminists is that the stereotype of the 'good girl' who will help male ex-offenders 'go straight' does not have a direct equivalent (Leverentz 2006). There are more male ex-prisoners than female ex-prisoners in society generally, and it has been argued that stereotypes of appropriate female behaviour make it undesirable for men to form relationships with women who have been imprisoned: they are less attractive as partners because of their criminality. This means that the 'pool' of men available to female ex-prisoners may involve a high proportion of men who have a history of criminality and/or imprisonment.

Problematizing the data about women in prison

There are currently 14 women's prisons in England and none in Wales, which means that all Welsh women prisoners are held outside their home country. Many women's prisons began life as men's prisons or were built for completely different purposes (Carlen and Worrall 2004). Due to the pressure of numbers and overcrowding in men's prisons, a number of women's establishments, such as Bullwood Hall in Essex, have recently been re-rolled to take men instead of women. Most women's prisons are not overcrowded although recent performance statistics show that both New Hall and Styal are (Prison Service 2009).[5]

The number of women held in prison in England and Wales is now at the highest level since the mid-nineteenth century (New Economics Foundation 2008). The female prison population in England has risen sharply since 2000, having grown more than twice as fast as that of men. Since 1991 the number of women in prison in England and Wales has nearly trebled and women now make up 6 per cent of the total prison population. Figures from the Prison Reform Trust (2009), however, indicate that there were 236 fewer women prisoners in June 2009 than the previous year, but it remains to be seen whether this represents the beginning of a bigger fall in the female prison population, a settling down of the numbers at this level, or a statistical anomaly which will in the future be followed by yet more rises. At the time of writing (16 October 2009) there were 4279 women in prison. The increase up until 2008–9, as research has demonstrated, does not reflect a shift towards women committing more serious offences, but reflects a decline in usage of non-custodial penalties and fines for women by magistrates and an associated rise in the use of short custodial sentences. In 1996 10 per cent of women convicted of an indictable offence were sent to prison: by 2006 15 per cent were.

Over a third of all adult women in prison have no previous convictions, which is more than double the number of men (Ministry of Justice 2008a). There has also been a near 80 per cent increase between 1996 and 2006 in the number of women in custody on remand. Most women sentenced to imprisonment are sentenced for non-violent offences, with the largest group being sentenced for drug offences. Theft and handling offences and violence against the person also account for a high proportion of offences. Women are often sentenced to short sentences with 63 per cent of those sentenced to custodial sentences in 2006 being given six months or less. Statistics are, however, limited when, for example, talking about women's paths into 'crime' and custody, and whether or not their offending was committed alone or in conjunction with partners, other family members and friends (see Figure 3.1). Anecdotally it is common to find women 'fencing' stolen goods for their burgling family members, or women helping their partners in selling drugs. This information, however, is not readily available.

Women prisoners are five times more likely to have mental health problems than women in the general population (Plugge et al. 2006). Seventy-five per cent had taken an illegal drug in the six months before prison and 58 per cent of women prisoners had used illegal drugs daily during that period. Thirty-seven per cent have attempted 'suicide' at some point in their lives (Corston 2007a). Over half have experienced domestic violence and a third sexual abuse (Social Exclusion Unit 2002). They are,

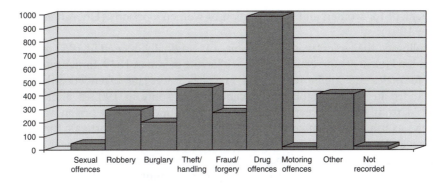

Figure 3.1 Women offender profiles 2008

Source: Offender management caseload statistics (2008e)

on the whole, poor, vulnerable and with a high likelihood of having low educational attainment, nearly 40 per cent having left school before 16 and 10 per cent aged 13 or younger (Social Exclusion Unit 2002). Around 65 per cent are mothers of children under the age of 16, nearly half being single parents. Around a quarter spent time in local authority care during childhood. The women's prison population, therefore, is characterized by experiences of social exclusion, abuse, mental health difficulties and substance use or dependency. Around 30 per cent are members of BME groups.

Historical context

Historically, women rule-breakers have been dealt with differently to men, through both formal and, more commonly, informal patriarchal social controls. Where women stepped out of line, for example, by being bossy or argumentative towards men, they could find themselves punished. Institutions for the confinement of women began as religious institutions and held not only pious women but women who were there against their will. The most apparent precursors of today's female prisons were the Magdalen penitentiaries or asylums for 'fallen' women, i.e. prostitutes, or those thought or assumed to be prostitutes or morally in need of reform. Although the Irish versions of these institutions are perhaps most famous, some of which operated up until the 1990s, there were many in England and Wales too (Finnegan 2004). Under a mantle of benevolence, women who were deemed 'fallen' would be rehabilitated, spiritually and morally, and trained in domestic tasks so they could then find 'respectable' posts as servants. Research, however, has shown that many of these institutions were brutal in their surveillance and control of women, and the women resident in these institutions suffered profound social stigma (Finnegan 2004). In some, women had their hair cropped, were physically and sexually humiliated and made to work long hours in the laundries. Indeed, the dehumanization of these 'penitents' sometimes led to these women being renamed, rendering the removal of their identity and agency complete. The history of these institutions overlapped with the emergence of other institutions of confinement for women and the evolution of women's prisons (Dobash et al. 1986; Zedner 1991).

Holloway, the largest women's prison, was originally opened in 1852 as the City of London House of Correction, work on it having begun in 1849. Initially it had three wings for males and one for females and juveniles. It was later extended and a hospital wing added in 1883–4. Holloway became women-only in 1902–3 after Newgate closed.[6] During the early years of the twentieth century Holloway prison was often in the news as it held women convicted of offences linked to the struggle for women's suffrage, and it was in Holloway that a number of women went on hunger strike and were subsequently force fed. Indeed, the repeated imprisonment of many female suffragists between 1905 and 1914 meant that a number of educated, influential women gained direct personal experience of prison, and they gave huge amounts of publicity to controversial issues, especially humiliating and degrading practices such as the requirement that women have all their hair cut off, and relentlessly challenged the Home Office over the treatment of women in prison (Zedner 1991).

It is tempting to laud nineteenth-century reformers such as Elizabeth Fry or the less well-known Sarah Martin for their humanitarian attempts to improve conditions for women, but it is important to remember that the work of these reformers was heavily linked towards not only 'reforming' institutions but also 're-forming' women to fit into a particular conception of femininity.[7] As Prochaska (1980: 145) puts it, 'within this framework of cleanliness, godliness and needlework the visiting scheme sought to prepare prisoners for a return to society'.

Elizabeth Fry and John Howard before her were keen to separate men from women, which was achieved by the middle of the nineteenth century. It is enticing to view the reforms initiated by Fry, and propounded in texts such as her *Observations* (Fry 1827), that women were not subject to the same disciplinary and surveillance techniques as men, that they were somehow treated more 'gently'. As Carlen and Worrall (2004: 8) point out, however, 'her later blueprints for women's prison regimes prescribed several of the disciplinary techniques which became hallmarks of the mid to late-twentieth century institutions'.

Thus women became subject to constant surveillance, erasure of individuality and strict discipline. As Dobash et al. (1986: 61) remark, patriarchal conceptions 'played a crucial role from the beginning'. Women's work was based on assumptions about domesticity and the 'nature' of women and women were always more closely regulated than men. Although by 1850 women and men were not sharing the same accommodation, regimes for women in the nineteenth century differed little from those for men, except women were not whipped and sometimes were allowed slightly longer periods of association. The concept of women as breaching both the codes of criminal law and also societal expectations about gender – that they were not simply offending people but offending *women* – however, echoes in today's prison standards for women, where prisons are being encouraged to make reception areas more pleasant by including pot plants and women are encouraged to engage in craft activities such as cross-stitch.

Holloway was rebuilt on the same site during the 1970s and early 1980s, a major undertaking in itself, and Paul Rock, in his account of the redevelopment, writes that its physical design 'would bear the impress of a new penology':

Externally the new institution was to be a prison that would not look like a prison. It was instead to be a 'secure hospital' that might eventually be surrendered to the Health Service when the supply of delinquent women dwindled altogether. The new Holloway was to be slipped unobtrusively into its urban setting, a place to which the local community might come, an out-patients clinic to which former prisoners and women on bail might be referred.

(Rock 1996: 10)

There were so many delays that during its building the entire landscape of penal policy shifted and the possibility of the abolition of women's imprisonment, combined with the concept of prison as a therapeutic community, no longer seemed appropriate, practical or politically attractive. Consequently it never fulfilled its original purpose. That said, whether or not it would have been desirable to maintain it as a medicalized environment is a moot point, as it would simply have shifted from one form of discipline and governance of 'deviant' women, i.e. that of the prison, to the psychiatrized and medicalized techniques of the hospital. As women are more likely to have their offending linked to pathological, individualized explanations and psycho-medical responses, this would simply have changed the manifestation whilst retaining the same emphasis on controlling women. The rebuilding of Holloway with this goal 'brought to the fore an ideological strand of discourse that had been present in women's imprisonment since the birth of psychiatry' (Medlicott 2007: 260).

Within a year of the opening of the rebuilt Holloway there was a highly critical inspection report (Home Office 1985) which highlighted the overcrowding, the boredom and frustration of women being locked up for all but an hour per day; the unsanitary and vermin-infested conditions and the particular hardships and suffering of women held in C1 wing, which was for women experiencing mental health and behavioural problems. The women held there were harming themselves at a high level and there were many incidents of vandalism, flooding and violence. In the aftermath of this report the new governor, Colin Allen, tried to introduce a regime involving more time out of cells, more purposeful activity and more public scrutiny (Medlicott 2007). His efforts, however, were not supported by the Prison Officer's Association. Although the conditions in Holloway and, to a lesser extent, some of the other women's prisons caused occasional public controversies, often through the efforts of campaigning groups such as WIP, from then until 1995 the prison response to women, especially in Holloway, continued to be inadequate and frequently harmful. It was only in 1995 that the matter became one of pressing concern, when the Chief Inspector of Prisons carried out an unannounced inspection:

It was overcrowded and filthy dirty, its staff overstretched and demoralized and the vast majority of its prisoners locked up in their cells all day, doing nothing. There were wholly inadequate arrangements for caring for the large numbers of mentally disordered women. Rates of self-harm were alarmingly high. In the Mother and Baby Unit new mothers asked me whether it was right that they had been chained to prison officers while they were in labour. There was no induction programme, no sentence planning and no preparation for release. What I found particularly concerning was that there was no one in Prison Service Headquarters responsible for women in prison, merely a civil servant who wrote policy. The Prison Service's attitude was exemplified by the fact that injuries to women were recorded on a diagram of a man's body.

(Ramsbotham 2002: ix)

This led into the period when, as Baroness Corston remarked, more has been written about women and less has been done than with any other issue (Medlicott 2007).

Contemporary penal policy

Following David Ramsbotham's highly-publicized withdrawal from Holloway in 1995 standards of cleanliness and the environment appear to have improved. Colin Allen made significant changes in Holloway leading to women being out of their cells for longer. The focus of the debate has shifted from the near-invisibility of women in discussions of prisons in the 1980s and the failure to comprehend their particular needs and experiences, to additionally incorporate concern about sheer numbers. Several reports have highlighted the needs of women prisoners and their experiences of prison, the most significant recent report being that of Baroness Corston, which published its final report in 2007. The work of Baroness Corston followed other reports such as that by the Fawcett Society led by Vera Baird (2004). Most of the recent policy developments in relation to women's imprisonment have been prompted by the Corston report (2007a).

Case Study 3.3 The Corston Report

In March 2006 Baroness Jean Corston was commissioned by the Home Secretary, to carry out 'a review of women with particular vulnerabilities in the criminal justice system of England and Wales' (Corston 2007a), against a background of concern about the number of self-inflicted deaths in women's prisons in the previous two years. The report was published in March 2007. It contained 43 recommendations and included a detailed blueprint 'for a distinct, radically different, visibly led, strategic, proportionate, holistic, woman-centred approach' (Corston 2007a: 79). At the core of this blueprint were the creation of an Inter-Departmental Ministerial Group for women who offend or who are at risk of offending; creation of a Commission for women who offend or who are at risk of offending; the extension of a network of women's community centres, some with residential provision and the development of smaller local units to (over time) replace prisons. The report contains a detailed vision of the structure, aims, purposes and relationship between the ministerial group and the commission. The women's centres would provide a real alternative to custody, supervise community sentences and support women offenders and women at risk of offending. They could also offer other forms of support such as drop in facilities. The emphasis here was on strong relationships between these centres and health social care and criminal justice agencies encouraging women to access early support and intervention.

Residential women's centres could also be established which could provide safe and suitable accommodation for women and their children in addition to the kinds of support services already described. They could also be used for women on bail and for those leaving prison with no suitable accommodation, and would serve women at risk of being, for example, remanded into custody or for those who would otherwise be given short prison sentences of less than twelve months, or for those who may receive longer sentences but who are not dangerous or at risk of offending. These centres would be staffed by women, be accessible, offer support and adopt a holistic approach to a woman's well-being including trained staff and volunteers with an awareness of gender issues, abuse and mental health. Corston also recommended small custodial units to replace women's prisons. These should be easily accessible for visitors and eventually should be removed from Prison Service control and run under the direction of the proposed Commission for women who offend or who are at risk of offending. These should house 20–30 women and be targeted at those who have been sentenced to two years' custody or more.

The Corston Report is not without its critics. The suggested smaller prisons are *still prisons* perpetuating the structured pains of confinement. The proliferation of smaller and localized centres of confinement may facilitate the 'punitive city' and what Foucault (1977) described as the 'carceral continuum'. Despite all the holistic woman-centred rhetoric such a strategy could still be mutated into the responsibilization of women (and their siblings) rather than lead to their empowerment. Finally, the review is detached from wider innovation around the actualization of social justice.

Despite its limitations, the Corston Report (2007a) was distinctive in its holistic approach and emphasis on the need for a cross-government response to address women offenders' multiple and complex needs. The government agreed with most of the recommendations and committed to take many of them forward. Thus the government committed by June 2008 to establish an Inter-Ministerial Group; appoint a Ministerial Champion for Women and Criminal Justice; set up a new cross-departmental Criminal Justice Women's Unit; produce a more detailed Delivery Plan for taking forward the commitments; publish and begin implementation of the NOMS Equality and Diversity Action Plan (to implement the Gender Equality Duty); to publish the Ministry of Justice Gender Equality Scheme and to set up a project to review generic women's centre provision and identify how to build on existing services, and another project to review the women's prison estate and the merits of smaller units for women, and to introduce gender specific standards for women in prison. In June 2008 the Ministry of Justice published its progress report on *Delivering the Government Response to the Corston Report* (Ministry of Justice 2008f) and there was a later written update early in 2009.

Some progress has been made towards some of these objectives. The *National Service Framework for Women* sets measurable strategic outcomes. The government has developed community provision, recognizing pro-active steps are needed to reduce the number of women going into custody. Thus £40 million in additional funding was given to NOMS for promoting effective community sentences. The *Offender Management Guide to Working with Women Offenders* has also been published (National Offender Management Service 2008). Moves are also being made to consider provision for a women's centre combining residential and day care somewhere in the South West.

The government response, however, has been criticized. In her opening speech in the House of Lords debate on which reforms were likely to be in place by the end of 2009 (House of Lords 2009), Baroness Howe of Idlicote quoted and approved the view of the Howard League for Penal Reform that 'the visionary, radical proposals at the heart of the Corston review have either been sidelined or completely abandoned'. After similar questions and queries raised by other members of the House, Lord Bach, the Government Whip, responded and identified a number of significant developments. He pointed out that the government view is that 'women should not end up in prison unless it is absolutely necessary' and that the government is committed to providing additional resources to divert women from custody. Linked to this are additional services in the community for women offenders and women at risk of offending. The second principle he identifies in the government response is that 'the services we provide to women prisoners should reflect the nature and characteristics of that group and meet their gender-specific needs'. He pointed out that new arrangements for searching women have been introduced so that in the absence of specific intelligence or suspicion that something has been concealed women do not routinely have to remove their underwear. Full search arrangements have been amended in order to reduce the frequency of full searches. He then briefly mentions 'pathways to resettlement'; the new offender health strategy; improved specific staff training and identifies new units at several prisons including an independent living unit outside the main prison at Morton Hall.

Many of the government's responses appear positive although the most radical and visionary recommendation, that of small custodial units, has not been taken forward. The government project Working Group concluded that the principles underlying the concept of small custodial units should be accepted and, as far as possible, taken into account when developing the women's prison estate (Ministry of Justice 2008f). The model of small custodial units, however, was not accepted as the best way of embedding the principles because of weaknesses identified by the Working Group. The Working Group argued that it would be difficult to deliver the full range of services, including kitchens, education, drug treatment, training and offending behaviour programmes on such a small scale as recommended in the report. They concluded that a model of a range of smaller units *within* existing women's prisons should be developed to provide a more supportive environment for vulnerable women.[8]

The Working Group argued that small custodial units would be of most benefit to lower-risk, short-sentences women, but these are the women whom Corston (2007a) proposed should be dealt with in the community. They argued that more serious offenders would have a different set of needs and requirements which may not be served by small custodial units. Curiously, the Group also suggested that for such women the closeness to home issue was not so pressing. Finally, they concluded that the need to reconfigure the women's estate, including a range of approaches for family visits, be considered further in the light of Corston's recommendations. The new wing at HMP Bronzefield, to be completed in 2009, was suggested as an opportunity to implement and test a new approach to the physical environment and regimes for women. There are also pilots at HMP Downview and HMP Askham Grange which provide accommodation next to the prison for women to spend time with their children.

The Working Group (Ministry of Justice 2008f: 11) referred to 'research from Canada' which showed that training of staff was more important than the physical environment. It is clear, however, that Corston's most fundamental recommendation has been rejected. In addition, the problems of smaller units on the same site as larger units are challenging. For example if the smaller units have a different regime and ethos, and all-female, women-centred staff, then arguably this means that the staff would have to be dedicated to that unit. Otherwise if staff must move between the Unit and the general women's prison around it, the differences between regimes and attitudes of staff may mean that the Unit simply becomes a miniature version of the bigger prison surrounding it.

The Dóchas centre in Dublin offers a new vision of women's imprisonment, endorsed by Baroness Corston in her report. The Dóchas centre (named after the Irish word for 'hope') aimed to create a different environment for women and to operate in a women-centred way.[9] The difficulty with this initiative is that its women-centred ethos could be manipulated to work against the interests of women (Hannah-Moffat 2001). Either way this approach has been rejected by the British government. By refusing to implement the radical suggestions of Corston (2007a) women's specific needs in the penal setting have yet again been ignored.

The Prison Service's latest set of standards specifically for women's prisons have been implemented from April 2009 (*Prison Service Order No. 4800*). Some of these reflect current good practice in male prisons, such as 'first night' provision and support for buddy and listener schemes. Some of the old criticisms, however, about the utilization of gender in imprisoning women still echo. For example, knitting and cross-stitch are commended as in-cell activities for women. That is not to say that some women do not want to knit nor do cross-stitch but these seem almost archaically gendered.[10]

Legitimacy

The situation in which we now find ourselves is one of a female prison population which has undergone massive expansion, increased prevalence of self-inflicted deaths and self-harm, and a growing realization that as a society we need to question both the imprisonment of women and the prison environment as a whole. The Corston Report (2007a) reiterated the unsuitability of prison for women and thus it would be timely to challenge the prison building programme and seek selective abolition (Carlen 1990). Many women offenders are not dangerous, and it is inappropriate to continue to imprison them within a penal model which has evolved for men, and which, indeed, does not seem to work for men either. We need to consider if and how it is possible to assess and implement equality of impact for men and women and to create a just and caring response to women who break the law.

It is disappointing that as yet no UK government has grasped the nettle of truly challenging women's imprisonment.[11] The New Economics Foundation (2008) contend that for every £1 invested in support-focused alternatives to prison for women, £14 worth of social value is created over a ten-year period. Thus there are sound social and economic arguments for *decarceration* strategies for women. In place of the prison, local community support centres could be developed which would help women address the causes of their offending, an idea supported by 86 per cent of the respondents in a recent survey (SmartJustice 2007). These centres could adopt a 'woman-wise' approach to women's offending, recognizing the socio-economic circumstances of most female offenders and also offering help in dealing with substance abuse and coping with life histories of violence and abuse. Woman-centred facilities, including accommodation if needed, drug detoxification and rehabilitation programmes and initiatives at helping women move on from abuse, could offer a realistic *immediate* alternative to imprisonment. The report by the New Economics Foundation (2008) highlights the work of two centres, centre 218 in Glasgow and the Asha Centre in Worcester, which engage with women's needs and, as demonstrated in the report, increase women's self-esteem and self-confidence more successfully than imprisonment. Alongside this we should also need to consider the possibilities of decriminalization, particularly for some drug offences.

Eaton (1993) argued that women offenders would only be able to turn their lives around when they have access to housing, employment and health facilities. However, as Eaton says, in addition women need to feel that they are people of worth who can sustain, and be sustained in, meaningful and not exploitative relationships. This combined notion of redistribution *and* recognition lead us to the demand for social justice and the safeguarding of human rights. Imprisonment is unnecessary and damaging to women who may already have significant and severe vulnerabilities. The ultimate consequence of the current incarceration binge of certain (lower class, unrespectable) women lawbreakers is nothing less than the systematic sexualized abuse of women at the hands of the Capitalist State. It is a social harm that should not be tolerated.

Further reading

Bosworth, M. (1999) *Engendering Resistance: Agency and Power in Women's Prisons.* Aldershot: Ashgate.

Carlen, P. (1983) *Women's Imprisonment.* London: Routledge and Kegan Paul.

Carlen, P., Hicks, J., O'Dwyer, J., Christina, D. and Tchaikovsky, C. (1985) *Criminal Women.* Cambridge: Polity Press.

Carlen, P. and Worrall, A. (2004) *Analysing Women's Imprisonment.* Cullompton: Willan.

Corston, J. (2007) *A Review of Women with Particular Vulnerabilities in the Criminal Justice System.* London: Home Office.

New Economics Foundation (2008) *Unlocking Value: How we All Benefit from Investing in Alternatives to Prison for Women Offenders*. London: New Economics Foundation.

We also recommend that students regularly check the websites of pressure groups such as Women In Prison, The Howard League for Penal Reform, and No More Prison for details of latest data, reports and debates on women in custody.

4

Children and young people in custody

Common sense assumptions and media portrayals often give the impression that young people are becoming increasingly irresponsible and disrespectful and are engaging in unprecedented levels of criminal activity, especially in relation to knives and guns. Public and media panics about youth 'crime', however, are far from new and indeed, every generation believes its children and young people are out of control, invoking a historically myopic vision of a 'golden age' when you could 'leave your front door open, where everyone knew everyone else, and children respected their parents' (Pearson 1983; Scraton 1997; Muncie 1999; Wills 2007). The idea that society is undergoing some sort of inexorable moral decline holds enormous power which has been exploited by government rhetoric in order to justify new criminal justice policies – while simultaneously denying that this is what they are doing.[1] Critical thinkers challenge the assumptions of 'enlightened modernity' which seek to portray a historical progression from barbarism to a more caring and human-focused approach to young offenders, pointing out how punitive our attitudes to children who offend have become (Wills 2007).[2] Indeed the 'peculiarly British addiction to punishment of the young and resort to their custody' (Morgan 2009, citing Morgan 2007: 201–8) is reflected in the government's continued emphasis on punishing young people.[3]

The experiences of children in prison have failed to create the kind of scandal which might be expected as a consequence of exposures of the high numbers of deaths, accounts of violent restraint techniques, and verbal, physical and emotional abuse and neglect (Drakeford and Butler 2007). Children are some of the most vulnerable members of our society, and yet there seems to be an increasing public and political acceptance of their incarceration. This 'institutional child abuse' of children in custody illuminates a system lacking in policies and procedures based on human rights principles (Goldson and Coles 2005). In addition, as we know, children in custody are often the most socially excluded, deprived and abused youth in our communities even before they are sent to prison.

This chapter outlines what we know about children in custody, considering the increasing numbers of young people detained. Current policies in relation to custody for young people are situated in the social, historical and political context of the battle between punitive and welfarist approaches to children who break the law. The chapter critically assesses the current custodial detention of children, arguing that it amounts to state-sponsored institutional child abuse, and concludes with arguments supporting the abolition of custody for children.[4] Interspersed in this chapter are three case studies on contemporary penal controversies.

Thinking critically about children in custody

Childhood is a social construction with a relatively short history, with current understandings dating back to as recently as the nineteenth century. Legally, childhood in England and Wales is a contradictory phenomenon, as on the one hand there are various legal restrictions placed upon children undertaking certain behaviours, such as drinking alcohol, whereas on the other hand children can be held legally responsible for their actions from the age of 10. Bizarrely, under the *Pet Animals Act* 1951, children under 12 are not even deemed legally entitled to buy a pet but they are regarded as being equally as responsible as adults in court (Goldson and Peters 2000: Gillen 2007). There exist, then, two very different constructions of children: 'innocent' and 'evil'. This false dichotomy entails the application of emotive value judgements, determining between the 'respectable' children that we should protect, and those 'undesirables' that we should punish. Young people are, until they turn 18, usually dealt with in the Youth Court. As the age of majority is 18, legally they are children until that age. Younger children, however, can be held in local authority secure accommodation. From the age of 18 to 20 offenders are deemed to be 'young adult offenders' and are held in Young Offender Institutions (YOI). From the age of 21 offenders can be held in adult prisons.

The language of child imprisonment is one of 'doublespeak', where child prisoners are not children but 'young offenders', which implies that they could be expected to develop into 'older' or 'adult' offenders. These 'young offenders' are held not in 'prisons', but in specialist separate institutions which, while sharing many of the characteristics of prisons in terms of containment and coercion, are named and identified as not being prisons. The language of 'restraint' and 'physical control in custody' obfuscates the fact that adults can in some circumstances assault children. By referring to such custodial institutions as Secure Training Centres, for example, the false impression is given that such settings for young people are 'not real prisons' or not places where 'people suffer extremes of desperation and despair' (Medlicott 2001: 9).

Imprisoning children is ineffective in reducing future criminal behaviour, despite s37(1) of the *Crime and Disorder Act* 1998 setting out that the principal aim of the youth justice system 'is to prevent offending by children and young persons'. The costs are extremely high while the benefits are low: the Youth Justice Board (YJB) has two thirds of its budget swallowed up by the costs of custody, spending over ten times more on custody than it does on crime prevention programmes (YJB 2006). It costs £185,780 to keep a young person in a secure children's home for a year, which would pay for a child's education at Eton College (if that were to be considered desirable) for six years at current fee rates (Glover and Hibbert 2008).

There is a substantial body of published literature which offers a powerful critique of child imprisonment in England and Wales – especially in the international human rights context (Detrick et al. 2008) – and challenges how we treat young people in conflict with the law, such as in relation to the application of the *Children Act* 1989 (Goldson 2009).[5] Debates about young offenders are often discussed in terms of a tension between 'justice' and 'welfare', although John Muncie (2009: 301) argues that in the light of the development of managerialism this may be 'particularly moribund'. The debate, however, is still relevant and both justice and welfare can be contrasted with abolitionism. The justice model adopts a classicist, punishment-focused approach which treats young offenders as responsible for their actions. It thus places more emphasis on the criminal act than on the child's needs. The justice model recognizes the special situation of children by setting a statutory minimum age of criminal responsibility after which children are assumed to be rational actors. This approach involves the use of the penal law to ensure due process and 'just deserts'. Liberal justice-based approaches stress rights, accountability and due process whereas more conservative approaches stress just deserts and responsibility. The justice model justifies imprisonment as a proportionate response to wrongdoing and has a key role in making children who offend recognize the consequences of their actions. The justice model is highly consistent with the legalism interpretive frame.

In contrast, the 'welfare' approach adopts a more positivistic interpretation and sees the young person as the product of individual, social or environmental factors, who thus should be helped rather than punished. This approach includes psycho-medical approaches to responding to young offenders, including psychological, neurological and nutritional factors offering explanations for offending. Within this perspective a range of psychological explanations for 'crime' dominate, such as those focused upon maternal attachment. The welfare model can, however, also draw on social pathologies, rooting explanations within environmental circumstances. Under the welfare model, imprisonment provides an opportunity for reform, for education and for young people to undertake programmes in response to their needs.

The third approach is that of critical perspectives proposing, to varying extents, the abolition of custodial penalties for children and young people. Abolitionism in its broadest sense does not simply involve the abolition of custody for young people but also a challenge to the criminalization of children and the raising of the age of criminal responsibility. The imprisonment of children is a prime candidate for immediate abolition. If the powers that be believe that a child is so dangerous that they need to be contained for public protection, this child clearly has a range of needs which require a social work-based or welfare-based response, not a penal response.

Problematizing the data about children in custody

The number of children in custody in England and Wales is now the highest in Western Europe (Muncie 2009) and has been attributed to the courts adopting a more punitive approach, sending proportionately more children into custody and for longer periods (Blyth et al. 2009). A particular concern relates to the more-than-doubling of the number of indeterminate sentences (Blyth et al. 2009). The average number of children and young people in custody increased by 13 per cent between 1997 and 2007 (Morgan 2009, citing Morgan 2007) (see Box 4.1). This rate of increase has slackened

---

Box 4.1 How many children are in custody?

In March 2009 there were:

- 255 12–15-year-olds in secure training centres in England and Wales
- 198 children in local authority secure children's homes

In September 2008 there were:

- 156 children aged 14 and under in the secure estate (28 were 13 and five were 12)
- 2133 15–17-year-olds in custody

In 2008, 5165 young people aged 15–17 entered prison.

- Just under half were serving sentences up to and including six months.
- 117 were there for sentences of four years or longer.
- 90 were serving indeterminate sentences.

There was an eightfold increase in the custodial detention of children between 1992 and 2006. The number of girls sentenced to custody by magistrates increased by 181% between 1996 and 2006. The use of custody for 10–14-year-olds increased by 550% between 1996 and 2006, mainly for breaching community orders such as by failing to keep weekly appointments with the Youth Offending Team. Reconviction rates are high: around 75% reoffend within twelve months after release. Nearly 80% of 10–14-year-olds reoffend within 12 months of release.

Source: Glover and Hibbert (2008); Prison Reform Trust (2009); Ministry of Justice (2009a)

---

compared to the increase in the final years of the Conservative administration prior to the election of New Labour in 1997. Between 1997 and 2007 the number of young people held in secure children's homes more than doubled while those held in secure training centres increased fivefold (Morgan 2009).

Imprisoned children's lives are already characterized by poverty, family instability and difficulties; emotional, physical and sexual abuse; homelessness, isolation, loneliness, self-harm and disadvantage (Goldson 2005). Further details of the social background of children and young people in custody are detailed in Box 4.2.

There are currently 19 YOIs (Rose 2009) often housing more than 300 detainees each and with the majority being for males. Most of these establishments are in older buildings. They form part of the general management structure of the prison estate although there is a specific regime and rules. Secure Training Centres are privately owned, constructed and managed under contract to the YJB. They are smaller than YOIs, usually holding 1–80 places. One has a mother and baby unit (Rose 2009). Secure Children's Homes are run by local authorities and some involve the voluntary and private healthcare sectors. These hold 16–32 children and provide places not only for children remanded or sentenced but for children who are detained on other welfare grounds and for whom a secure setting is felt to be necessary. These are not,

---

Box 4.2 Children and young people in custody

Children and young people in custody are

- 16–17 years old (average age)
- male (93%)
- increasingly likely to be imprisoned for breach of community orders
- not persistent offenders, with many having only one or two previous offences (37%)
- likely to have committed robbery, violence against the person or vehicle theft.

Children and young people in custody are likely to have a history of:

- truancy
- school exclusion (79% of young men on average)
- being in care (37% of young women)
- bereavement of a parent or close relative
- mental health problems (31% of young men)
- using alcohol (81% of young men and 74% of young women)
- take illegal drugs (82% of young men)
- smoking (83% of young men)

In addition

- 25% have learning difficulties (further 33% borderline)
- 10% of the young men and 9% of the young women have children themselves
- 20% have been placed on a child protection register

Young women are likely to

- have some level of psychiatric disturbance (71%–86% depending on calculation)
- have self-harmed in the last month (36%: of these 92% had cut themselves)
- have been paid for sex (10%)

Source: Harrington and Bailey (2005); Youth Justice Board (2006); Glover and Hibbert (2008); Morgan (2009); Parke (2009)

---

primarily, penal establishments per se, although their residents may have committed offences and be detained there as a consequence of their sentence.

It is essential to note the different historical traditions from which the present structure and system of secure accommodation has emerged:

> The extent to which history shapes culture may be debateable; but, undeniably, the formal and informal narratives that make up the history of a particular establishment have a continuing part to play in the way that staff interpret their experiences and understand the establishment's role and purpose. This, in turn, impacts on the young people who pass through the establishment and contributes significantly to how they experience custody.
>
> (Rose 2009: 23)

Thus Secure Children's Homes have emerged from a different context of service for young people in contrast with YOIs, which are within the Prison Service and have historically developed as penal institutions. There are, therefore, significant disparities including questions of staff uniforms, prison vocabulary and the use of first names (Rose 2009). Questions can also be raised as to the nature and effectiveness of these regimes:

> The costs of secure accommodation cannot be measured solely in financial terms. There are human costs that ensue from the wasted potential of the lives of young people who, without skilled help and support, are likely to remain enmeshed in criminal activity. While the use of custody retains a role in the youth justice system, it is essential to ensure that the daily routine in every establishment offers each young person the appropriate level of safety, security and well-planned, positive experiences.
>
> (Rose 2009: 33)

One of the most valuable sources of information on the experiences of imprisoned children can be found in the quantitative surveys carried out over a two-year period and published jointly with the Youth Justice Board (Parke 2009). The most recent is the fourth to be published, which allows an assessment to be made of changes, progress and improvements in the system. It covers both males and females aged 15 to 18, although it does not cover the youngest age group of juvenile detainees. The most recent report shows there has not been a great deal of change in young men's custodial environments, but significantly more young men (80 per cent) reported feeling safe on their first night in custody and fewer than previously reported victimization by other young people (25 per cent). For young women the situation has changed significantly. Young women are no longer held with adult women in adult prisons, and all were held in units completely separate from the women's prisons in which they were situated. The number of those feeling unsafe dropped from 30 per cent to 22 per cent.[6]

A quarter of the young men surveyed said they had been victimized by other young men in their current setting, which was an improvement on the previous survey's figure of 31 per cent. Fifteen per cent had experienced insulting remarks and 10 per cent physical violence. Although two units had incidents of sexual abuse (4 per cent), seven others had none reported. Nineteen per cent reported they had been victimized by members of staff but this varied widely from 0 per cent in the Carlford Unit to 33 per cent at Stoke Heath. The highest percentage of those reporting physical abuse by staff was 8 per cent in one unit. It is interesting to link this to the question of whether young men would tell anyone if they were being victimized and if so who they would tell: 63 per cent overall said they would tell someone with 31 per cent saying they would tell their personal officer and 31 per cent they would tell family or friends. More worryingly, only 40 per cent on average said they felt staff would take them seriously if they reported victimization. Where there were higher levels of belief that staff would take such reports seriously, there were higher levels of willingness to report victimization. Of the young women 19 per cent said they had been victimized by other young women, ranging from 5 per cent to 36 per cent depending on the unit, but with the numbers of individuals affected being small. As for young men, insulting remarks were the most common form of abuse, with physical abuse being less likely for young women than for young men. Nine (12 per cent) reported victimization by staff, with one young women reporting sexual abuse. Seventy-five per cent said they would tell someone if they were being victimized: interestingly, young women were far more likely to tell their personal officer (46 per cent) than their families and friends (34 per cent). Many more young women (61 per cent) than young men (40 per cent) felt they would be taken seriously by staff if they reported victimization.

Historical context

For nearly two hundred years a range of penal institutions have been created aimed specifically at children: from the Parkhurst Prison for Boys in 1838[7] to Secure Training Centres, via Industrial Schools, Borstals, Approved Schools, Remand Centres and Young Offender Institutions. It is only relatively recently, then, that incarceration has involved children being treated differently from adults. Children were usually dealt with as miniature adults once they had reached the age of 7 and were subject to the same penalties as adults (Newburn 2003). In the early nineteenth century there were a number of attempts to reform criminal procedure and penal policies so as to differentiate between children and adults, but reform was slow. 'Change came slowly, partly because children were generally regarded as miniature adults, expected to cope with the hardships of life from a tender age, and partly because the state had not yet developed for itself the role of child protector' (Morgan 2007: 201).

A number of people, including Lord Shaftesbury and Thomas Barnardo, lobbied for improving one aspect or another of children's lives (Williams 1944). A prominent group of 'child savers' campaigned to protect children from danger and exploitation and to separate children from adults in the context of punishment. These included Mary Carpenter who founded Kingswood School in Bristol in 1852 (Morgan 2007) and whose advocacy of separation of juvenile offenders from adults partly led to the passing of the *Youthful Offenders Act* 1854 (Rutherford 1986). Indeed, Mary Carpenter (1851, cited in Rutherford 1986: 28) had 'great objection to calling them [children] even semi-criminal because the word has moral meaning. I consider the condition they are in as that of extreme neglect'. This recognition of children as different from adults has been acknowledged as a key element of the evolution of modern childhood (May 1973).

At around the same time there were other attempts to create schools with a reformist agenda, such as that established by Peter Bedford (the 'Spitalfields Philanthropist') and Matthew Davenport Hill, who developed an early form of probation for young offenders which became known as the 'Warwickshire Plan', which involved an early and voluntary example of an industrial school. The *Youthful Offenders Act* 1854 established reformatories where children could be sent after serving a prison sentence of between two and five years, then in 1857 industrial schools were established. Thus began the long history of the imprisonment of children in 'specialist institutions' which, as Barry Goldson (2005a: 79) puts it, casts 'its shadow over the best part of two centuries'.

Initially these institutions were separate, with reformatories existing for young offenders and industrial schools for those deemed to be likely to offend. They had, however, similar regimes and similar young people contained in them. By the end of the nineteenth century the requirement of spending time in prison before going to the reformatory or industrial school was abolished.

In the early years of the twentieth century the Probation Service was formally created, as was the juvenile court. *The Children Act* 1908 removed those aged under 14 from prison and made it mandatory that for a court to send a young person to prison an 'unruly certificate' must be issued (Newburn 2003). Although imprisonment for children was abolished, at around the same time the *Crime Prevention Act* (1909) created specific correctional establishments for young offenders, which had been piloted at prisons in Bedford and, famously, at Borstal in Kent. As a consequence, the name of 'Borstal' came to be used for all subsequent similar institutions. This was seen at the time as 'a major liberal breakthrough' (Muncie 2004: 283). The sentence of Borstal training was an indeterminate sentence lasting for not less than one and not more than three years, within a regime based on discipline, hard work and drill. Offenders aged 16 to 21 were given industrial or agricultural trade training, discipline and exercise in a countryside rather than urban setting. After the time spent in the Borstal the young people would be supervised in the community with privileges and early release being earned by good behaviour. Alexander Paterson viewed the system as being akin to an adaptation of the public school system experienced by many wealthier children, involving 'housemasters' who could realize the potential of those in their charge (Morgan 2007).[8]

The system was criticized from its inception on the grounds that young people could be detained for longer periods in the name of 'reform' than they would under the previous system. It could not, in addition, deal with those deemed to be 'incorrigible' or incapable of benefiting from the system. These young people continued to be sentenced to, or transferred to, adult prisons (Morgan 2007). That said, it claimed high levels of success in preventing reoffending, in 1915 reporting reconviction rates of 27–35 per cent (Muncie 2004). Not all commentators view these reform efforts and the Borstal system as motivated by humanitarian ends. The 'child savers' were the precursors of twentieth-century social workers and these middle-class reformers heralded 'what was arguably a new form of paternalistic authoritarianism':

'Juvenile delinquency' was socially constructed. The concept suggested new forms of punishment and intervention in order that delinquents be saved from the allegedly corrupting influences of families, peers and neighbourhoods. Delinquents were invariably working class. A whole network of specialized closed institutions was created to instil in them the discipline which their imputed pathology was held to require.

(Morgan 2007: 202)

During the First World War recorded juvenile crime increased significantly, which put pressure on the reformatories and industrial schools. As Stephen Humphries (1981, cited in Newburn 2003: 190) points out the issue that dominated public debates and government reports was that of the control and reformation of rebellious working class youth . . . From the turn of the century onwards reformatories were controlled by a professional body of penal administrators who attempted to infuse the system with the public school ethos of Christian manliness and patriotic duty.

The next high point in terms of policy was the *Children and Young Persons Act* 1933, which prohibited capital punishment for those aged under 18 (although in reality this was standard practice by this time) and required that the juvenile court be staffed by specially selected magistrates and have regard to the 'welfare of the child'. The reformatory and industrial schools were reorganized and became known as 'Schools approved by the Secretary of State', i.e. 'approved schools.' In the 1930s the reformatory Borstal system was at its peak, with outdoor activities, camps and physical activities similar to the ethos of the Boy Scout movement (Harding et al. 1985).[9]

Indictable offences rose in the early 1940s and after the Second World War the incoming Labour government introduced the *Criminal Justice Act* 1948, which, while restricting the use of imprisonment, also created the precursor of the 'short sharp shock' sentence which came later. Gradually the Borstal institutions became more punitive, with short term detention sentences being introduced in 1948, Portland being designated a punishment Borstal in 1950 and tougher regimes being recommended throughout the whole system (Morgan 2007). In 1961 the minimum age for Borstal training was lowered to 15 and it was also made easier to transfer young people into the prison system. Gradually a more and more welfare-focused approach prevailed, leading to the high point of the welfarist orientation, the *Children and Young Persons Act* 1969. This allowed young offenders aged 10–14 who had committed offences to be subject to 'care and protection proceedings' as an alternative to court, unless they had committed homicide. In addition, for those aged 14–16 there was to be mandatory consultation between police and social services before criminal proceedings were brought and approved schools were abolished. The emphasis was on the court as a welfare-providing agency.

Between the passage of the Act and its implementation, however, there was a change of government and the incoming Conservative government did not implement some key sections of the Act. Thus the juvenile courts continued to operate much as they had prior to the Act and although it became possible to use care proceedings throughout the 1970s the juvenile courts increasingly used punitive disposals (Newburn 2003). The Act was criticized for being 'soft' (Muncie 2004) and became 'the scapegoat for all the perceived ills of juvenile crime and juvenile justice in the 1970s' (p. 195).

By the end of the 1970s the use of custody for juveniles had doubled and the Conservative government elected in 1979 promised to provide a 'short sharp shock' to young offenders through the creation of new detention centres, and also created more attendance centres for 'hooligans' (Morgan 2007). Following a White Paper a new, tougher regime was introduced at Send and New Hall detention centres. The *Criminal Justice Act* 1982 shortened the detention centre sentence from three months to 21 days and the maximum from six months down to four. Imprisonment for those aged under 21 was abolished and the new determinate-length Youth Custody Order was created. This represented 'a move away from treatment and lack of personal responsibility to notions of punishment and individual and parental responsibility' (Gelsthorpe and Morris 1994: 972).

The use of custody for young people fell as a consequence of innovative attempts to divert young offenders away from the youth justice system during the period known as the 'decade of diversion' or 'the successful revolution' in youth justice. A policy of 'bifurcation' distinguished between minor and occasional offenders and more serious, persistent, offenders. Thus the number of young offenders sentenced to custody halved during the 1980s so that by the end of the decade the average daily population in custody was below what it was in 1970 (Morgan 2002). The 'short sharp shock' approach was deemed to be a failure, with more than half of those being sent there being reconvicted within a year. Thus the separate detention centre sentence was replaced in 1988 by 'detention in a Young Offender institution' and youth custody centres and detention centres were amalgamated to form Young Offender Institutions which became available for those aged 15 or over. In 1989 the juvenile court lost its powers to make care orders and there is now a clear separation between civil and criminal proceedings involving children.

In the early 1990s the *Criminal Justice Act* 1991 extended the remit of the juvenile court to include 17-year-olds and renamed it the Youth Court. This reflected an intention to expand the approaches which had been successful with young offenders to include older offenders, recognizing the dangers of defining young people as criminals when, statistically, they were likely to mature out of crime. This continued the bifurcatory or 'twin track' approach which differentiated between young offenders in need of welfare intervention and persistent or committed young offenders in need of punishment. Again, the importance of multi-agency working and consultation was emphasized.

In the early 1990s, from about 1991 onwards, there was a change in the tone of official concern about juvenile offending (Newburn 2003). The public disorder at estates such as Blackbird Leys in Oxford and Meadowell on Tyneside shifted attention to young, usually white men in conflict with the police. The concerns focused not only on the behaviour but on the alleged powerlessness of the police to stop activities which were harming communities. Gradually, panics emerged about 'persistent young offenders' who terrorized their communities, such as so-called 'one boy crime waves', for example, who were given nicknames by the popular press such as 'Rat boy' or 'Balaclava boy', which dehumanized them and presented them as a pest or a threat. On the afternoon of 12 February 1993, and in the weeks which followed, developments took place which changed the landscape of youth justice in the UK.

Case Study 4.1 The abduction and murder of James Bulger

On the afternoon of 12 February 1993, 2-year-old James Bulger was abducted from the Strand shopping centre in Bootle, Liverpool. CCTV footage from the shopping centre showed him walking with, or being led away by, two young people. Two days later his battered and mutilated body was found near a local railway line, two miles away. Two local 10-year-olds, Robert Thompson and Jon Venables, were arrested and charged with the murder and were remanded in custody, amid angry and violent scenes outside the court which led to several arrests. The trial was held at Preston Crown Court in November 1993 amid huge national and international media interest. The media coverage was highly hostile and punitive and took no account of the age of the offenders, one of the most famous examples being the headline of the *Daily Star* which, below a picture of the boys who had been convicted, said 'How Do You Feel Now, You Little Bastards?' (*Daily Star* 1993). The boys were not named during the trial, being simply referred to as 'Child A' and 'Child B' but were named after they had been found guilty.

The trial judge initially recommended that they serve at least eight years in custody, entitling them to a review of their sentence after five years. The Lord Chief Justice set the tariff at ten years with review after seven. However, as a consequence of a petition and a campaign by the *Sun* newspaper, which encouraged readers to send coupons to the Home Secretary which stated that the killers 'should stay in prison for LIFE', the Home Secretary fixed the tariff at fifteen years with review after twelve. After a number of legal challenges under English law Thompson and Venables applied to the European Court of Human Rights arguing that the UK government had committed six breaches of the Convention. The Court held that there had been three breaches; first because their public trial in an adult court had breached the Convention; second, the Home Secretary had violated the Convention in setting the tariff because, as an elected politician, he was neither independent nor impartial. Finally, there had also been a breach because the tariff-fixing process denied the right to a periodic review of detention by a judicial body. The case led to the new Home Secretary to recommend the tariff be reduced from ten to eight years.

After a six-month review by the parole board they were released on a life licence in June 2001 after serving eight years. An injunction was imposed prohibiting details about the boys, their location and their new identities. Since then occasional information about them has surfaced, including the fact that, after an anonymous tip-off, Denise Fergus, James Bulger's mother, had located Robert Thompson, saw him but was unable to confront him. The *Manchester Evening News* was fined in 2001 for releasing information about where they were held and in 2007 the Home Office brought an injunction against a magazine based outside the UK which wanted to reveal their identities.

The moral panic (Cohen 1972) that arose after the death of James Bulger focused on youth criminality and a sense that previous policies had failed to deal with a society where children were becoming out of control (Haydon and Scraton 2000). Although this was not the first killing of a child by other children (Sereny 1997), it was portrayed as a new, dangerous and threatening possibility; that of children who were out of control and amoral, who had 'the Mark of the Beast imprinted' on them (*Sunday Times* 1993) or who had 'the Satan bug inside them' (Ellis 1993). James and Jenks (1996: 321) perceptively analysed the case in relation to the meaning of childhood and the 'nature' of children: 'society struggled to comprehend a growing disillusionment with what children are or might become in the modern world. It was not, as we suggest, just two children who were on trial for the murder of a third but childhood itself.'

Other commentators described children spending their time truanting from school smoking cannabis, watching violent films on video, lacking in morality, responsibility and parental guidance. Indeed 'what followed in the mass media was a kind of outbreak of moral condemnation usually reserved for the enemy in times of war' (King 1995: 3). This fed into ongoing concerns so that an incredibly rare incident became linked to a more general 'crisis of the family' which in turn led to a perceived 'crisis in authority' (Haydon and Scraton 2000). As John Muncie wrote, the death of James Bulger 'came to signify more than an isolated tragic event . . . Demons had invaded the innocents' (Muncie 1999: 7).

In 1994 the maximum sentence of detention in a Young Offender Institution was increased from 12 to 24 months and the government introduced Secure Training Orders for 12–15-year-olds who had been convicted of three or more offences which would be imprisonable in the case of an adult: these orders were to be served in privately built and run Secure Training Centres (STCs). These were aimed at 'that comparatively small group of very persistent juvenile offenders whose repeated offending makes them a menace to the community' (Hansard 1993). In addition to the requirement of three or more convictions they must have also proved 'unwilling or unable to comply with the requirements of supervision while in the community while on remand or under sentence' (Hansard 1993). The age limit was later restricted to 12–14-year-olds. These secure training orders would involve a determinate sentence being set by the court with half to be served in the Secure Training Centre and half under supervision while in the community. Although academic and social commentators criticized the new orders, largely because 'locking up children' was seen as an undesirable and retrograde step in youth justice terms, there was little political debate because the Conservatives and the opposition at that time were keen to be seen to be 'in touch' in relation to law and order issues.

When Kenneth Clarke, the then Home Secretary, was succeeded by Michael Howard, the new swing towards populist punitiveness continued. After a visit to Texas in January 1994 Home Secretary Howard became obsessed with the idea of introducing USA style 'boot camps' into the United Kingdom. Two 'Howard Camps' (Fletcher, cited in *The Guardian* 8 May 1995) were planned to be opened in 1996 to instil discipline into child volunteers from other custodial institutions, although critics were convinced that all they would produce were 'young criminals who can run faster than the police' (*The Guardian* 14 March 1995). In practice the regimes in the two 'Howard Camps' were much more diluted than originally envisaged, making them barely distinguishable from other correctional sites. The real insight comes through exploring the rationale behind this initiative: if the present forms of punishing and disciplining young people are failing, it is because they are not harsh enough.

The solution to such failure in punishment is more punishment (Foucault 1977). Proposed responses to children with troubles are tougher and harsher regimes: they should be disciplined or be damned.

Contemporary penal policy

Within the first few months of the election of the Labour government in 1997 they embarked upon what Morgan and Newburn (2007) call 'a flurry of activity', publishing six consultation documents on youth crime within six months. The *Crime and Disorder Act* 1998 established the Youth Justice Board (YJB) and set up local Youth Offending Teams, along with reforming community penalties. For the first time, it set out a principal aim of the youth justice system, that is, to prevent offending by children and young persons. The concept of *doli incapax* – i.e. the presumption that from the ages of 10 to 13 a young person does not know the difference between right and wrong, and if facing prosecution that it must be ascertained that they knew what they were being accused of was wrong – was abolished, despite its long history (Gillen 2007). We thus have one of the lowest ages of criminal responsibility in Europe, 10-year-olds now being just as liable as adults.

The *Crime and Disorder Act* introduced the Detention and Training Order, combining secure training orders and detention in a YOI for those aged 15, 16 or 17, into one 'hybrid' sentence, half of which is served in an institution. The Act lowered the minimum age for conferral of the order to 10, although for those under 12 the order

---

Case Study 4.2 Education for young people in custody

Custody may allow young offenders to engage with valuable programmes and to develop literacy and numeracy skills; life skills and thinking skills. Of those in custody of school age over a quarter have the literacy and numeracy skills expected of a 7-year-old. The number of hours' learning engaged in by each learner each week varies widely from 11.38 hours at Stoke Heath to 22.71 hours at Feltham. The YJB requires 25 hours per week. Eighty-one per cent of 15–18-year-old males in custody are in education, and over half are learning a skill in some establishments with the highest levels of involvement in education and skills training; less than two thirds said they benefited from it. For young women nearly all are involved in education and 60 per cent are learning a skill. There is little available information on qualifications achieved. In 2006/7 there were 68 GCSE achievements by those aged 15, 16 or 17, with 19 achieving one GCSE; five achieving 2 and 13 achieving 3. There are low levels of achievement by YOI detainees and there is no evidence that prison education is revitalizing the educational achievements or motivation of those in custody.

Source: Batchelor (2005); Hansard (2009a); Parke (2009); Prison Reform Trust (2009)

must be necessary to protect the public and there are currently no designated institutions for children of this age under this order. Young people who have committed serious offences can become liable to 'long term detention' for which the maximum period for a young person is the same as that for an adult, or mandatory detention according to Her Majesty's Pleasure for murder.[10] One area of emergent concern is that of the operation of sentences of 'Detention for Public Protection' which is the juvenile version of the indeterminate sentences for adults created by the *Criminal Justice Act* 2003.

The regimes experienced by child prisoners have been labelled by Barry Goldson (2005a: 80) as 'organised hurt' which leads to thousands of children being physically, psychologically and emotionally harmed (Goldson 2006). Two of the most significant controversial aspects of child imprisonment are educational provision for children in prison, and deaths in custody. Thirty children died in penal custody in the UK between 1990 and 2008, most were self-inflicted but some following restraint (Epstein and Foster 2008).[11] The recent deaths of Adam Rickwood and Gareth Myatt took place in Secure Training Centres during or following the use of physical restraint by staff. Physical restraint techniques have been highly controversial, in the past, allowing adults to assault children by punching them on the nose or, until recently, by pulling their nostrils up, in order to distract them when using violent and uncooperative behaviour: 'despite the use of euphemistic language and sanitised descriptions, approved "control" techniques would almost certainly be described as child abuse in any other context' (Goldson 2006: 457).[12]

The deaths of Gareth and Adam led to the introduction of the Secure Training Centre (Amendment) Rules 2007, which were later quashed by the Court of Appeal as violating detainees' human rights.[13] The Rules were found to be in violation of Article 3 and 8 of the European Convention on Human Rights, which guarantee freedom from inhuman and degrading treatment and respect for private life.

Case Study 4.3 The death of Gareth Myatt

On 19 April 2004 Gareth Myatt, aged 15, died under restraint at Rainsbrook STC where he was being held, the first child ever to die in a privately-run STC. Gareth was small for his age, was only 4' 10" tall and weighed 6.5 stone. He was from a mixed race background. He was three days into a twelve month detention and training order for assault and theft; he refused to clean a sandwich toaster and went to his room. Two members of staff followed him and began moving items from his room. When one tried to remove a piece of paper from a shelf, later found to be his mother's new mobile phone number, Gareth became upset and staff said he lunged at them. He was then restrained by three members of staff using a technique called the 'seated double embrace'. He tried to tell the staff that he could not breathe but they didn't release him, one member of staff saying 'well, if you are shouting, you can breathe' (Smith 2007). He choked on his own vomit and died.

His death prompted three inquiries and in June 2004 the seated double embrace hold was withdrawn from use in juvenile facilities. The inquest heard that at least four other children had complained of being unable to breathe while held in the seated double embrace. The inquest jury returned a verdict of accidental death and made a number of criticisms of the YJB. The Coroner, Richard Pollard, wrote to Jack Straw to outline 34 recommendations needed in order to prevent similar deaths. The CPS did not prosecute anybody involved in Gareth Myatt's death.

This case, along with that of Adam Rickwood who was found hanging in his room at Hassockfield STC after he had been restrained and subjected to the controversial nose distraction technique, formed the basis for the Carlile review of restraint. However, these have not been the last deaths of young people in custody: Gareth Price and Liam McManus hanged themselves in Lancaster Farms, the inquest verdict on Gareth Price identifying the collective failures of multiple agencies.

Source: INQUEST (2007)

The Carlile Report was published in February 2006 following his inquiry into the use of strip-searching, physical restraint and segregation of children in custody, methods which would, in other circumstances, trigger a child protection investigation and could even result in criminal charges (Epstein and Foster 2008). Physical restraint measures were often counter-productive due to the feelings of anger and resentment generated in the children. In July 2008 the Court of Appeal addressed the question of the use of physical restraints on persons who are detained in STCs all of which are run by private contractors in accordance with the *Prison Act* 1952 and the STC Rules.[14] The case is interesting not only for legal reasons but because of its illuminating discussion of the nature and practice of 'physical control in care' (to which the Rules refer as 'restraint'). The case explains the difference between 'restraint', which includes a variety of holds, and 'distraction techniques' which are founded on the infliction of pain, such as by delivering a blow to the nose or pulling an inmate's thumb.

After many criticisms, the nose distraction technique was withdrawn by the Secretary of State in December 2007. There were several legal grounds for the appeal. The Court of Appeal held that the introduction of these Rules without prior consultation with the Children's Commissioner was unlawful. The Court then considered whether there had been a breach of Article 3, the test being 'whether the act or treatment was such as to arouse feelings of fear, anguish and inferiority capable of humiliating and debasing the person' (cited in Epstein and Foster 2008). Where a person has been deprived of his liberty, resort to physical force which has not been made strictly necessary by his own conduct is a breach of Article 3. The fact that those involved were children also meant that the government was under an obligation, under the UN Convention on the Rights of the Child, to treat them with humanity and in a manner which takes account of the needs of persons of their age.[15] The Court had rejected the Secretary of State's argument that the amendment was necessary to allow STCs to adopt an effective range of discipline, so it could not be said to be necessary and was quashed as being in violation of Article 3.

The debate about restraint continues: a quarter of young men and a fifth of young women surveyed reported that they had been physically restrained (Parke 2009). Interestingly, those units in which higher levels of use of force were reported also had the highest level of formal adjudications, which reflects different regimes and staff-inmate cultures. For young women, as for young men, experience of the use of force varied from one in ten to over a third, and high levels of adjudications were linked to high levels of use of physical restraint. Significantly, despite the fact that the Ministry of Justice accepted the recommendation of the review of restraint, in June 2009 Anne Owers, the Chief Inspector of Prisons, highlighted what she called an 'unacceptably high' level of serious injuries at Castington YOI, in which over the course of two years there had been seven confirmed fractures and three other suspected: one offender had both his wrists broken and another had a fractured knee (Travis 2009). The number of uses of restraint was comparable with similar institutions but the level of serious injuries meant that control and restraint techniques were not being applied correctly, and because staff were rushing during implementation. Although an inquiry and review is to take place, this was criticized by the Prison Reform Trust, a spokesperson for which commenting that 'another prison service internal review would be an inadequate response to such a dreadful record of injury' (Casciani 2009).

Legitimacy

It is important to note the breadth and depth of national and international concern, criticism and condemnation of current child imprisonment policies in England and Wales, which has focused on both the scale of child imprisonment and also on what Barry Goldson (2006: 450) calls 'the corrosive impact of penal regimes on children'. Indeed 'why does a nation with so many admirable qualities have such a punitive attitude to the most vulnerable members of society, our children?' (Mather 2004: 500). Children who commit offences are thought of as offenders first and children second, in contrast with concerns about other vulnerable children as evidenced by the media and public concern surrounding other forms of institutional abuse of children, such as the furore about alleged abuses in residential care in Jersey or recent scrutiny of the Ryan Report into long-term and endemic child physical and sexual abuse linked to the Roman Catholic church in Ireland (Commission to Inquire into Child Abuse 2009). Rather than being confronted with a 'childhood of crisis' we are, in the words of Phil Scraton (1997), in fact faced with a 'crisis of adultism' and a denial of the harms perpetrated against young people. Here we are seeing a divided response to children. That is, they are either 'innocent children who need help, support, love and stability' or 'baby criminals'. As 'adult-criminals-in-waiting' their status as an offender is a master status in the eyes of the criminal justice system, which dominates and outweighs all other identities and status roles.

There can be no rational justification for child imprisonment on the scale at which it is currently used in England and Wales and thus a case should be made for its abolition (Goldson and Coles 2005). Even if child imprisonment is not abolished completely, in the short term a pilot project in north Hampshire has cut the number of custodial sentences imposed on young people by 42 per cent, after a panel was set up to assess cases where children were imprisoned (Rayner 2009). The panel members were drawn from the Youth Offending Team, children's services and the voluntary sector, although judges and magistrates declined to take part. Through assessing cases where young people had received custodial sentences, and evaluating how things could have been done differently, lessons learnt included writing pre-sentence reports to encourage community penalties rather than custody and encouraging the children's services and Youth Offending Team (YOT) representatives to work together to find alternatives to imprisonment.

Glover and Hibbert (2008) make a case for partial abolition of custody for 10–14-year-olds in particular, arguing that in England and Wales there should be a change in sentencing thresholds so that only those 10–14-year-olds convicted of 'grave crimes' or violent offences are locked up. They also argue for more timely support for children, young people and their families in order to address problems at an early stage before they become out of control, asserting that children who offend or who are at risk of offending and their families respond well to early intervention initiatives such as family therapy, restorative justice and targeted support in relation to education, housing and mental health services.

As Abigail Wills (2007) points out, in historical terms we are not witnessing an unprecedented increase in youth crime or unprecedented concern about abuse in custodial institutions; rather, what is unprecedented is the punitive turn since the 1990s and the lack of political commitment to challenging this approach to young people. This stands in contrast with the situation in Scotland, where the children's hearings system has, since 1971, taken over responsibility for dealing with children and young people under 16 (and in some cases under 18) who commit offences or are in need of care and protection. Within the Scottish welfare-based system children who commit offences are often recognized as also in need of help and support. What is highly significant is that the Scottish Chief Inspector of Prisons has gone one step further and recommended an end to the detention of children in Scotland's prisons, the justice minister announcing that he did not believe that 'in the long run Scotland will be well served by jailing children' (Allison 2009).

In England and Wales, however, there seems little or no political will to challenge the situation, even though the evidence shows that imprisoning children perpetuates a range of harms and does little to prevent crime and protect the public. Alongside abolition of child imprisonment, the age of criminal responsibility needs to be raised to at least 16, which would bring the UK in line with most European countries (4children 2008). Non-punitive solutions to young peoples' offending need to be introduced, including activities aimed at enabling and empowering young people to resist peer pressure, such as that to carry knives, and to promote self-esteem and confidence in young people so that they can build non-criminal lives for themselves. For some young people whose home lives contribute to their offending, alternative accommodation including supportive mentoring and foster care could work. We need to listen to young people themselves and support and empower rather than punish, aiming at social inclusion rather than exclusion (Scraton 1997; Smith 2007). The interests of children who are likely to be already experiencing profound social exclusion, educational and social marginalization and abuse, are being sacrificed in the name of political rhetoric, and we can only wonder how many more children have to die in custody before the profound harms caused by child imprisonment are recognized as one of the most controversial issues in contemporary society.

Further reading

4Children (2008) *Unlocking Potential: Alternatives to Custody for Young People*. London: 4Children.

Morgan, R. (2007) Children and young persons, in Y. Jewkes (ed.) *Handbook on Prisons*. Cullompton: Willan Publishing, pp. 201–23.

Morgan, R. and Newburn, T. (2007) Young people, crime and youth justice, in M. Maguire, R. Morgan and R. Reiner (eds) *The Oxford Handbook of Criminology (4th edn)*. Oxford: OUP, pp. 1024–60.

Muncie, J. (2008) The 'punitive turn' in juvenile justice: cultures of control and rights compliance in Western Europe and the USA, *Youth Justice*, 8(2): 107–21.

Muncie, J. (2009) *Youth and Crime (3rd edn)*. London: Sage.

Smith, R. (2007) *Youth Justice: Ideas, Policy, Practice (2nd edn)*. Cullompton: Willan.

We would also recommend that students keep up-to-date with the Youth Justice Board website and publications and also follow debates highlighted by penal pressure groups The Howard League and No More Prison.

5

'Race', racism and foreign national prisoners

There is no such thing as 'race'. There are simply human beings. All humans are unique and yet share so much in common no matter where they were born, who their ancestors were, what language they speak, or the colour of their skin. Tragically, however, there is much historical and contemporary evidence indicating a widespread failure to recognize such a simple fact in the prison place (Gordon 1983; Wilson and Moore 2003). Though 'race' is a highly problematic social construct with no credible proof of existence, the idea of racial differences and subsequent hierarchies of power remain deeply embedded in common sense assumptions about the social world and continue to exert significant influence over human actions, interpretations and meanings. As indicated in previous chapters, prisoners' social backgrounds are often presented as a key element of the explanation for their subsequent criminal activity and penalization. Prisoners from certain believed culturally or biologically determined 'racial groups' are understood as being genetically, intellectually or socially inferior beings, thus contributing to their own poverty of life experiences and criminal identity (Herrnstein and Murray 1994; Steiner and Wooldredge 2009). Dividing practices separating one perceived 'race' from another have significant consequences. Talk of 'race' renders prisoners as 'other', increases conflict and intensifies the subjugation of solitary and vulnerable individuals. Inevitably the application of the construct of 'race' can breed only one thing: racism. In the prison place racism is a key dimension of the expression of power, shaping prejudicial decisions, exclusionary practices and the physical manifestation of violence, bullying and intimidation. This penal terror goes even further for some, such as foreign national prisoners, as it can exacerbate the structured pains of the prison place itself. 'Race' and racism undermine solidarity, create barriers for those wishing to embrace collective forms of resistance and means of support against the wasting processes of incarceration and deepen the profound sense of isolation, loneliness and loss.

In this chapter we critically examine the highly topical and emotive issues of the implication of 'racial' classifications in the prison setting. We start with a consideration of the meaning and definition of 'race' and its close connection with the imagined community of nation and then consider the four main typologies and competing ways of thinking about racism in prison. The chapter then proceeds to provide an overview of the available data on BME groups and foreign nationals in prison before proceeding to outline 'race relations' and the day-to-day manifest-ations of racism in prisons in both historical and contemporary contexts. Adopting an abolitionist perspective, we conclude with a critical discussion of the legitimacy of current penal policies and an exploration of how prison practices embody state racism through their role in the control of migrant populations. Interspersed in this chapter are case studies outlining three recent pertinent penal controversies.

Case Study 5.1 The death of Alton Manning

Alton died on 8 December 1995 at HMP Blakenhurst. He was aged 33. While on remand, he was strip-searched. When he was ordered to squat for an anal and genital examination, he refused. The inquest heard that he was then thrown to the floor, restrained face down while officers held his head and legs. He was taken out of his cell and carried down the corridor, held in a neck hold. He was then put on the floor: some prisoners said they saw officers knock him down. There was a pool of blood by his mouth and his body went limp. Although a nurse was called, it was too late. The post-mortem examination found that he died of restraint-related asphyxia, and had bruising to his neck and back, blood spots in his eyes, face and neck, and abrasions to his arms and legs. Despite their claims that he had resisted violently, no officers sustained any significant injuries. An inquest jury in 1998 concluded unanimously on the basis of patho-logical and eye witness evidence from prison officers and prisoners that he had been unlawfully killed. The Crown Prosecution Service (CPS), however, announced that no criminal charges were to be brought against any of the officers involved, on the grounds of 'insufficient evidence'. The family and their supporters campaigned tirelessly and challenged this decision in the High Court, which forced the CPS to reconsider, but in 2002 the CPS again refused to initiate criminal charges. Disturbingly, such deaths of members of BME groups in custody continue to occur, one of the most recent being that of Godfrey Moyo who died in 2005 in HMP Belmarsh as a result of restraint-related positional asphyxia and epilepsy. The inquest in July 2009 found his death was caused by restraint and neglect.

Source: INQUEST (1995)

Thinking critically about 'race' and racism in prison

'Race' is a blaming language that is rooted in a rationale of exclusion, exploitation, persecution, and justification of inferior treatment.[1] 'Race' has been authoritatively defined as a 'socially constructed categorisation which specifies rules for the identi-fication of members' (Husband 1984: 19) and in common day practice 'race' is used to differentiate people based upon distinctive physical variations. Although there are no actual racial divisions between humans, a phenomenon does not have to be *real* for it to have very real social consequences. All it takes is for people to define something as having a factual existence and act accordingly (Baxter and Sampson 1972).[2] Use of the concept of 'race' today often also incorporates the concept of ethnicity and contemporary racialized ideologies have both biological and cultural variants, although advocates of 'race' hoping to legitimate claims of biological differentiation or evidence of lesser intelligence face considerable obstacles.[3] Most notably, psychomedical scientific evidence of biological or intellectual hierarchies has been entirely dismissed (Tobics 1972). It is now established, for example, that of the 50,000 genes that human beings possess only 10 genes determine skin colour, reinforcing the claim that whatever the apparent physical differences, humans are much more similar than not (Tobic 1972).

Despite obvious limitations, most societies continue to classify identifiable groups. The most widely adopted phrase used today in England and Wales to describe 'race' is Black or Minority Ethnic (BME) groups (Bowling and Phillips 2001). Although we adopt this term throughout this chapter we acknowledge that it does have some significant limitations: it implicitly accepts whiteness as the norm; it can lead to the establishment of essentialisms around cultural differences; it cannot adequately distinguish differences between the collectivized 'minority groups'; and it cannot recognize or challenge power differentials within or outside its classificatory framework (Sivanandan 1990). Precisely because people *remain* people whatever their backgrounds, paradoxically sharing both similarities and differences, the most important thing to emphasize throughout is our subjects' shared humanity and the diversity of human life.

The term racism is one that has nothing but negative connotations and is something, in various guises, which continues to plague our society and the institutions that constitute it. Racism is all about power and dehumanization and 'implies some races are inherently superior to others physically, mentally, or in some other way' (Richmond 1972: 2).[4] Attempts to identify the specific forms of racism in prisons have not been without its difficulties (Edgar 2007). Kimmit Edgar (2007) identified what he believes are the four main types of racial incidents in prison. The first type he calls the 'blatant or malicious act or decision' (p. 280). This includes the use of racist language, physical abuse or harassment, and abuse of power. Citing research by Edgar and Martin (2004), Edgar (2007) argues that this kind of overt discrimination is relatively rare and of those who had disclosed that they had experienced racism in prison in the above study (52 per cent of the BME prisoners interviewed) only 16 per cent said they had been subjected to this kind of racism by a prison officer. Critical research, by contrast, such as that by Wilson and Moore (2003: 4), identifies the significant presence of blatant and direct racism in contemporary prisons and the overuse of violent control and restraint techniques against young black male prisoners.

I've been called a chimp before. I was also called a golliwog by one of these officers. I ended up getting into trouble for that, and I was put on adjudication.

One of the officers said to me – 'you're a piece of shit. When I wipe my arse it looks like you'.

I was coming back from the library and I saw a poster that had graffiti on it – it said 'I hate Niggers'. I waited for weeks for someone to take that poster down. No one seemed to be bothered. We kept walking back and forth and pointing out what it said and we kept asking why it was still there a month later. It was there because they either don't care or they hate niggers too.

The second type of racism is 'direct racial discrimination', which involved decisions being made which are racially biased, disadvantaging either individuals or a group. For Edgar (2007) this involves the misuse of prison officer discretion. He argues that this is very hard to identify as decisions which may not appear to be racist in the individual context may create apparent racist outcomes when they begin to affect a group disproportionately harmfully in comparison with another. This latter point is very important, but it should be remembered that discretion itself is never based on total unfettered freedom of choice: rather, discretion is shaped and structured by wider social and organizational conventions, which direct what is seen as the appropriate response to certain situations. In other words discretion is patterned. This means that the exercise of power can be equally predictable whether it is based on legal rules or the interpretive frames of alternative social and organizational rules, thus making it possible to conceptualize and critique structured racist decision-making (Baumgartner 1992; Scott 2008c).

The third type is 'informal partiality', which Edgar argues is the most widespread form of racism. Informal partiality involves actions by officers who do not realize that their behaviour and decisions are biased. The difficulty here is that this category could be used to excuse officers' racism, as their actions are defined as unwitting or unintentional (Scarman 1981). The fourth type Edgar (2007) suggests involve situations which appear ambiguous, which may or may not be racially biased. Edgar (2007: 283) argues that these all differ in intensity and outcomes but 'all are serious for the victim and none should be seen as trivial', arguing that the Prison Service has taken a strong stance against blatant, malicious racism but has neglected informal partiality. Once again prisoners may perceive mistreatment and racism which are impossible to prove, fuelling feelings of frustration and injustice which ultimately cannot be resolved. While Edgar (2007) is correct to identify that there are differences in the form that racist abuse takes, and the difficulties in proving intention, racism is conceived as an individualized or 'personal trouble' and his analysis fails to consider the manner in which state penal policies, laws and rules themselves can be racist. For various reasons all four manifestations of racism continue to plague the prison place more than official data suggests, and it remains likely that many racist actions are being 'explained away' and denied with the claim that they were mistaken for something else.

When conceptualizing racism in prison, four approaches characterize contemporary debates: the *individual pathology or 'bad apple' thesis; institutional racism; 'race' as a determining historical and structural context;* and *state racism* (see Box 5.1). Let us here briefly examine each one in turn. In the individual pathology or 'bad apple' interpretive frame, racism is restricted to the actions of a small number of racist prison officers. These problematic officers hold racist opinions which are contrary to their colleagues, Prison Service policies, the law and the wider population in society. Through the construction of racism as an abnormality (pathological), the

Box 5.1 Four different approaches to racism

1 Individual pathology or 'bad apple thesis'

- In this interpretive frame discriminatory and prejudiced behaviour is blamed on a few racist prison officers.
- Understandings of individual racism are closely associated with the report of Lord Scarman (1981) who believed it was largely 'unwitting' and individually-based. Racism is a matter of lack of awareness or deliberate wrongdoing, but not culturally or structurally embedded (Scarman 1981).
- The solution to racism in prison is straightforward. Racist members of staff should be sacked and careful selection criteria should be adopted when making new appointments.
- The limitation is that it ignores the role of power, social structure and the mediating role of the Capitalist State and that all the evidence indicates that problem is much more widespread than this explanation allows (Gordon 1983).

2 Institutional racism

- There are two influential approaches to institutional racism. The first is by Lord Macpherson (1999: 28) who defined institutional racism as:

    [T]he collective failure of an organization to provide an appropriate and profes-sional service to people because of their colour, culture or ethnic origin. It can be seen or detected in processes, attitudes and behaviour which amount to discrimination through unwitting prejudice, ignorance, thoughtlessness and racist stereotyping which disadvantage minority ethnic people.

- For Macpherson (1999) racism is culturally entrenched within criminal justice organizations and cultures.
- Solutions to racism in prison revolve around challenging staff; promoting 'race' awareness and diversity training; supporting 'race-relations' liaison officers; and promoting policy initiatives such as diversity and decency.
- Although significantly different from Scarman (1981), both Scarman and Macpherson worked within the assumptions of the Capitalist State and adopted a legalistic rather than experiential or critical approach to the issue of racism. While Macpherson identified the collective failure of the organization, he did not link racism to the broader structural problems of society (Bourne 2001).
- Carmichael and Hamilton (1967: 112) provide a second way to approach institutional racism:

    Institutional racism relies on the active and pervasive operation of anti-black attitudes and practices. A sense of superior group position prevails: whites are better than blacks; therefore blacks should be subordinated to whites . . . Institutional racism has been maintained deliberately by the power structure and through indifference, inertia and lack of courage on the part of the white masses.

- Abuse of BME groups is condoned, normalizing existing hierarchies and legitimating the dominance of 'whiteness': 'Racist assumptions have become so deeply engrained into the fibre of society that they infuse the entire functioning of the national sub consciousness' (p. 111).
- This understanding of racism has not been utilized by the Prison Service, but is consistent with the two following critical perspectives.

3 'Race' as a determining historical and structural context

- Racism has ideological and structural roots deriving from the legacy of British Imperialism.
- Whiteness, economic prosperity and adherence to law are culturally embedded as characteristic of the English nation (aka 'Englishness').
- The non-English (foreign national/migrant/settler) are conceived as lawless, morally suspect, potentially dangerous and economically unproductive.
- Biologically derived justifications of racism still exist but are marginal to the development of the 'new racism' (cultural racism) which 'others' migrant and foreign populations who are scapegoated as *the problem*, especially in times of economic crisis.
- Solutions engender a commitment to shared humanity which radically addresses issues around global justice and recognition of the role of imprisonment in perpetuating injustice.

4 State racism

- This conceptualizes the problem as a combination of popular, institutional and state racism.
- The focus is on exclusionary penal policies and the developing role of the prison as a means of controlling migrant populations (Gordon 1983).
- Racism is conceived as an expression of power and effective solutions require a radical redistribution of the social product, recognition of shared humanity, and a commitment to cosmopolitan justice.

phenomena is problematized and it is implicit that the racist officer's behaviour should be challenged (Scarman 1981). Significantly, racism is presented as isolated incidents that can be understood on an individualized basis (Edgar 2007). This model in effect absolves the Prison Service and the Capitalist State of wider responsibility, as long as obvious abuses by officers are confronted. Considerations of power and social inequality are painfully missing from this analysis, which conceives of racism as a personal trouble rather than a social issue (Mills 1959). To speak metaphorically, the difficulty is that rather than there being a few 'bad apples' in the barrel it is more likely that the barrel itself and the warehouse in which it is housed are themselves tarnished and contribute to the perpetuation of the problem.

Since the early 2000s the individual pathology explanation has been rarely used by penal practitioners or government representatives with the institutional racism interpretive frame much more likely to be adopted. As we see below, the increasing proportion of members of minority ethnic groups and foreign national people in prisons, combined with high profile incidents such as the racist murder of Zahid

Mubarek and the death of Alton Manning, have 'elevated prison racism to an issue of primary importance in the Prison Service's Agenda in recent years' (Cheliotis and Liebling 2006: 286). Speaking in 1999 the then Director General of the Prison Service, Martin Narey, acknowledged that it was 'institutionally racist' and that 'pockets of blatant racism still existed' (cited in Wilson and Moore 2003: 3).

When making his claim Narey drew inspiration from the highly influential Macpherson Report (1999) into the murder of the black teenager Stephen Lawrence which understood racism in criminal justice agencies as something institutionally embedded. The problem of racism is not individual, but cultural and institutional, and to address racism requires new policies, guidelines and training. While this interpretive frame is undoubtedly a considerable improvement in the previous recognition of racism in prison, it is not without its limitations. The notion of institutional racism places highly restrictive parameters on the understanding of the phenomena, effectively limiting it to a discussion of occupational cultures and the internal workings of the prison. As a result it cannot accommodate the wider structural factors underpinning racism or their intimate links to state policies; the social and political factors which shape the constitution of the prison population; nor the very meanings attributed to the idea of 'race' itself. In other words, the focus may have shifted from the 'bad apple' to recognition that the 'rotten barrel' needs major repairs, but doesn't seem to consider if the warehouse in which it is contained might have a leaky roof or broken windows that ultimately allowed the rot to set in.

More radical approaches have located racism within wider historical and structural contexts and pointed to the influence of 'neo-colonialism' on the application of the penal law (Bowling and Phillips 2001).[5] For writers such as Stuart Hall et al. (1978), Paul Gordon (1983) and Paul Gilroy (1987) the material and ideological legacies of British colonialism from the seventeenth to the twentieth century continue to influence contemporary culture and socio-economic realities. Ideologically, it is argued that the historical legacies constructing 'non-white' people as inferior beings remain as a cultural deposit in the contemporary 'English' imagination. Crucially, Hall et al. (1978) identify that lawfulness is one of the central lay ideologies of *Englishness* and that 'crime' is conceived as an action undertaken by the non-English other. With respect to imprisonment, this analysis implies that ideologies of nationhood and the construction of the non-national lawbreaker become entrenched within everyday practices and institutional cultures of the penal system.

One way to examine the manner in which such ideologies shape racism is through the prison 'racial' classification processes. Both popular and official classifications of 'race' have been closely tied to the concepts of religion (such as Judaism, Islam, Rastafarianism, Hinduism and marginalized doctrines of the Christian church) and nationality, leading to considerable confusion and the proliferation of subcategories charting differences. Roger Matthews (2009) points out that the official classifications of 'race' conflate differences around skin colour, such as identification as black or white, with nationality or a person's country of origin, such as the categories of Asian or Chinese. The current categorizations of 'race' in the Prison Service are divided between White, Black (African, Caribbean and Other), South Asian (Indian, Bangladeshi, Pakistani) and Chinese (Other Asian and Other). While such distinctions initially appear banal, a classification system openly conflating 'race' and nation raises concerns about the relationship between the 'non-white' other, nationhood and the factors which influence *who* is placed in custody (Bosworth and Guild 2008; Symonds 2008).

In recent years the links between 'race' and nationhood have become increasingly culturally, legally and politically important, especially when considering foreign national prisoners. Even the adopted terminology in this chapter, Black or Minority Ethnic (BME) groups, implies such a link, derived as it is partially from the Greek word 'ethnos', which means nation. The category of the 'foreign national' prisoner is a catch all classification that appears to include people as diverse as asylum seekers, economic migrants, refugees and citizens of non-British nationality. While the foreign national label is not a particularly illuminating insight into the lawbreaker's social background, its theoretical significance is in the combination of the prisoner's *foreign* status with subsequent cultural constructions of 'crime'. Crucially, notions of foreignness transcend conceptions of the prisoner (Bosworth 2008; Matthews 2009). Common sense assumptions around Englishness utilize dividing practices to distinguish the 'foreign national' as a dangerous and threatening criminal who should be removed from society rather than reintegrated and allowed to settle.[6] Consideration, then, of racism through its historical and structural contexts can allow us to gain a better understanding of the assumptions influencing the wider filtering and focus of the penal law. To return to our earlier metaphor, in this critical analysis the focus shifts from the rotten apple barrel to the structural problems of the apple warehouse in which it is housed. The only way forward is to dismantle and rebuild with new more appropriate foundations.

More recently, and selectively building on the insights from previous critical debates, Sivanandan (2001) has identified three kinds of contemporary racism – state, institutional and popular racism – which he argues must be contextualized within the broader functioning of the Capitalist State. Here 'institutional racism and popular racism are woven into state racism' (Sivanandan 2001: 3). State racism acknowledges the existence of structural and institutional racism but also adds another dimension to the debate: the manner in which government policies and laws reflect and reproduce certain racist ideologies. State racism can be explored through, for example, immigration laws focusing on xenophobia or the development of certain criminal 'justice' laws and policies. Thus, in a time when it appears that the government is taking racism seriously in some ways, such as in its response to the Macpherson report, in others, such as in its punitive new immigration laws that discriminate against people because of their nationality, it is perpetuating it (Bourne 2001). Our metaphor is therefore now extended to consider the role of the 'managers' of the apple warehouse and how they conceive and deploy policies which reflect the specific interests of the owners of the apple production process.

Case Study 5.2 The foreign national prisoners political scandal, 2006

On 26 April 2006 it came to light that 1023 foreign prisoners had been released since 1999 without their deportation being considered. In 160 of the cases the Judge had recommended deportation. Two hundred and eighty-eight of the offenders in question had been released from prison after Home Secretary Charles Clarke became aware of the situation. It took three weeks for him to inform the Prime Minister. Clarke stated that of the 1023 who had been released without their deportation being considered, 79 were in the category of most serious offenders: that is, they were convicted of murder, rape or manslaughter. For 103 offenders their 'crimes' were unknown. Seventy of these ex-offenders were to be deported. It was not known where some of the ex-offenders were and so the police and other CJS and Immigration agencies had to undertake a large-scale operation in order to locate them. On 3 May, Clarke announced that the number of serious offenders had increased to 90. On 5 May Clarke was sacked and John Reid was appointed as Home Secretary. John Reid then announced that the figure of most serious offenders was considered to be at least 150. On 9 May 2006 he warned that if armed robbers were included – thought to be 93 – then the number of serious offenders involved could be 'several hundred'. It was initially reported that 5 ex-prisoners had reoffended with serious offences but this was a gross underestimation and as Reid himself said, reoffending was 'happening as we speak' (Reid 9/5/06).

Immediately, a new *presumption of deportation* was introduced for foreign nationals convicted of imprisonable offences. The scandal demonstrated administrative failures but also the scope for the political manipulation of statistics. The rhetoric of fear and danger employed, and of the need to protect the British 'nation', meant that it was easy to implement new, draconian immigration laws and procedures due to a lack of resistance. Since April 2006 foreign national prisoners have spent longer in detention after their sentences while immigration decisions are taken. The numbers transferred to Immigration Removal Centres (IRCs) has risen and there has also been a rise in foreign national prisoners being recalled.

For some foreign prisoners, deportation may lead to torture, execution and human rights abuses in their country of origin. On 8 May 2006, however, Tony Blair argued that new legislation would be necessary 'to override the human rights' of foreign nationals so they could be deported. In practice it was not so easy for the government to convince the judiciary that human rights should be overruled, as demonstrated in the 'Afghan hijackers' case (see Symonds 2008), leading the government to implement the racist and xenophobic *Criminal Justice and Immigration Act* (2008) (CJA, 2008).

Source: Home Office (2007); Bhui (2007); Symonds (2008)

Problematizing data on 'race' and racism

The very collation of data on 'race' and racism, never mind the methodologies deployed or their perceived validity or accuracy, is profoundly controversial. On the one hand, it is argued that the statistical classification of false racial categories is likely to legitimate assumptions of racial difference and perpetuate racial discrimination (Simpson 2002).[7] On the other hand, it is believed that statistical data can help identify racist hotspots and be used as a form of knowledge to challenge discriminatory practices. In this sense official data could be used to facilitate a 'crisis of visibility' and provide damning evidence of state racism (Fitzgerald and Sim 1979). Despite the difficulties associated with official data generally, and statistics on 'race' and racism in particular, it is clear that we need data on BME prisoners (Scott 2008a).[8] Information on the ethnic composition of the prison population in England and Wales has only been published since 1986, but concerns about members of BME groups being over-represented in the criminal justice system and the prison population in comparison with the general population have been expressed since the late 1960s (Bottoms 1967). In 1985 8 per cent of men and 12 per cent of women in prison were from BME groups although they constituted only 1 per cent of the general population. It is difficult to draw long term comparisons as the classification system used by the Prison Service changed in 1992, but broadly speaking there has been an increase in the total prison population coupled with an increased number and proportion of members of BME groups. In 2008 21 per cent of sentenced offenders came from a BME group,[9] while in July 2009 foreign national prisoners collectively constituted 14 per cent of the overall prison population (11,400 of an 83,900 ADP) (Ministry of Justice 2009b).

Data on racism in prison is much less developed and is likely to be a significant under-estimate. For contemporary official data see Box 5.2. Because of difficulties in proving racist intent, 'interpretative denials' (Cohen 2001) of racist incidents in prison are common, resulting in their invisibility in official data. Racist incidents may also not be recorded because there is reluctance from prisoners to make use of official complaints or grievance procedures. Prisoner testimonies cited in Wilson and Moore (2003: 6) detail prisoner scepticism as 'all the screws stick together' and 'when you fill in a complaint form they don't do shit anyway'. There is also fear or reprisals: 'I don't make complaints because at a later date the screws get back at you. You start to lose your privileges, like they take away your association or they take away your gym and so it's not worth it' (Wilson and Moore 2003: 6).

Box 5.2 Official data on 'race', religion and nationality in prison in 2008

- 27% of the total prison population (sentenced and remand) are members of black or minority ethnic groups.
- BME prisoners are not evenly geographically distributed across the country and constitute between 25%–50% of the populations in South East England.
- 38% of BME prisoners are foreign nationals.
- Numbers of foreign national prisoners increased by 144% from 1997 to 2007.
- Nearly 20% of women in prison are foreign nationals. Seventy-three per cent of the foreign national women prisoner population are in prison for the first time.
- In prison 42% of Muslims are Asian, 34% are 'black' and 14% white.

Source: Ministry of Justice (2008c, 2009b); Her Majesty's Chief Inspector of Prisons (2009a); Prison Reform Trust (2009)

Controversy also reigns regarding the interpretation of data on BME prisoners with mental health problems. While BME people have been identified as over-represented in prison and secure psychiatric facilities, the numbers of BME prisoners diagnosed with mental health problems has historically been relatively low. Coid et al. (2002) believe that this phenomenon can be explained because: (1) there is racism among mental health workers who ignore the mental health needs of BME prisoners and (2) BME prisoners are more reluctant to admit to their mental health problems with psychiatric professionals in prison. If BME prisoners are perceived as being control problems and racially stereotyped as 'big, black and dangerous', trust between BME prisoners and mental health staff is likely to be seriously eroded (Shaw and Sampson 1991). Today people from BME communities with mental health problems represent about 10 per cent of the UK BME population but in prison this rises to around 20 per cent. Indeed, the Bradley Report (2009) indicates that the prison system is now a major pathway for BME groups into mental health services as members of BME groups are 40 per cent more likely to access mental services via a criminal justice route.

Historical context

It was not until the 1970s that long held concerns about policing BME groups began to develop into broader critiques of the role of law and legal agencies in the context of a racist society. Only then were concerted efforts made to address the historic 'invisibility' of the experiences of BME groups in British prisons. Early critical researchers, such as Paul Gordon (1983), found extensive and highly disturbing evidence of widespread and endemic racist abuse. BME prisoners faced brutal treatment and the neglect of their cultural or religious needs.[10] There was considerable evidence of individual and institutional racism in terms of work allocation and responses to disciplinary infractions, and where prisoners complained of racism it was either ignored or often inadequately dealt with (Gordon 1983; Genders and Player 1989). Indeed, like today, many racist incidents went unreported (Burnett and Farrell 1994).

In the early years of concern the focus of researchers was primarily on those categorized as 'African-Caribbean'. Gordon (1983) details prisoner testimonies reporting orchestrated violence and beatings; being subjected to regular racist verbal abuse and taunting; being referred to as 'wogs' and 'niggers'; forced into solitary confinement; and officers openly being active members of racist organizations such as the National Front.[11] Racism was so overt that it was witnessed by external researchers to prisons at the time, one of whom was asked if she had 'come to view the wogs' (Gordon 1983: 127). At the same time, due to the bombing campaign conducted by the provisional IRA on the English mainland during the 1970s and 1980s, Irish people came under suspicion and prisoners faced extreme hostility from some prison staff (Hillyard 1993).

The initial steps towards acknowledgement of the problem came in 1981 when the Prison Service issued its first instructions to governors on 'race relations' closely followed by the development of its first 'race relations' policy in 1983 (NACRO 2000). Genders and Player (1989), in an important early study of 'race relations' in prisons, found that many officers were less tolerant and more wary of BME prisoners than 'white' prisoners. Staff used racist terminology and the study uncovered significant evidence of direct racial discrimination. To help combat racist officer cultures the Prison Service made a largely unsuccessful attempt to recruit more BME officers in 1990 and in 1991 it launched a 'comprehensive' 'race relations' manual.[12] Alongside this it introduced new training events, a staff pocket guidebook and created the role of the 'race relations' liaison officer. Despite these initiatives problems still persisted throughout the 1990s. Evidence was accumulated regarding how British-born black women were subjected to manhandling, heavier supervision, harsher punishment, cultural stereotyping, and constructed as 'troublemakers' (Devlin 1998; Chigwada-Bailey 2003). Male BME prisoners continued to be seen as a *problem* and labelled as a dangerous and lawless other by prison staff. Detailed research also indicated that members of prison staff often over-reacted to disruptive behaviour by 'African-Caribbeans', operating racist stereotypes and negative reputations to effectively distance and dehumanize the prisoner (Chigwada-Bailey 2003; IRR 2005).

Evidence of racism was also apparent when BME prisoners looked to the Prison Service for protection from physical assaults, racist abuse and harassment. Serious concerns began to be raised about the high number of BME deaths in custody (Ryan 1996). The Prison Service failed to learn the lessons from the tragic deaths of Edita Pommell, Cheryl Hartman, Anthony Mahony and many others. Indeed, rather than taking BME deaths in custody seriously, attempts were made to 'explain away' the phenomena. For example, in 1998, Richard Tilt, the then Director-General of the Prison Service, suggested that black prisoners are more likely to die from positional asphyxia while being restrained because of their genetic disposition to sickle cell anaemia (*Independent*, 28 March 1998). It seems likely that self-inflicted deaths of BME prisoners can be aggravated by a lack of concern for their fears and physical, mental health needs or by ignoring previous 'suicide' attempts (Ryan 1996; Bowling and Phillips 2001). This underlines the twin fallacies that imprisonment protects innocent victims and reforms offenders: where members of BME groups are concerned it does neither. They are more likely to be victimized and then defined as a problem.

In the early 1990s Burnett and Farrell (1994) surveyed 501 prisoners in eight prisons, measuring verbal abuse, threats, assault and harassment. Fifty-eight per cent of black prisoners felt they had been victimized by staff; 39 per cent of those of 'other' nationalities; 36 per cent of Asians; and 33 per cent of white prisoners. Interestingly, 44 per cent of black prisoners perceived a racial element to their victimization in contrast with only 2 per cent of white prisoners. Black prisoners were less likely to view relations between staff and prisoners favourably although nearly three-quarters of officers described staff-prisoner relations as 'generally good'. In 1995 the Commission for Racial Equality (CRE) and the Prison Service published a report on the *Management of Race Relations in Prison Establishments*, which led to a revised draft of the 'race relations' manual and racial abuse becoming a specific staff disciplinary offence. In 1997 a new streamlined policy on 'race relations' was issued which included a set of standards covering legal obligations; management structures and performance assessment; ethnic monitoring; facilities and services; complaints and racial incidents, external contacts, training and information. Two years later a new programme (RESPOND) was launched and in 2000 the Prison Service introduced a new BME staff support network (RESPECT). The Prison Reform Trust (2001) conducted a survey of 29 of its members and found that covert and structural racism were more widespread causes of concern than blatant direct racism. Sixty-one per cent of those interviewed said they had experienced direct racism while employed in prisons while two thirds felt that 'race relations' were valued. There were, however, concerns that those who experienced racism did not report it.

Contemporary penal policy

The contours of Prison Service policy today are shaped by official responses to the controversial death of Zahid Mubarek in HMP/YOI Feltham in March 2000. Three years after the death the CRE (2003a and b) published two reports on the murder. Part one identified 20 failings in how Feltham was being run and concluded that Zahid Mubarek had not been given the equivalent protection of that available to white prisoners. Part two focused on the evidence from all other parts of the investigation that were not directly related to Zahid Mubarek's death and the report identified fourteen areas of failure. The 2003 reports led to a partnership between the CRE and the Prison Service and the publication of an action plan, *Shared Agenda for Change*. The CRE reports and action plan, however, did not go far enough and, after a long hard legal struggle brought by Imtiaz Amin, the Uncle of Zahid Mubarek, culminating in the House of Lords Ruling on 16 October 2003, a public inquiry was established on 29 April 2004. *Regina v. Secretary of State for the Home Department ex parte Amin* found that the existing inquiries into the death had not met the requirements of Articles 1 and 2 (1) of the European Convention of Human Rights and Lord Justice Keith was commissioned to head up the report.

Case Study 5.3 The racist murders of Zahid Mubarek and Shahid Aziz

Zahid Mubarek (1980–2000) died after a violent attack by his cellmate Robert Stewart in HMP Feltham on the night before he was to be released. Zahid, who was in prison for the first time for a number of petty property offences, was beaten to death by a known racist with a table leg that had been detached a number of days before the incident. Zahid Mubarek went into a coma as a result of the attack and died seven days later on 28 March 2000. Zahid Mubarek's murderer Robert Stewart was defined as having a personality disorder and in the Keith Report (2006) 25 of the 63 chapters in volume one are focused exclusively on the catalogue of failures to acknowledge or address Stewart's personal troubles. While Robert Stewart was 'a very strange young man' (p. 75) with a swastika tattooed to his forehead, the circumstances leading up to Zahid Mubarek's tragic death and his family's struggle for justice also tells us a great deal about the operational practices and culture of the Prison Service as well as how seriously the government takes the problem of racism in prison.

There were clear omissions on the part of the Prison Service in the lead up to Zahid Mubarek's murder. From 1990 to 2001 there were 26 prisoner-on-prisoner homicides, 12 of which were in shared cells. Serious concerns were consequently raised around the decision for the two young men to share a cell[13] and the failure of prison authorities to act upon a racist letter written by Robert Stewart less than a month before his violent assault. Here is a brief extract from the letter (cited in CRE 2003: 3): 'Cannot see it stickin in ere, If I don't get bail on the 7th, I'll take xtreme measures to get shipped out, kill me fuckin padmate if I have to, bleach me pillowcase white + make a klu Klux klan outfit + walkout me pad wiv a flaming cruxifix'.

A less well known, but equally disturbing case is the death of Shahid Aziz in 2004. Shahid Aziz was 25 when convicted of criminal damage and sent to HMP Armley Leeds to await sentence. Only two days later, however, he was murdered by his cellmate Peter McCann for speaking Urdu. Shahid had also been outspoken the previous day about racism in Armley. He was beaten to death with a chair, where his skull and jaw were broken, and then he had his throat cut. In May 2007 the Inquest into the death gave a verdict of 'unlawful killing' and a critical narrative stating that the Prison Service was partially responsible for his death. Despite it occurring four years after the death of Zahid Mubarek, the Prison Service does not appear to have learnt any lessons regarding protecting vulnerable BME prisoners.

Source: CRE (2003a); Keith (2006); Scott (2008b)

Before the Keith Report was completed, however, the HMCIP (2005a) published *Parallel Worlds*, a thematic review of 'race relations' in prisons. The review began from a recognition that processes for addressing racism were in place, but that surveys routinely found that BME prisoners had worse perceptions of their treatment than white prisoners. The report found that 'there is no shared understanding of race issues within prisons: instead, there are a series of parallel worlds inhabited by different groups of staff and prisoners, with widely divergent views and experiences' (HMCIP 2005a: 2). Thus there was a huge difference between governors and white race relations liaison officers, who felt the regime operated fairly, and BME staff members, who found it difficult to influence change, felt lack of direction and support and were less likely to believe the prison was tackling 'race' effectively. A significant aspect of the report, however, was that it challenged an assumption of homogeneity of experience, with 'parallel worlds' existing between different ages, genders and minority groups. Respect was the primary concern for 'Black' prisoners, for example, but for 'Asian' prisoners the key concern was safety.

On 29 June 2006 the long awaited Keith Report was published. The inquiry operated within the interpretive frame of institutional racism adopted by Macpherson (1999). Keith (2006: 30–1) 'saw no reason not to accept the conclusion that institutional racism existed in the prison service . . . [this was] attributable to a collective organizational failure which was informed and shaped by the institutional racism with which Feltham was infected'. The Keith Report (2006) provides a highly damning account of the systemic failings of the Prison Service to adhere to its procedural guidelines, where they existed, and the dominance of a culture rooted in moral indifference, neglect and insensitivity to racial and religious differences. Keith (2006) made 88 recommendations in total but conveyed the reassuring message that much of what he would have recommended had been subsequently put in place and that many of the systematic shortcomings his review had identified had, by the time of reporting, been removed (Scott 2008b). Ultimately the most high profile recommendation was to expand Macpherson's definition of institutional racism to include 'institutional religious intolerance' (Keith 2006: 546). Though the report is significant for its emphasis on accountability and the responsibility of prison officers for the wellbeing of prisoners, it cloaked its analysis with more familiar arguments. Keith's main concerns were with addressing resources; failures in the transfer of prisoner information; under-staffing and the need for 'decency'. Crucially it omits any attempt to expand the analysis to consider the legitimacy of imprisonment when understood within the nature of state racism. There was no attempt to locate racism in prison within current policies of social exclusion for asylum seekers and refugees, immigration policies, racial bias in the criminal justice system as a whole, or the experiences of foreign national prisoners.

So, the question must be asked as to what progress, if any, has been made since the CRE (2003), HMCIP (2005) and Keith (2006) reports? In December 2008 the Ministry of Justice published *Implementing Race Equality in Prisons – Five Years On* (Ministry of Justice 2008c) and in his foreword current National Offender Management Service Director General Phil Wheatley maintains,

> Race is an integral part of managing prisons – it is a key part of our work and a key part of how we make everything else work. Getting race wrong is dangerous to society, duplicates resources and wastes time and money. It also sours relations between prisoners and staff – the key component in securing control, order and a reduction in re-offending.
>
> (p.1)

The Ministry of Justice report stresses how much the Prison Service has progressed in delivering 'race' equality since 2003, and how many systems and processes have been introduced, although it also emphasizes the need for strong and effective leadership and a shift in culture. Yet this report also acknowledges that 'despite considerable investment in procedural changes, the experience of BME prisoners and staff has not been transformed' (Ministry of Justice 2008c: 9). The Prison Service has also tried to improve employee diversity, with recruitment and retention of staff from BME groups improving from 3.5 per cent in 2000 up to 6.2 per cent in April 2008. Each prison or YOI now has a Race Equality officer and the handling of racist incident reporting forms has been made more rigorous in order to ensure access, tracking and investigation. The report also identifies, however, that BME prisoners are more likely to be on the basic rather than enhanced regime, to be in segregation for reasons of Good Order or Discipline or to have force used against them (Ministry of Justice 2008c). The complaints system seems more able to deal with open, blatant racism than more subtle and covert forms, and BME prisoners continue to view the complaints system more negatively than white prisoners.

Following on from the five-year plan the Prison Service has attempted to shift from a narrow focus on 'race relations' to a broader focus on a range of equality issues under the new 'single equality duty'. The emphasis here on diversity is *not* based on a commitment to equality for prisoners, but to ensure that the goals of protecting the public and reducing reoffending are met. As Phil Wheatley (Ministry of Justice 2008c) puts it:

> Right relationships and fair service delivery are crucial to our business. They are the key to safety in prisons, to reducing reoffending and to public protection. Offenders must be provided with a chance to reform, and that means being able to gain access to the services they need.

Other fundamental contradictions also remain. The Prison Service is increasingly committed to policies differentiating, monitoring and excluding individuals on the grounds of their 'nationhood'. There has been a clear assimilation of prison and immigration controls (Bosworth and Guild 2008).[14] This blurring of the boundaries means both systems now aim to house the unwanted 'non-English' other. Migrants are conceived as a threat and danger whether they have broken the law or not and the increasing number of foreign nationals in prison appears to justify increasingly repressive and exclusionary government immigration control practices. Consequently, while there appears to be some progress on the one hand, such as the Diversity policy, on the other hand, the Capitalist State claws it back with its punitive policies towards foreign nationals and migrants. Thus while the Diversity policy prohibits discrimination on the basis of national origin (HM Prison Service 2004) dividing practices based on the surveillance, identification and categorization of the foreign other are increasing entrenched in penal practices. As the Prison Service must only tackle discrimination that is against the law there is no obvious conflict of interests here, yet this simple example demonstrates the significance of analysing the legitimacy of government policies rather than reducing accounts to legality and institutional practices alone.

Legitimacy

To understand the insidious nature of 'race' and racism in prison we need to use our sociological imagination to look beyond the interpretive frames of individual or institutional racism towards understandings that locate the phenomena at the level of social structure and the workings of the Capitalist State. Mechanisms of state racism can be subtle: they involve decisions and policies which appear 'race-neutral' but impact disproportionately on BME groups and crucially perform a key role in the constitution of prisoner populations. The most obvious example of this today concerns foreign national prisoners. Matthews (2009) argues that there has been an exponential growth in foreign national prisoner populations for two reasons: (1) there has been an internationalization of 'crime', and (2) it is intimately linked with attempts to control migration. Matthews (2009) also points out that migrants are likely to have limited financial resources, and, as it is the poor who provide the main pool from which prison populations are drawn, we should not be surprised that foreign nationals are now flooding the penal system. Significantly, foreign nationals are not going to be reintegrated back into the community, and so by default the prison's role for this population must be one of containment rather than normalization.

> The net effect of the growing racial disproportionality in prisons is that there appears to be developing a two-tier system of imprisonment in Western Europe: one for citizens and one for foreign nationals. These two systems of imprisonment, although occurring in the same building, mean that the experiences, purposes and effects of incarceration are likely to be very different for the two groups.
>
> (Matthews 2009: 229)

With the focus on 'protecting the public' and deportation of non-citizens (PSI 42/ 2007) it is perhaps no surprise that the treatment of foreign nationals is at times nothing short of appalling. Foreign national prisoners experience the usual 'pains of imprisonment' but these are exacerbated by being imprisoned in a foreign country. The three most serious problems relate to family contact, communication and isolation (Bhui 2007). The chances of being granted bail are also greatly diminished. Additional stress and challenges are faced by foreign nationals in relation to uncertainty about their immigration status and fear of deportation, especially where the offending behaviour leads to stigmatization and hostility on return to their 'home' country. It is perhaps significant to note that in 2008 16 per cent of self-inflicted deaths in prisons were of foreign national prisoners (HMCIP 2009a).[15]

Immigration controls and laws, such as the new points-based system (PBS) can also constitute forms of state racism as they are predicated on public support for the view that immigration should be limited, tapping into latent ideologies of the UK being 'swamped' by large numbers of incoming migrants. The *Criminal Justice and Immigration Act* 2008 (CJIA 2008) creates a new power to designate certain people as 'foreign criminals' and render them subject to controls. The CJIA 2008 can also remove access to welfare support until the foreign national agrees to leave. The CJIA 2008 must be read in conjunction with the powers extant under the 2007 *UK Borders Act* (UKBA) which came into force on 1 August 2008. From that date the UK Borders Agency is able to deport any non-British and non-EEA citizen who has been sentenced to a prison term of 12 months or more, unless they can demonstrate that deportation breaches their human rights.

The new provisions, justified by political rhetoric of preventing terrorism and avoiding giving sanctuary to overseas criminals, allows for the designation of 'foreign criminals' and their family members as having 'special immigration status' (Pantazis and Pemberton 2009). This status is aimed at those people who would be deported under the UKBA 2007 but who cannot be deported for human rights reasons. This status leaves those subject to it in an indefinite form of limbo. People so designated have been described as being in a 'twilight zone' (Symonds 2008). Once somebody is given this status, they are subject to immigration control, but not to be treated as an asylum seeker and are not in breach of immigration laws. This legislation it is not only potentially discriminatory and harmful to those who have committed offences, but also to their non-convicted family member. This is clearly state racism operating under the justificatory guise of public protection, and it has major implications for future detained populations.[16]

'Black' and 'Asian' communities, and increasingly communities from across Europe, become inextricably linked in the popular, media and public imagination of 'crime' and disorder. Instead of racism being seen as the problem, it is the members of these communities that become defined as 'the problem', drawing attention away from the racist abuses perpetrated by 'white English' people. Prison provides us with a snapshot of the denial, exclusion and discrimination against members of BME groups in Britain today, yet all of the initiatives in the world to improve 'race relations' will ultimately come to nothing unless the inherent racism of the Capitalist State and its agencies is challenged. The Capitalist State needs to stop considering BME prisoners as 'the problem' and instead focus on tackling racism head on.

One obvious way forward is to abolish the increasingly punitive and racist government policies controlling migrant populations and bring an end to immigration detention. There should also be an immediate end to penal sanctions for migration transgressions and indeed, much current immigration law could be substantially reformed and amended so as not to stigmatize and criminalize foreign nationals and their families. Further, foreign national prison populations would be drastically reduced if migrants were given greater support to settle in the community and if the prison sanction for drug possession and low-level dealing was abolished. These selective abolitions of the emerging penal-immigration complex would be a first step towards embracing the principles of human rights and social and cosmopolitan justice (Hudson 2009). Central is the recognition of rights of others and the need to treat *all* people, whatever their social backgrounds or wherever they are from, with dignity, respect and a little hospitality.

Further reading

Bowling, B. and Phillips, C. (2001) *Racism, Crime and Criminal Justice*. London: Longman.
Genders, E. and Player, E. (1989) *Race Relations in Prison*. Oxford: Clarendon Press.
Gilroy, P. (2001) *Between Camps*. London: Verso.
Gordon, P. (1983) *White Law*. London: Pluto Press.
Sivanandan, A. (1990) *Communities of Resistance: Writings on Black Struggles for Socialism*. London: Verso.
Wilson, D. and Moore, S. (2003) *Playing the Game – The Experiences of Young Black Men in Custody*. London: The Children's Society.

Alongside keeping a keen eye on the latest of official reports and policies we also recommend that students follow closely the important critical debates raised in journals such as *Race and Class* and *New Left Review* as well as regularly checking the website and related publications of the Institute for Race Relations (IRR).

6
Self-inflicted deaths

Self-inflicted deaths in prison are one of the most disturbing features of the confinement project. It is estimated that around 200 people die in prison each year (Forum for Preventing Deaths in Custody 2007). Approximately three prisoners kill themselves every two weeks, with a slightly higher number of 'natural' deaths in custody over the same period. The likelihood of a prisoner taking their own life is between four and eleven times higher than the general population (Themeli 2006). Many others come perilously close to taking their own lives and for at least one penal commentator the criminal justice system 'has rapidly become our secret death penalty' (Wilson 2005: 1).[1] A self-inflicted death occurs when somebody takes their own life but only becomes a suicide if the person *intended* to die. As it is very difficult to determine intention we adopt the term self-inflicted deaths in this chapter. In recent decades such deaths have been reasonably high on the Prison Service agenda but they have not always received major public, political or media interest. In the 1940s, 1950s and 1960s few people paid much attention and prisoner deaths were largely unreported. By the early 1980s, however, deaths in prison once again became recognized as a serious cause for concern, largely because of consistent lobbying from prisoners' families and friends, often channelled through the pressure group INQUEST (Sim 1990; Ryan 1996).[2]

The death of Christine Scott, aged 19, who died from a subdural haemorrhage at Holloway in 1982, was one of the first self-inflicted deaths to receive major media attention in recent times. In this tragic case Christine died from throwing herself repeatedly around her cell. The prison officer who found her stated that 'there was not a single part of her body without a bruise' (cited in Scraton and Chadwick 1987a: 136). While isolated deaths continued to create controversy, media and political attention gained serious momentum from the 1980s through focusing on the clustering of deaths in particular penal institutions. In 1984 HMP Brixton recorded ten deaths in a period of just over 12 months while the same prison grabbed the headlines again in 1989 when it was revealed that 11 prisoners had died that year, eight being self-inflicted. In a period of less than 30 months from 1987–89 11 self-inflicted deaths were recorded at Risley Remand Centre, earning it the nickname 'Grisly Risley'. Five young men aged from 17 to 19 died while on remand at HMP Armley between

May 1988 and February 1989. A further teenager died at Armley prison in 1990 while between August 1991 and March 1992 four young offenders, including a 15-year-old, took their lives at Feltham YOI (Ryan 1996).

Cluster deaths have not been restricted to young male offenders but plague all aspects of the penal estate. Six women hanged themselves in a three-year period from 2002 to 2005 at HMP Durham H wing, while from August 2002 and September 2003 six women took their lives at HMP Styal, the latter sad events leading to the commissioning of the Corston Report (2007a). There have also been cluster deaths among adult male prisoners. In one recent example five prisoners killed themselves at HMP Whitemoor between 19 November 2006 and 10 December 2007. Presented in numerical form this data hardly reflects the tragedy of such circumstances but public exposure, after years of being hidden from view, has meant that the Prison Service is now confronted with a 'crisis of visibility' (Fitzgerald and Sim 1979).

For some writers there exists a *continuum of self-destructive behaviour* (Liebling 1992) encompassing a range of self-injurious acts. It is argued that self-harm and 'suicide' arise from psychological pain and operate as 'a continuum along which one step may prove to be the first stage of a pathway to despair' (p. 67). Self-harm in prison includes cutting, scratching, suffocation, overdosing, head-bashing, swallowing foreign objects, burning, refusing food, inserting items into the body and jumping from wing landings (Rickford and Edgar 2005). Most acts of self-harm do not endanger life and it seems more appropriate to understand this action as primarily a means to release pain (Howard League 2001). A prisoner who self-harms is probably trying to find a way of dealing with negative feelings by turning mental pain into physical pain. Self-harm then is a step on the 'road to survival' (p. 3) rather than the pathway to suicide. We consequently focus on prisoners who have taken or attempted to take their life, with consideration though that some self-inflicted deaths may have been acts of self-harm gone wrong.

This chapter starts with a critical overview of the definition and four main ways of thinking about self-inflicted deaths in prison and then proceeds to discuss the difficulties of adopting a 'scientific' approach to assess the extent of the problem. Utilizing an abolitionist interpretive frame we highlight the fundamental limitations of official data and then question a number of assumptions about how prisoners cope, or not, with the prison place. The chapter then reviews critically the historical and contemporary development of Prison Service policies on self-inflicted deaths and concludes with a discussion of their legitimacy and possible alternative means of responding to wrong-doers vulnerable to suicidal ideation. Interspersed in this chapter are case studies outlining three controversial deaths.

Thinking critically about self-inflicted deaths

Whether a self-inflicted death is defined as a 'suicide' is influenced by the circumstances leading up to the death, the manner in which the person has died, their social background and the location where the act occurred. A self-inflicted death in prison is more likely to be defined as a 'suicide' if it is undertaken by a man, occurs during the night and happens at the weekend (Dooley 1990). Around 90 per cent of prison 'suicides' are accomplished by hanging and historically 'suicide' verdicts are more likely to be reached if the death occurs in the healthcare centre (prison hospital) or segregation unit (Topp 1979; Lloyd 1990). According to Alison Liebling (1992) a 'suicide' verdict is more likely if the dead prisoner has previously self-harmed, attempted 'suicide' or has a history of psychiatric treatment. Generally there has to be a communication of intent, such as through a suicide note. Under the *Suicide Act* (1961) it must be proved beyond all reasonable doubt that the act was 'suicide'. If there is ambiguity or the death could be understood as an accident then it cannot be officially defined as suicide (Maxwell Atkinson 1978; Dooley 1994). In short it is only 'suicides which "look like" suicides, [that] become suicides' (Liebling 1992: 85–6).[3]

Deaths in custody have been largely framed through the psycho-medical model resulting in a focus upon individual pathologies rather than penal institutions (Sim 1990). The deployment of this interpretive lens informs dividing practices which attempt to identify, classify and profile suicidal risk, often linking self-inflicted deaths with 'abnormal' people with serious mental health problems. Yet, the analytical purchase gained from such assumptions is remarkably limited (Williams 2001). Even if a person who takes their life has mental health problems this cannot tell us why they took their life at that specific time or provide any insight into the distinct set of interpersonal dynamics leading up to the act (Kobler and Stotland 1964).

It has proved exceptionally difficult to identify the manner in which mental health problems actually relate to suicidal attempts or to differentiate the 'suicidal' from the rest of the prison population (Lloyd 1990). One of the key issues here is evidence of the prevalence of suicidal thoughts among prisoners, with a number of studies identifying high levels of suicidal ideation. Singleton et al. (1998) found that 46 per cent of male remand prisoners had thought of 'suicide' in their lifetime, 35 per cent in the past year and 12 per cent in the week prior to interview. Jenkins et al. (2005) found that 40 per cent of male prisoners and 55 per cent of female prisoners had experienced suicidal thoughts in their lifetime compared with 14 per cent of men and 4 per cent of women living in the wider community. Liebling (2007) found that 34.6 per cent of male remand prisoners, 19.4 per cent of male sentenced prisoners, 49 per cent of female remand prisoners and 33.9 per cent of female sentenced prisoners have thought about suicide during the past year. It seems then that somewhere between one third and one half of the prison population have suicidal thoughts, and that many have recently thought about taking their lives. If such figures are accurate this would involve somewhere in the region of 42,000 people in prison on any given day. This number is so large that it raises serious doubts about explanations rooted in individual pathologies.

While many people in prison do have mental health problems, those who commit 'suicide' are less likely to have a psychiatric history than those on the outside who take their own lives (Liebling 1992). Recognizing the weakness of the mental health–suicide connection one public health psychologist has gone as far as to claim prison 'suicides' should be understood as a means of communicating violence. For David Crighton (2006b: 65) suicidal ideation is 'based on aggressive impulses, deriving from the emotion of anger' as violent offenders, when prevented from being violent to others in the prison environment, are more likely to be violent to the self. This suggestion is of course fundamentally flawed, condemned through commitments to positivistic methodologies, individualized assumptions and a general denial that emotional disturbances can be created by the prison place itself.

It seems much more plausible to focus on how self-inflicted deaths are a socially negotiated process where the final decision to end life is influenced by the interpretations and expectations of significant others. For Kobler and Stotland (1964: 1) an apparent suicidal attempt may be a frantic and desperate attempt to 'solve problems of living'. If the response to this situation is hopeless and there is an explicit or implicit expectation that the individual will take their life, this negative communication may erode any sense of hope and facilitate a suicide attempt. Self-inflicted deaths then should be conceived as a social problem where those who take their own lives respond to 'a set of fluctuating capacities which will wax and wane in relation to time, place and social relations' (Medlicott 2001: 13).

Case Study 6.1 Adam Rickwood

Adam died on 9 August 2004, at Hassockfield Secure Training Centre. He was aged 14. Adam grew up in Burnley, Lancashire. He had strong attachments to his grandparents, but was severely shaken when three of them died during an 18-month period. After this Adam was excluded from school and had a history of self-harming behaviour, including on one occasion an attempted overdose of tablets. In July 2004, Adam was accused of stabbing 19-year-old Stephen McNally and was sent to Hassockfield Secure Training Centre, near Consett, County Durham. It was Adam's first time in custody and he had told his mother that he intended to kill himself a few days before he died. After an argument with a member of staff, Adam was severely restrained by three male members of staff. Adam was 5ft 1inch tall and weighed seven and a half stone but staff used the 'nose distraction' restraint technique. The sense of injustice was unbearable and later that evening Adam made a ligature from his shoelaces and hung himself from a curtain rail. Before he died he wrote a detailed account of what had happened.

> When the other staff came they all jumped on me and started to put my arms up my back and hitting me in the nose. I then tried to bite one of the staff because they were really hurting my nose. My nose started bleeding and swelled up and it didn't stop bleeding for about one hour and afterwards it was really sore. When I calmed down I asked them why they hit me in the nose and jumped on me. They said it was because I wouldn't go in my room so I said what gives them the right to hit a 14 year old child in the nose and they said it was restraint
>
> (cited in Allison and Hattenstone 2007: 2)

Adam is the youngest ever person to die in penal custody.

Source: Goldson and Coles (2005); Scott (2008a)

Official discourse has generally privileged explanations where the person who died is understood as being personally culpable for their own death (Topp 1979; HMCIP 1999). The individual character and social background of the person who died is identified as pathological: they were 'weak' or 'high risk inadequates' who would have committed 'suicide' whether they were in prison or not. Their death is directly linked to vulnerabilities and risk factors that existed prior to imprisonment such as unemployment, substance misuse, mental health problems, child abuse and social isolation, or to the nature of their offence, or sentence length (Paton and Borrill 2004; Wool and Pont 2006). In other words the Prison Service 'believes that the continuing high levels of apparent self-inflicted deaths are a product of the high proportion of prisoners with key risk factors' (HM Government 2005: 10).

Alongside this there exists an even cruder notion of individual inadequacy that is closely associated with the traditional prison officer working personality. This understanding is founded through the institutionalization of negative reputations and dividing practices categorizing prisoners as deserving or non-deserving of care and attention (Scraton and Chadwick 1987a). Prisoners are placed at great psychic distance and successfully 'othered', thus preventing any possible empathy and acknowledgement of prisoner suffering (Malloch 2000; Cohen 2001). Negative categorizations justify hostility, neglect and moral indifference, and lead to the blame of prisoners for their own dreadful predicament (Coles and Ward 1994). Those who harm themselves or attempt to take their own lives are labelled as childish and pathetic manipulators whose harming act is part of a 'general display of attention-seeking behaviour' (Topp 1979: 26). For Liebling (1992: 233) both the staff and prisoner argot is a 'language of contempt', referring to self-harmers as 'slashers' and 'cutters'. When they die it is interpreted as a manipulative gesture gone wrong.

Self-inflicted deaths have also been explained as an inability to cope with degrading prison conditions (Dooley 1994; Paton and Borrill 2004; Themeli 2006; Allison 2007). From this perspective the prison environment can be healthy and safe for people with vulnerabilities but becomes dangerous when it falls below certain standards. Particular focus has been on prison crowding. It has long been recognized that most self-inflicted deaths take place in the most crowded prisons (Wool and Dooley 1987; Stewart 2007). Prison crowding is seen as exacerbating the structural deprivations of imprisonment, leading to idleness; limited constructive activities; difficulties in carrying out risk assessments; shortages of essential resources; greater unpredictability of daily life; increases in situational induced stress; increased opportunities for violence and intimidation; and increased staff/prisoner ratios. It may also lead to more vulnerable people being imprisoned (Cox et al. 1984; Bernheim 1994; McCarthy 2003; Huey and McNulty 2005).

The official line is that prison crowding does not increase self-inflicted deaths. In fact, it is argued that it does the opposite as it is believed that cell sharing can be used as a preventative strategy (Hancock 2003). For example, a Ministry of Justice spokesperson (cited in Woodward 2008: 1) stated in January 2008: 'A high proportion of prisoners arrive in prison with known factors that we know increase the risk of them harming themselves. However, there is no agreed evidence that overcrowding exacerbates levels of self-harm in prison. In fact cell sharing is a known protective factor against suicide.' While it is important to consider the situational context, reducing the debate to crowding and physical conditions alone may be unhelpful. Crowding is something that can be easily identified but surviving the prison place is much more complex than this (Medlicott 2001).

It has also been argued that self-inflicted deaths arise from a combination of 'risky prisoners', who may or may not be psychiatrically ill, with an inability to cope with the stress of confinement (Zamble and Porporino 1988; Liebling 1992; Blaauw and Kerkhof 2006; Harvey 2007). For Liebling (1998: 68), some prisoners are 'suicide prone', as 'the prison population is carefully selected to be at risk of suicide'. The suicidal prisoner is considered to suffer from fear, depression, despondency and hopelessness and a general inability to adapt to prison life. The poorly managed prison is conceived as highly stressful turning already existing emotional disturbances into suicidal ideation (Dear 2006). Suicidal prisoners simply do not have the personal resources to cope with the deprivations of an 'unhealthy' and poorly performing prison. Further, for Liebling (1996) it would be wrong to see all 'suicides' as the same. Rather they should be divided into three categories with the 'poor coper' grouping constituting more than half of all 'suicides' (see Table 6.1).

It is argued that the pains of imprisonment are concentrated at particular points in the prison sentence, with the start of a prison sentence entailing the greatest levels of stress. As time goes by, however, most prisoners learn to adjust (Zamble and Porporino 1988). Adaptation is linear, not easily reversible and dependent upon the ability to effectively develop mechanisms of support. Joel Harvey (2007) has elaborated upon this, arguing that prisoners who cannot adapt are more likely to attempt to take their own lives. 'Harmers' have poor relationships; spend large amounts of time in their cells alone; are averse to physical education, bored, inactive; suffer from sleeplessness and generally find the prison place more painful than 'copers' (Harvey 2007).

Some of these assumptions have been taken to task by abolitionists, who

Table 6.1 Liebling's suicide typology

Type of suicide	Proportion of total suicides	Age	Important features
Psychiatrically Ill	25–30%	30+	Infrequent previous self-injury; single; motivation = fear, loss of control, alienation, etc.
Life sentence prisoners	10–15%	30+	Infrequent previous self-injury; often on remand; some well into sentence; motivation = guilt/no future
Poor copers	50–60%	Under 26	More impulsive, situation-specific, previous self-injury frequent; motivation = fear, helplessness, distress

Source: Liebling (1996: 43)

understand the prison place as a highly toxic environment undermining constructions of the self for all prisoners. Life in the prison place is seen as a humiliating and unsafe experience perpetuating fear and loathing on a daily basis. Dividing prisoners between 'copers' and 'non-copers' provides only false assumptions about who may be suicide prone (Medlicott 2001). Most prisoners only just cope as the prison place fosters an existential crisis, ultimately leaving some shattered (Cohen and Taylor 1972). For abolitionists there is no linear adaptation to the prison environment. Rather, coping is a tenuous, relative and fluid concept that ebbs and flows over time. The real pains of imprisonment are not to be found in the given quality of living conditions, relationships with staff or levels of crowding, but in the denial of personal autonomy, feelings of time consciousness, and the lack of an effective vocabulary to express the hardship of watching life waste away.

> Non-copers keep returning to the issue of time: *they are saturated in now-time awareness:* they cannot move through time but must endure the feeling of its slow passing as a kind of personal torture . . . Stretches of empty time can produce the breakthrough into consciousness of much material which the prisoner would rather not revisit . . . The difficulty of time management is in no way related to the longevity of sentence, and the length of time spent in prison does not have a direct relationship with the pain suffered, *because the ability of inmates to handle time varies so markedly from person to person.*
>
> (Medlicott 2001: 143, original emphasis)

Deaths in prison should not then be considered as aberrations or malfunctions of the system but rather traced back to the daily processes of imprisonment itself (Ryan 1996). Such recognition should not lead to impossiblism, nihilism, 'defeatism' or an acceptance of current rates of self-inflicted deaths in custody as inevitable (Coles and Ward 1994: 140–1). It should instead foster scepticism of our reliance upon confinement, alongside a commitment to exploit the contradictions in the penal apparatus of the Capitalist State and find humanitarian policies for those currently incarcerated (Ryan and Sim 2007; Sim 2009).

Problematizing data on self-inflicted deaths

The first major official survey of 'suicides' in prisons in England and Wales was undertaken by RM Gover (1880, cited in Liebling 1992: 17), the first medical inspector of prisons in the 1870s. Gover found that there were 91 official verdicts on prison 'suicides' over the seven year period 1873 to 1879. Eighty-one 'suicides' had occurred in local prisons and his findings appeared to indicate that first time prisoners and those on remand had a greater vulnerability to suicidal ideation. Another medical officer (Smalley 1911, cited in Liebling 1992: 18) undertook a follow-up study of the 86 men and nine women officially recorded as 'suicides' between 1902 and 1911. This also found that those at the start of sentence were most vulnerable, with 36 people taking their lives within a week of admission, and five on the day of reception.[4] In 1913 Charles Goring's (1913) study *The English Convict* also provided statistical data on prison 'suicides'. The most significant finding here was that the suicide rate amongst prisoners (178 per 1000 deaths) was over four times as great as that of the general population (73 per 1000 deaths).

Indicative of the low level of political significance given to deaths in custody, it was over sixty years before the next major study of prison 'suicides' was undertaken, this time by the Principal Medical Officer for South East England, D.O. Topp (1979). Topp (1979) examined 775 recorded suicides from 1880 to 1971 and overall found that the official suicide rate in this time had declined from 60 to around 40 per 100,000 Average Daily Population [ADP]. Topp (1979) also made a detailed study of a subsample of 186 deaths covering the period 1958–1971. Significantly this figure was derived from the official suicide records and some open verdicts that Topp (1979) felt were 'suicides'. He found that on average 13 people took their own lives every year in prison in the period 1958–1971 and that there was an official suicide rate of 42 per 100,000 ADP.

While there is then evidence that the recorded rate of self-inflicted deaths in prisons in England and Wales was in decline for much of the twentieth century, the officially recorded figure has reached record highs at the beginning of the twenty-first century (see Table 6.2). In 1983 there were 27 recorded 'suicides' in prison. The 'suicide' toll stood at 23 in 1984, 29 in 1985 and 21 in 1986. The number of recorded 'suicides', however, leapt by over 100 per cent in 1987 to 46 (88.79 per 100,000). This exorbitant increase was explained by then Chief Inspector of Prisons, Judge

Table 6.2 Self-inflicted deaths in HM prisons in England and Wales 1988–2008

Year	Total SID	Male SID	Female SID
1988	37	37	0
1989	48	46	2
1990	50	49	1
1991	42	42	0
1992	41	39	2
1993	47	46	1
1994	62	61	1
1995	59	57	2
1996	64	62	2
1997	70	67	3
1998	82	79	3
1999	91	86	5
2000	82	74	8
2001	73	67	6
2002	95	86	9
2003	94	80	14
2004	95	82	13
2005	78	74	4
2006	67	64	3
2007	92	84	8
2008	61	60	1

Source: Medlicott (2001); INQUEST (2009)

Stephen Tumin (Her Majesty's Chief Inspector of Prisons 1990), as arising through an increase in 'mentally disordered' prisoners, new screening procedures, and changes in the working arrangements of officers following the introduction of Fresh Start in 1987. Other data places the rise within a longer time frame. Enda Dooley (1990, 1994) undertook a retrospective analysis of all unnatural deaths in prisons in England and Wales during the years 1972–1987.[5] Dooley noted that the prison suicide rate between 1972 and 1987 increased from 31 per 100,000 prisoners in the Average Daily Population per year in 1972–5, to 56 per 100,000 in 1984–7. This was an overall increase of 81 per cent, compared with an increase in the ADP of 22 per cent.

Official data show that there was another major incline of recorded self-inflicted deaths only seven years later in 1994, when there were more than 60 recorded deaths for the first time, and yet again four years after in 1998, when data recorded the self-inflicted deaths of more than 80 people in prison (HMCIP 1999). This number was to rise to consistently over 90 in the following decade.

There was a partial reversal of this trend between 2008 and 2009. Sixty-one people took their own lives in 2008, which is a significant decline on the previous year, when there were 92 such deaths. Yet the number of self-inflicted deaths in recent years remains alarming. From 1994–2004 804 prisoners were officially recorded as committing 'suicide': 55 per cent were on remand, 739 were men, 65 were women and 17 were children (Forum for Preventing Deaths in Custody 2007). These figures would appear to indicate the people most at risk of self-inflicted deaths in prison are *white male adult offenders on remand*. These assumptions are not quite as reliable as they first seem. According to official data nine women committed 'suicide' in prison from 1973 to 1990. This figure is undoubtedly a significant underestimate (Scraton and Chadwick 1987b). Dooley (1990) points out that while women's deaths made up only 1.7 per cent of the official suicide figures, out of the other 142 unnatural prison deaths in the period 1972 to 1987, Dooley (1990) believes that 52 of these were 'consciously self-inflicted'. Even taking into consideration previous underestimates it would appear that the number of women who take their lives in prison has increased dramatically. There were 65 recorded self-inflicted deaths of women from 1994 to 2004. In 2003 there were a staggering 14 female self-inflicted deaths in prison. The average female prison population increased by approximately 165 per cent between 1993 and 2003, while the rate of female self-inflicted deaths (per 100,000 of the ADP) increased by almost 500 per cent (Borrill et al. 2005). Women in prison today are 40 times more likely to kill themselves than women in the community (Wilson 2005: 63). It is estimated that between 37 per cent and 50 per cent of female sentenced prisoners have made previous 'suicide' attempts (Social Exclusion Unit 2002; Themeli 2006).

It is also clear that custody is experienced differently by young people. Young people are emotionally vulnerable and more likely to find the loss of personal relationships on the outside harder to cope with than adults (Goldson and Coles 2005). Although there are high levels of mental health problems among young people in prison (Harvey 2007), it has been maintained that the deaths of young people in custody may be more situationally specific to the prison place than those by adults (Wool and Dooley 1987; Greve et al. 2006). Young people also have less life experience on which to rely to help to deal with problems associated with prison life, or to manage a suicidal impulse when things are looking bleak (Liebling 1992). From 1990 to 2007 there were 30 child deaths in custody. 1695 incidents of self-injury or attempted suicide by children were recorded from 1998 to 2002. There are also concerns that child deaths are more likely to cluster in particular establishments. One leading commentator links this with 'impulsivity and the influence of contagion' (Liebling 1992: 120). Further, in prison 'the presence of "suicide fever", organizational changes, low morale, a harsh subculture and common domestic problems have been found to be associated with clusters of young prisoner suicides' (Liebling 1992: 80).

There are significant concerns that BME communities are over-represented in prison. Interestingly, although there are still a large number of cases of BME self-inflicted deaths (INQUEST 2009) 'Black' prisoners are proportionately under-represented (6 per cent of SIDS compared with 13 per cent of the prison population) while self-inflicted deaths among 'Asian' prisoners are proportionate (5 per cent of SIDS compared with 5 per cent of the prison population) (Liebling 2007: 432).

As the Prison Service only began to release data on all self-inflicted deaths in the mid-1990s any discussion of increases or decreases in death rates must be approached with some caution. There are also a number of common methodological weaknesses with the above studies on deaths in prison. Most of the main reviews include deaths only when a verdict of 'suicide' has been officially established; utilize Prison Service records only; lack control groups; and are firmly rooted in the assumptions of individual pathologies (Medlicott 2001). Historically, coroners have erred on the side of caution leading to many open verdicts, while it also remains possible that some non-suicidal deaths might be deliberately re-designated to avoid an embarrassing scandal (Lloyd 1990). In short, 'the recorded data on suicide attempts and self injury are notoriously weak, and cannot be assumed to bear any valid resemblance to the "true incidence" of such behaviour' (Liebling 1992: 83).

Given such substantial limitations we should also be careful of what lessons we learn from official data. Official self-inflicted death rates are often interpreted as indicating that prisoners are more vulnerable to suicidal ideation at the early stages of custody, and it has long been taken as a given that one of the most vulnerable times is when on remand (Hobhouse and Brockway 1922; Paton and Borrill 2004). Approximately a half of all self-inflicted deaths occur within a month of the prisoner arriving at that establishment, with a third occurring in the first seven days (HMCIP 1999). This data implies that the more time a person spends in prison the lower the likelihood of them taking their own life. Risk of suicidal ideation is expected to be concentrated upon those people who have not yet adapted to incarceration, implying that the prisoner's ability to adapt is central to their survival (Harvey 2007).

A very different picture emerges, however, when alternative techniques of analysing the data are deployed. A study by Crighton (2006b) of 525 of the 600 self-inflicted deaths in prisons in England and Wales from 1988 to 1998 found that any changes to the prison place, irrespective of the amount of time spent in custody, gave rise to increased risk of suicidal ideation. While it should be acknowledged that the early period of imprisonment is a time of exceptional risk, transfers to a new prison, or even different parts of the same prison, also give rise to new problems.

For Crighton (2006a) it is the *time spent* in any given institution that is the key

Table 6.3 Remand prisoner's risk of self-inflicted deaths

Remand prisoners	Number	ADP 1988–1995	Rate per 100,000 per annum
Number of deaths by ADP	191	10,372	238
Number of deaths by reception	191	63,562	39

Source: Towl and Crighton (2002: 81)

to understanding 'suicides' and self-inflicted deaths. The shorter the period of time in a given prison environment, the greater the difficulty a person has in coping with everyday life. Therefore, to focus on remand prisoners at the expense of sentenced prisoners is 'fundamentally misguided' as people on remand are only at a higher degree of risk because they spend relatively short periods of time in a given prison (Towl 1999; Crighton 2006a). Crighton (2006a) argues that using death rates based upon the Average Daily Population gives an inflated risk for remand prisoners. He found that 10 per cent of those who took their own lives did so within 24 hours of being transferred from another establishment. Significantly, this figure accounts for just under half of all those who take their own lives within 24 hours of reception into prison (Crighton and Towl 2008).

When looking at ADPs, the rate of self-inflicted deaths by people on remand appears to be very high. Yet when the figures are calculated via reception into the Prison Service, the rate (39 per 100,000 receptions) is much lower and closely resembles the rate for sentenced prisoners, which stood at 31 per 100,000 receptions for the period 1988–1995 (see Table 6.3). These findings challenge the idea that prisoners develop coping skills and strategies as custody progresses. Adaptation is not a permanent state of affairs. Coping mechanisms are tenuous and easily eroded. Fear, anxiety of the unknown and the potential harms that imprisonment deliver have profound negative impacts that do not pass with time. Any notion that there exist stages in a person's adaption to 'prison life' is limited as any progress is reversible. Coping and non-coping with prison life are matters of degree that fluctuate over time and *all* prisoners are vulnerable to suicidal ideation (Medlicott 2001).[6]

The way in which the data is presented is also crucial. Figure 6.1 is from the

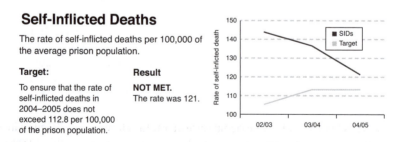

Self-Inflicted Deaths

The rate of self-inflicted deaths per 100,000 of the average prison population.

Target:
To ensure that the rate of self-inflicted deaths in 2004–2005 does not exceed 112.8 per 100,000 of the prison population.

Result
NOT MET.
The rate was 121.

Figure 6.1 Prison Service 2005 Annual Report table

Source: HM Prison Service (2005)

Prison Service *2004–05 Annual Report and Accounts*. In this year there had been a record number of 95 self-inflicted deaths. Yet the graph appears to show that self-inflicted deaths are falling. This is because the baseline measure adopted is the number of deaths per 100,000 of the prison population, which showed a decline from baseline rate of 140.4 in 2000 to a rate of 125 in 2005 (HM Prison Service 2005: 24). The trick here is that the numbers of deaths are compared to an exorbitant rise in the prison population as a whole. The data tells us that in a time of massive rises in the overall prison population self-inflicted deaths have not matched the increase. Indeed in times of record Average Daily Populations the death rate is in decline. Locating the data within three year trends the Prison Service was able to use the graph to reassuringly point to a 'stabilisation in the figures over recent years' (HM Prison Service 2005: 24). This is ultimately an example of interpretive denial, where disturbing data is re-contextualized to appear more palatable and less controversial (Cohen 2001).

Case Study 6.2 Sarah Campbell

Sarah died on 18 January 2003, at HMP Styal. She was aged 18. Sarah had been sentenced to three years imprisonment for manslaughter after accosting a man with serious heart problems who then died. On 17 January 2003 Sarah arrived at HMP Styal for a second time and was placed alone in the segregation unit. Her only means of communicating was through a crack in the door. On the morning of her death Sarah swallowed 120 Dothiepen anti-depressant tablets and then told staff what she had done. Left unattended and locked in her cell Sarah vomited blood. There was an avoidable delay of around 40 minutes between the reporting of the overdose and the arrival of the ambulance. At her inquest in January 2005 the jury returned a narrative verdict stating that there had been a failure in the 'duty of care'. In an out of court settlement the government later admitted liability for the breach of Sarah's human rights under article 8 of the European Convention on Human Rights. Sarah's mother, Pauline Campbell, became one of the most active campaigners for radical penal change this century. She was arrested 15 times between 2003 and 2008 for protesting outside prisons where women had recently died. Tragically Pauline never recovered from the loss of her daughter and was found dead at the entrance to the cemetery that held Sarah's grave on 15 May 2008.

Source: Scott (2008a)

Historical context

Prison has always been deadly. The penal reformer John Howard (1777, cited in Scott 2008a: 69) in his comprehensive survey the *State of the Prisons* identified that in the 1770s more people were dying in detention than were being executed by the death penalty. Certain penal institutions were notorious for the loss of life. At Coldbath

Fields 376 prisoners died in the space of 34 years (1795–1829), an average of around 11 people every year (Sim 1990). The medical journal *The Lancet* (July 1840, cited in Sim 1990: 24) stated that between 1826 and 1831, the death rate in 93 prisons was 16 per 1000 compared with 10 per 1000 for the general population. In the 15 years from 1848 to 1863 423 prisoners were officially recorded as dying in prison, an average of around 28 each year. In 1848 the large number of self-inflicted deaths in HMP Pentonville left prison authorities short of an answer. Indeed the Prison Commissioners admitted that 'it may be difficult to offer a certain explanation of the great number of cases of death and insanity that have occurred within the past year' (cited in Coggan and Walker 1982: 203). At Chatham Convict Prison eleven deaths were recorded in 1865 and a further 14 at the same institution in 1866 (Sim 1990: 20–38).

While the high numbers of deaths in prisons in the nineteenth century were largely overlooked, media attention was given to some tragic cases.[7] For example, controversy raged after John Rawlings, a 'lunatic' murderer, hanged himself in an underground cell at Lancaster Castle prison following a serious assault by a prison warder (Medlicott 2001). Another death that attracted great attention was that of Edward Andrews, a 15-year-old boy who had been sentenced to three months hard labour at Birmingham Prison in 1854.

> Imprisoned for stealing four pounds of beef and placed on the crank, which he was required to turn 10,000 times every day. This was divided into a number of periods: 2000 turns before breakfast, 4000 between breakfast and dinner and 4000 between dinner and supper. If the task was incomplete he was placed on bread and water while the shortcomings had to be made up. In addition, he was not permitted to go to bed until one and a half hours after other prisoners.
>
> (*The Lancet*, 1854, cited in Sim 1990: 29)

To achieve his targets Andrews would have had to exert a force equal to 'one fourth of the ordinary work of a draught horse' (cited in Sim 1990). In response to such intolerable conditions the boy hanged himself. Following widespread condemnation the government established a commission to investigate the circumstances of the death and the Birmingham prison governor was jailed for three months for assault.

Although there was no explicit policy on self-inflicted deaths in prison until the early 1970s procedures were in place from at least the mid-nineteenth century. According to the Royal Commission on Penal Servitude (1878, cited in Coles and Ward 1994: 128) prisoners showing 'suicidal tendencies' at HMP Pentonville in the 1870s were 'sent to a medical observation cell, the trap door of which is kept constantly open, and certain directions are given to the officers that the prisoner is to be specially watched . . . The furniture of his cell is always removed'.

By the early 1920s a large number of situational precautions were operative in prisons in England and Wales. Initiatives included strong wire netting to prevent prisoners jumping from the wing landings to their deaths, which was first introduced in nine prisons in 1896. In addition,

> cell furniture and utensils are so devised as to render extremely difficult any attempt at self destruction. The knife provided for prisoner's meals is such as

would make extremely slow and painful any suicide attempted by its means; cord and other articles which might be used for self-strangulation are kept as far as possible from the prisoner's possession. The artificial lighting in the cells is apt to be very defective largely on account of the arrangements adopted to prevent the inhalation of gas.

(Hobhouse and Brockway 1922: 550)

Suicide risk was understood as being tied to time spent in prison, and focus for prevention was upon the early stages of imprisonment. Standing Order (SO) 317 (cited in Hobhouse and Brockway 1922: 555) explicitly stated:

Precautions, therefore, are especially necessary during the earlier weeks of imprisonment, and those who are in prison for the first or second time are more likely to suffer from the state of mind which tends to suicide than those who have been many times in prison, and are hardened to crime.

In 1973 the first explicit prison suicide policy was introduced in the guise of Circular Instruction (CI) 39/73 (cited in McHugh and Snow 2002: 6). Primarily an exercise in suicide awareness, CI 39/73 established the use of what became known as the 'F' marking system, where prisoners identified as a potential suicidal risk had a large red 'F' placed on their files.[8] Responsibility for perceived suicidal prisoners lay firmly with the medical officer and the primary response was to isolate them in the prison medical centre (McHugh and Snow 2002).

Following the hangings of three prisoners within twelve months at HMP Swansea and an Inquest verdict of 'lack of care' after the self-inflicted death of 18-year-old remand prisoner Jim Heather-Hayes at Ashford Remand Centre, the prison department came under concerted pressure to significantly revise the 'F' marking system (Ryan 1996). In 1984 The HMCIP was commissioned to undertake a thematic review of *Suicides in Prison* and while this reaffirmed that 'suicide' was the responsibility of the medical officer, it did criticize CI 39/73 for being too vague. In response the government established a Working Group on Suicide Prevention (1986, cited in Ryan 1996), whose main recommendations informed a new Circular Instruction (CI) 3/87. This stated that staff must, 'take all reasonable steps to identify prisoners who are developing suicidal feelings: to treat and manage them in ways that are humane and are most likely to prevent suicide; and to promote recovery from suicidal crisis' (HM Prison Service 1987: 3).

CI 3/87 ended the F marking system and introduced standardized referral forms to facilitate communication about high risk prisoners. It aimed to improve reception screening and staff training and placed greater emphasis on isolating the perceived suicidal in special locations, such as the prison healthcare centre. CI 3/87 also created a Suicide Prevention Management Group (SPMG), later renamed as Suicide Awareness Teams (McHugh and Snow 2002). A new Circular Instruction (CI 20/89) superseded CI 3/87 but was plagued with failures of communication and implementation and operated in a culture that was unable to conceive of 'high risk' prisoners as anything other than discipline problems (Coles and Ward 1994).

Contemporary penal policy

Current policies on self-inflicted deaths find their roots in the 1990 HMCIP thematic review of 'suicide and self-harm', widely known as the Tumin Report. The Tumin Report was a major break with previous official reports and stated that current policy,

> fails to communicate the social dimension to self-harm and self-inflicted death. It does not stress sufficiently the significance of the environment in which prisoners and staff are expected to live and work, or the importance of constructive activities in helping inmates cope with anxiety and stress.
>
> (HMCIP 1990: 7)

The Tumin Report also challenged the myths around the connections with mental health problems, stipulating that the 'majority of suicides are not mentally disordered within the meaning of the Mental Health Act 1983; and suicide prevention in prison is not essentially a medical predicament but rather a social problem' (p. 14).

In 1991 the Prison Service established the 'Suicide Awareness Support Unit' (SASU) and in the same year the first Listener/Buddy Scheme, where selected prisoners are trained by the Samaritans, was established at HMP Swansea. A guidance pack, 'Caring for the Suicidal in Custody' was also published in 1991 and a revised strategy introduced in 1992 utilizing a new form, F2052SH (Self-Harm at Risk) (McHugh and Snow 2002). The F2052SH could be activated by any member of staff rather than being the exclusive domain of healthcare staff. These moves were consolidated in April 1994 with Instruction to Governor (IG) 1/94 which issued strategy document *Guide to Policy and Procedures – Caring for the Suicidal in Custody* (HM Prison Service 1994a, 1994b).

In 1999 HMCIP published the thematic review *Suicide is Everyone's Concern*, which maintained that while the current policies were largely well conceived for adult male prisons they had been poorly implemented for and neglected the needs of women, young prisoners and those on remand in local prisons. The HMCIP also pointed to management failings, inadequate training of staff and poor communication about prisoners who were suicidal and placed much greater emphasis on environmental factors. This highly influential report wished to facilitate safe and 'healthy prisons' and in response the newly established Safer Custody Group appointed 30 full-time suicide prevention coordinators at 30 of the highest risk penal establishments in November 2000 as part of its new Safer Locals Strategy (Posen 2001). This initiative was followed up in November 2002 with a new Prison Service Order (PSO 2007) entitled *Suicide and Self-Harm Prevention* which aimed to provide a 'holistic approach' rooted in risk reduction. Overall the aim was to develop 'safer' prisons by improving design and architecture, including the introduction of 'safer cells' (Goldson and Coles 2005). For David Wilson, however, these

> procedures are as much about demonstrating that Prison Service Headquarters has taken the issue seriously – that they are 'working hard', rather than actually

making any impact on the number of prisoners who take their own lives. In short, if the numbers of prisoners killing themselves continues to rise it is not their fault and that blame lies elsewhere.[9]

(Wilson 2005: 26)

These concerns are echoed elsewhere.

> Officers described it [F2052SH] to me as a discipline document, in the sense that there would be disciplinary consequences for them if the associated procedures and paperwork were not carried out properly. Prisoners regarded it as a device to absolve the service of responsibility in the event of a death.
>
> (Medlicott 2001: 215)

The F2052SH proved to be inflexible, mechanistic, poorly implemented, and under-resourced. Notions of 'shared responsibility' in practice led to 'diminished responsibility' (Crighton 2003). It focused on observing rather than actively caring for prisoners and only heightened surveillance and prisoners' sense of shame. Prisoner input was marginalized and constructions of 'suicidal risk' focused on past behaviour rather than present needs (Denham 2005). In practice the scheme became swamped by prisoners who saw it as the only way that their needs would be addressed (Wilson 2005).

In 2002 F2052SH was evaluated by Manchester University Department of Health and as a result in January 2004 the Prison Service introduced its current strategy, the ACCT (Assessment, Care in Custody and Teamwork).[10] Its rationale is to 'work together to create a safe and caring environment, where distress is minimised and those who are distressed are able to ask for help. To identify individual need and offer individualised care and support before, during and after a crisis' (HM Prison Service Safer Custody Group 2004: 1). Consequently,

> Preventing suicide involves listening to the person at risk, engaging them in planning ways of reducing their problems, helping them to build up their own sources of support and thus helping them to choose life. **Watching and stopping can be important but it only works in the short-term**.
>
> (p. 1, emphasis in original)

The ACCT is based on three levels of risk (low, medium, high) and any member of staff that identifies a prisoner at risk can open an ACCT Plan. An 'Immediate Action Plan' is drawn up within 24 hours which aims to keep the prisoner safe until further assessments are undertaken (HM Prison Service 2007). A Care and Management Plan (CAREMAP) is then agreed with the prisoner and a case manager appointed. The aim is to identify warning signs of suicidal ideation as soon as possible. One of the key environmental aims of the ACCT is to introduce safer cells. Category A, B and local prisons should be fitted with 100 per cent safer cells and category C prisons should have 25 per cent safer cells.[11]

The design of safe cells are important to the establishment, the ACCT aims for a safe environment, minimising the factors and equipment that could be used for a person to commit suicide, and making sure the prisoner feels at ease with their surroundings, with other prisoners and staff alike.

(HM Prison Service 2007: 13)

A person at risk is now to be located in a safe environment, which is understood as anywhere the person at risk feels 'safe, comfortable and relaxed' which could be their own cell, a shared cell, a 'safer cell' or in the healthcare centre. Prisons, however, cannot be turned into truly safe environments as practices are shackled by the profoundly punitive nature of confinement.

> The concept of 'safer custody' or the 'caring prison' is, in essence, an oxymoron. There is little or no evidence to imply that the innumerable polices, practices, and procedures designed to provide safe environments . . . in penal custody have succeeded.
>
> (Goldson and Coles 2005: xviii)

Under the ACCT responsibility has moved from medical personnel to multi-disciplinary management but this has led to the removal of responsibility from specialist staff. Training has thus far been largely inadequate except for ACCT risk assessors and a clear gap has opened between the intended focus on teamwork, care and support and what actually happens on the ground (Rickford and Edgar 2005). There are also problems around information breakdown and concerns that the increased emphasis on monitoring may result in highly intrusive dividing practices serving institutional, rather than individual, need (Goldson and Coles 2005).

The ACCT is underscored by the logic on individual risk and it is assumed that if assessments can be made more accessible and delivered with greater haste, then self-inflicted deaths can be effectively managed. It is significant to note that only around a quarter of those who take their own lives have been identified by prison authorities as being at risk of suicide (Liebling 2007: 426). Subsequently the ACCT fails to acknowledge that the key problem is the potential vulnerability of *every prisoner* and such practices simply reinforce the labelling of certain prisoners as 'vulnerable', thus implying that the rest are 'invulnerable' (Medlicott 2001: 58). Only time will tell whether the ACCT can be an effective tool in substantially reducing the current record high number of self-inflicted deaths – we hope it will have a significant impact though we remain sceptical that the ACCT can actually get to the heart of the problem, and, as we discuss below, 'suicide' policies may not be the most constructive way forward. Without question situational preventions and safer cells cannot address psychological pains of imprisonment meaning that it is likely that the ACCT will only address the surface manifestations of the problem.

> **Case Study 6.3 Joseph Scholes**
>
> Joseph died on 24 March 2002, at Stoke Heath Young Offender Institution. He was aged 16. Joseph's parents divorced when he was young and from the age of 6 he was repeatedly sexually abused by a member of his father's family. Joseph was placed into the care of the Local Authority in 2001 and in December of that year, within a week of his arrival at the children's home, he became involved in a series of mobile phone robberies. Joseph had self-harmed in the past and it was known he had periodic suicidal thoughts. Two weeks before being sentenced he slashed his face 30 times. Despite calls that custody should not be used, Joseph was sent to Stoke Heath Young Offender Institution. Joseph told officers that he would take his own life if they attempted to move him from the Health Care Centre but shortly after this warning he was placed in a single cell with bars on its window. Nine days into his sentence, Joseph was found dead by a maintenance worker who had come to unblock a toilet. Joseph's final message read: 'I love you mum and dad. I'm sorry I just can't cope. Don't be sad. It's no one's fault. I just can't go on. None of it was your fault, sorry. Love you and family, Joe . . . I tried telling them and they just don't fucking listen' (cited in Goldson and Coles 2005: 64).
>
> *Source:* Goldson and Coles (2005); Scott (2008a)

Legitimacy

The number of different policies and procedures since the 1960s indicate just how badly the Prison Service is failing to protect people in prison. Indeed specific 'suicide' policies may be counter-productive. Kobler and Stotland (1964) identify how suicidal ideation is heavily influenced by the nature of responses by significant others. The more the situation is perceived as hopeless, the more likely that attempts to take life will occur. Death occurs 'only when, all significant hopeful relationships are broken' (Kobler and Stotland 1964: 262). This position is given some support in research by Kruttschnitt and Vuolo (2007) who point to the importance of focusing not on suicide risk and feelings of distress, but on engendering hope by keeping prisoners busy and preventing social isolation. The interactions between prisoners and staff were seen as crucial, but remarkably close relations with staff *increase* the risk of suicide ideation (Kruttschnitt and Vuolo 2007). Developing new suicide precaution policies is high risk as they explicitly label a person as a 'potential suicide'. In this sense 'suicide' precautions can represent the 'end of hope' with the prisoner considering their case as hopeless, therefore reinforcing the suicidal crisis.

While it would be unwise to over-state the above insights, such an understanding does place grave doubts about the possibilities of developing a legitimate policy solution within the prison setting. The problem is not to do with physical conditions and crowding but derives from the very workings of the prison regime itself. Interventions should be directed at helping people vulnerable to suicidal ideation to develop new meanings and alternative strategies that can help them take their lives forward. Central is the nurturing of hope and the prison is the very last place to try and do this. The most rational solution then seems to be for the adoption of social policies that can provide immediate humanitarian support to people who are suicidal and the diversion away from prison for wrongdoers who are especially vulnerable to the development of suicidal ideation. Given the high numbers of prisoners with suicidal thoughts, and their interconnection with other vulnerabilities, this raises key questions regarding the use of imprisonment at all. When understood in the context of its historical record it is clear that the prison place and self-inflicted deaths are intimately tied together. Nobody is truly safe in such a toxic environment. The penal apparatus of the Capitalist State has blood on its hands. They will not be washed clean easily.

Further reading

Goldson, B. and Coles, D. (2005) *In the Care of the State? Child Deaths in Penal Custody in England and Wales*. London: INQUEST.

Liebling, A. (1992) *Suicides in Prison*. London: Routledge.

Medlicott, D. (2001) *Surviving the Prison Place: Narratives of Suicidal Prisoners*. Aldershot: Ashgate.

Ryan, M. (1996) *Lobbying from Below: INQUEST in Defence of Civil Liberties*. London: UCL Press.

Towl, G., Snow, L. and McHugh, M. (eds) (2002) *Suicide in Prisons*. Oxford: Blackwell.

Wilson, D. (2005) *Death at the Hands of the State*. London: Howard League.

We recommend that students regularly check the websites of the Howard League, INQUEST and No More Prison alongside organizations such as the Forum for Preventing Deaths in Custody.

7

The treatment of people who sexually offend

It has been recognized for some time that people who sexually offend have become modern day folk devils (Sampson 1994; Lacombe 2008). Othered as 'demons', 'ogres' and 'beasts', people who sexually offend are portrayed as bad, sick or dangerous people beyond redemption and comprehension (Hudson 2005). They are not human but 'monsters'. These 'animals' do not have human rights and the only conception of 'justice' in this context is to lock them up and throw away the key. Stereotypes about these social pariahs are deeply ingrained. People who sexually offend are social inadequates who have poor interpersonal skills and cannot develop legitimate attachments with adults, possibly because they themselves were victims of child sexual abuse. They are emotional lepers unable to show empathy who only become sexually aroused through the maltreatment, degradation and exploitation of women or children (Prentky 1995).

The notion that the 'sex offender' is the 'worst of the worst' goes to the heart of modern day prison culture. People who have been sentenced to imprisonment for sexual offences are often confronted with violence or threats of violence.

> Some prisoners actively persecute those convicted of sexual crimes. Verbal abuse is ubiquitous, with threats and taunts forming the normal verbal backdrop for life as a sex offender in prison. Food is adulterated: mashed-up cockroaches are stirred into stew or potatoes. Tea is a favourite target: 'You can tell when they've pissed into it because it floats on top, oily like'.
>
> (Sampson 1994: 83)

Some prisoners avoid persecution by pretending they have committed a different offence, though even then they may be 'ratted out' by staff. In recent years there have been attempts to integrate prisoners who have sexually offended within mainstream wings, although historically the main policy was isolation in 'Vulnerable Prisoner Units' (VPUs). The VPU is 'a prison within a prison', with its own workshops, education classes, association and religious ceremonies. The difficulty is that such segregation leads to greater opportunities for paedophile networking and undermines attempts to bring about positive change (Sampson 1994).

Othering is counter-productive and may even facilitate the greater likelihood of sexual reoffending (Lacombe 2008). The pillorying of people who sexually offend leads only to dividing practices distancing the pathologized 'beast' from normal people and obfuscating sameness. People who sexually offend are unable to recognize themselves in the 'sex offender' stereotype and attempt to preserve a more acceptable identity. Ostracism and stigma through a dehumanized master status makes offenders less likely to ask for help and 'manage their own problems effectively' (Hudson 2005: 183). Ultimately the 'sex offender' stereotype facilitates denial and leads to offenders becoming unwilling to participate in treatment.

People who sexually offend may often be seen as 'abnormal beasts' but there are many more similarities than differences between perpetrators and 'normal' people (Marshall et al. 2006). Most people who sexually offend are known to their victims and many people who abuse children are close friends or relatives. Most people who sexually offend are not 'dangerous strangers' but ordinary people living 'normal lives'. There is no simple cycle of abuse where sexual victimization metamorphoses into sexual offending – most obviously, women are more likely to be abused but less likely to become adult abusers (Brown 2005). Nor is there any convincing evidence to suggest that people who sexually offend are psychiatrically ill or profoundly different from non-offenders.[1]

While some may be reassured by conceptions of the 'sex offender' as an easily identifiable enemy preying on the weak or vulnerable, this is a myth. Sexual offending is an *exaggeration* of social norms rather than a complete deviation and virtually all people who sexually offend 'engage in pro-social activities and hence are not "monsters" ' (Brown 2005: 1). This indicates the importance of recognizing the true nature and extent of the sexual offending and the need to challenge the processes of othering if we really want to take this major social problem seriously.

This chapter provides a critical overview of the definitions and understandings of sexual offending. This is followed by a discussion of the difficulties of constructing a knowledge base about people who sexually offend. The historical development of Prison Service policies on SOTPs are then reviewed, along with current policies, alongside a critical appraisal of the main assumptions of the believed radical differences between normal sexuality and sexual offending. The efficacy of cognitive behavioural therapies is then assessed and the chapter concludes with a discussion of current penal policies and possible alternative ways of responding to sexual abuse.

Thinking critically about people who sexually offend

The term 'sex offender' is a legal definition and refers to someone who has been sanctioned by the law for a sexual offence. Sexual offences are defined under the *Sexual Offences Act* (1956) and the *Sexual Offences Act* (2003), which came into force 1 May 2004. The term 'paedophile', which literally means 'lover of children', is broadly understood in its medical sense, which can be applied when an adult has had sexual fantasies about children for more than six months (Brown 2005). The terms 'paedophile' and 'sexual offender', however, have a much wider usage than merely their medical and legal applications, and are often used to refer to people who have neither been processed by the criminal law nor medically diagnosed. The label 'sex offender' is adopted in official treatment programmes, although it is closely associated with a master status rooted in deeply ingrained negative stereotypes (Lacombe 2008). In this chapter, where possible, we adopt the term 'people who sexually offend' to describe prisoners, sexual lawbreakers and perpetrators who have not been apprehended or convicted. The use of this term should be understood as devoid of stereotypes of radical differentiation.

Responses to people who sexually offend are influenced heavily by positivistic theories rooted in the psycho-medical model. Positivism is the assumption that the criminalized actor is radically different from the non-offender and that their pathological behaviour is determined by abnormal psychology, character, or background (Matza 1964). The early psycho-medical approaches to sexual abuse were rooted in Darwinian explanations of evolution. From this perspective, biological (somatic) factors such as brain abnormalities or hormonal imbalances were believed to be the causes of sexual abuse (Sampson 1994).[2]

Early psychological theories were behaviourist and operated on the assumption that as abusive behaviour was *learned* such problematic conduct could be unlearned (Barker and Morgan 1993). Sexual deviance was rooted in an inappropriate association of sexual desire with children. Initial cognitive approaches examined how people who sexually offended used techniques of denial to minimize their responsibility in the offence, and these insights had a major influence on the development of the SOTP in prisons. For David Finkelhor (1986) people who sexually offend have 'deviant sexual arousal' but must also find ways to gain access to their victims and overcome their own internal inhibitions through neutralizing their conventional morality.[3] Finkelhor's approach was groundbreaking but does have a number of significant limitations. Most notably the Finkelhor model is primarily descriptive, rooted in individual pathologies and unable to contextualize sexual abuse within wider concerns about the distribution and exercise of power. Further, as it falls in the trap of reflecting masculinist assumptions it can provide no explanation for sexual offending by women (Fisher 1994).

In a later theory integrating biological, psychological, cultural and sociological approaches to understand people who sexually offend, Marshall and Barbaree (1990) argue that men are biologically driven to fulfil their sexual desires and this can lead to confusion between sex and physical aggression. As a result men need positive psycho-social conditioning to control their natural urges. Young male children who are inadequately socialized fail to control their aggression and start to express their masculinity through violence. Men need to contain the beast within, and some either fail to do this or their normal inhibitions are temporarily weakened through alcohol or situationally derived anger. In a widely cited passage Marshall and Barbaree (1990: 272) summarize their approach as follows.

Biological inheritance confers upon males a ready capacity to sexually aggress which must be overcome by appropriate training to instil social inhibitions toward such behaviour. Variations in hormonal functioning make their task more or less difficult. Poor parenting, particularly the use of inconsistent and harsh discipline in the absence of love, typically fails to instil these constraints and may even serve to facilitate the fusion of sex and aggression rather than separate these two tendencies. Socio-cultural attitudes may negatively interact with poor parenting to enhance the likelihood of sexual offending, if these cultural beliefs express traditional patriarchal views.

Of central importance is a healthy attachment between the parent and male child. Insecure maternal attachments of a male child with their mother lead to antisocial behaviour, while poor relationships with fathers lead to sexual abuse. Poor attachments and a problematic childhood, especially physical, sexual and emotional abuse or neglect cause the boy to have low self-esteem, poor social skills and a tendency towards the over-sexualization of relationships. This is particularly evident with hormonal changes brought about through puberty. Unable to express his sexuality and male power via culturally accepted means, the under-socialized and inadequate male turns to sexual abuse.[4]

There are a number of limitations to Marshall and Barbaree's integrated theory. Their multi-factored and multi-disciplinary analysis can prove to be counterproductive, mystifying rather than providing insights. In the words of David Matza (1964: 23),

> when theories are cumbersome, this may be a sign of a rather fundamental misconception. When many factors matter rather than few, and no one can pretend to know how many is too many, this may be a signal that our model is not a truthful simplifying of reality but instead a complicated falsification. . . . When factors become too numerous, there is a tendency for them to be not factors at all, but rather contingencies. The term factor after all means something. A factor is a condition that is applicable to a given universe.

A further significant limitation is that its biological basis does not allow for the social construction of sexual interactions, norms and values. This draws parallels with other psychopathological models of rape and sexual abuse, as at the core 'are two basic assumptions, that rape is the result of mental illness and that this abnormality involves an uncontrollable sexual drive; which reflects the early biological theories of violence as innate and instinctual' (Mercer 1998: 115).

Laying blame squarely on parents, Marshall and Barbaree (1990) assume that all forms of sexual offending are expressions of aggression perpetrated by social inadequates. This results in a narrow focus on individual pathology rather than on patriarchies or cultural misogyny. The theory cannot differentiate between sexual offences and appears to ignore findings that people who sexually offend against children and are caught and prosecuted fall into two main groups: people who sexually abuse during their adolescence but desist as they get older; and people who do not sexually offend until their 30s or later when they have a position of responsibility, trust and authority over children (Smallbone 2006). This distinction appears to leave attachment theory in tatters as it is too deterministic for the first group and completely irrelevant for the second.

Abolitionist and feminist critiques have questioned the categorization of sex offenders and the development of orthodox positivistic systems of classification rooted in individual pathologies. They point to the way in which the psycho-medical model is rooted in control, regulation and surveillance (Sim 1990; Foucault 2006). Rather, people who sexually offend should be understood within the context of how masculinist hierarchies of power devalue the lives of women and children (Jagger 1983). From this perspective the similarities between the beliefs of people who sexually offend and wider non-offending populations become clear and point to the disturbing knowledge that rapists and child molesters are not 'monsters' but normal people. This banality of sexual abuse is one of the most difficult aspects of the debate to comprehend and to which to respond.

Women and children are commodified and portrayed as subordinate sexualized objects. On a cultural level there is an objectification of women for sexual gratification and youth and sexual desire are closely tied. There is an idealization of (later) teenage (female) bodies and there is undoubtedly societal legitimation of forms of misogyny and disempowerment of children. Yet the apparent human male preference for sexual partners is socially constructed rather than biologically determined.[5] Indeed, 'the fact that normal adult males are typically most attracted to youthful and physically beautiful sexual partners suggests that it is the *exploitation* rather than the *recognition* of young people's sexual appeal that characterises sexual offending behaviour' (Smallbone 2006: 99).

Problematizing data on sexual offenders

There are a number of significant difficulties when measuring the problem of sexual abuse. The perpetrator is often close to the victim and may be a spouse or family member. The victim may also fear the consequences of disclosure for either themselves or the abuser. Current theories about people who sexually offend are based almost exclusively on people who have been caught and convicted, yet sexual offences are largely under-reported and levels of conviction low. There is undoubtedly a very large pool of people who have sexually offended but who remain undetected. It is believed that less than 1 per cent of all people who sexually offend are sent to prison (Fisher 1994). Further, although people who sexually offend come from all socio-economic groups, those from lower socio-economic groups are more likely to be prosecuted and imprisoned (Barker and Morgan 1993; Brown 2005). Prosecutions are shaped through a wider emphasis on the surveillance and control of lower class people and those who are caught are largely not very good at concealing their abuse or controlling their victim(s). Consequently 'characteristics reported may simply be an artefact of the processes of detection, prosecution and conviction' (Crighton and Towl 2008: 218). Distance, respectability and social status all influence the likelihood of prosecution, but those penalized are not necessarily representative of people who perpetrate sexual abuse (Baumgartner 1992).

In 1980 4 per cent of sentenced male prisoners were convicted of a sexual offence but by 1989 this figure had increased to over 7 per cent of sentenced male prisoners. Indeed from 1979 to 1990 the number of sex offenders in prison doubled from 1500 to over 3000 (Sampson 1994). Today 8 per cent of the prison population are incarcerated for offences relating to sexual violence. The latest figures indicate that there are currently 3391 rapists in prison accounting for 56 per cent of the 6063 adult male sex offenders incarcerated.

Sexual offences comprise 0.9 per cent of all recorded 'crime' and as little as 5 per cent of sex offences against children reach court (Jewesbury et al. 1998). Yet it is estimated that 10 per cent of women have been adult victims of sexual offences and that 20 per cent of women and 10 per cent of men experience some form of child sexual abuse (Finkelhor 1986). The most likely location of sexual abuse is in the victim's home and from 20 per cent to 50 per cent of the total abuse committed against children is perpetrated by offenders under the age of 18 years of age (Renvoize 1993).[6] Evasion of the penal net is likely if the person who offends is a close relation, such as an elder brother or sister, or a trusted friend of the person abused. From 70 per cent to 90 per cent of child abuse is conducted by someone known to the child. It is also believed that 75 per cent of rapes are committed by someone close to the victim, with only 8 per cent of rapes of women committed by strangers (Brown 2005).

In a famous and widely cited study of male college students, Neil M. Malamuth (1981) found that 35 per cent of respondents, if given reassurances they would not be prosecuted, would consider raping a woman. In a further study of male college students by Brier and Runtz (1989, cited in Brown 2005: 12) 21 per cent of respondents admitted to having some sexual attraction to children and 7 per cent indicated they would abuse if they were given assurances they would not be penalized. Further studies have also found that high numbers of men (22 per cent) and some women (3 per cent) are sexually attracted to children (Hudson 2005: 28). For one leading commentator society's 'extreme antipathy towards sex offenders, and particularly paedophiles, thus to some extent represents our own vulnerabilities by displacing the fact that many adults find children disturbingly erotic' (p. 28).

People who sexually offend are not specialists and commit many different (non-sex-related) offences. They are also no more likely to reoffend. The recidivism rate for untreated people who sexually offend is 15 per cent over five years and 20 per cent over ten years, which is similar to other offenders (Brown 2005). In total, sexual offending involves less than 10 per cent of that person's time, and so for 90 per cent of the time people who sexually offend are undertaking 'normal' activities (Marshall et al. 2006). To say that people who sexually offend are closer to the normal population is of course to also say that normal people are closer to 'sex offenders'. This is not an argument likely to be welcomed, as it has implications for all of 'us'.

Historical context

The 1970s witnessed a general shift in psychology towards behaviourism, an environmental approach which aimed to shape behaviour through positive reinforcement and punishments (Brown 2005). People who sexually offended were expected to desist and alter their behaviour by coupling their deviant sexual arousal with negative stimuli. Behavioural based approaches, however, were deemed too simplistic and by the 1980s, reflecting another general shift in psychology, were replaced by 'cognitive-behavioural' treatments. Cognitive behavioural therapies (CBT) maintain that cognitive distortions can be challenged and offenders can learn new ways of thinking about sexual relations (Marshall et al. 1999). CBT aim to change an individual's internal cognitive functioning and ultimately to help them manage their future behaviour. The offender is understood as a rational decision maker who can develop strategies of self control and regulation. There is no talk of cure here, just self control (Hudson 2005). In the USA treatments for prisoners who had been convicted of sexual offences started to be developed in the 1980s by practitioners such as Bill Marshall. By the early 1990s not only had these programmes dramatically expanded in North America but enthusiasm had begun to spread to this side of the Atlantic (Marshall et al. 2006).

Pre-1980s developments in treatment programmes in prisons in the UK were fairly limited and most prisoners who had sexually offended spent their time in prison mixing with other perpetrators of sexual offences. By the late 1980s, however, there was increasing pressure for change, brought about through a combination of concerns about offenders networking in prison and growing confidence that treatments might actually have a positive impact (Sampson 1994). This pressure increased still further with the publication of the Woolf Report (1991 para 12.214) which highlighted the unsatisfactory situation of 'our current approach to sex offenders' and made it clear that 'more attention should be given to treatment'. Although the Prison Service was able to claim to the Woolf Inquiry that people who sexually offended were being offered treatment in 63 prisons in England and Wales, this ranged from individual counselling delivered on an ad hoc basis by untrained prison officers to more systematic initiatives at HMP Grendon and Wormwood Scrubs Hospital Annexe (Sampson 1994).

The first steps towards a major overhaul of sex offender treatments came with an announcement by the then Home Secretary, Kenneth Baker, in June 1991. Baker (cited in Sampson 1994: 108) claimed that new treatment programmes would be able to 'reduce sexual recidivism by about half'.[7] The following month, July 1991, the Prison Service introduced a new strategy document entitled *Treatment Programmes for Sex offenders in Custody: A Strategy*. The aim was now to:

> tackle offenders' distorted beliefs about relationships, enhance their awareness about sexual offences on the victim, and seek to get inmates to take responsibility for and face up to the consequences of their own offending behaviour. The programme will also get inmates to develop relapse prevention strategies, identifying the nature of their offence cycles and how high-risk situations can be avoided.
>
> (HM Prison Service 1991c, cited in Sampson 1994: 106)

Drawing on the insights of cognitive behaviouralism, and initially the writings of David Finkelhor, in 1992 two new SOTPs, the core and the extended programme, were established in 17 establishments. The core programmes aimed to challenge sexual beliefs and provide strategies to prevent relapses, while the extended programme was more individualized and aimed at the highest risk offenders. It was originally planned that 65 per cent of all sex offenders sentenced to over four years would complete the core programme but by 1998 the SOTP was running in 25 establishments covering prisoners serving more than two years (Brown 2005). Danny Lacombe (2008: 47) provides a very helpful metaphor for the SOTP: 'Experientially, treatment for sex offenders is not unlike the regimented modern school: offenders do in-class exercises, engage in active listening, challenge their peers, have guest lectures, see documentaries, have homework to do at night and are tested'. For Lacombe (2008) then, the SOTP is just like attending 'Sex Offender School' (see Box 7.1).

It became immediately apparent that there were a number of significant practical problems associated with the SOTP. Participation at 'sex offender school' was voluntary and dependent upon the prisoner's cooperation. Concerns were also raised regarding prisoner eligibility: people with mental health problems, those with low intelligence test scores, people considered to have personality disorders and those believed to be a serious suicide risk were, and still are, automatically excluded. This meant that some of the most serious offenders would not be dealt with by the SOTP.

Box 7.1 SOTP treatment stages

Pre-treatment: developing motivation for behaviour change

1   Denial
2   Minimization
3   Victim blame – victim empathy

Treatment planning

4   Understanding precursors to offending and the behaviour chain leading to the offence

Treatment: achieving behaviour change

Deviant sexual behaviour

5   Reducing deviant sexual arousal and fantasy
6   Reducing cognitive distortions
7   Addressing issues of their own victimization
8   Enhancing healthy sexuality, including increasing sexual knowledge

Nonsexual contributions to offending

9   Increasing social competence and anger control
10   Decreasing criminal thinking, lifestyle and behaviour
11   Substance abuse treatment (if required)
12   Treatment of mental disorder (if required)

Post-treatment: preventing the recurrence of sexual offending

13   Developing a relapse prevention plan
       • Internal self management
       • External supervision
14   Relapse prevention
15   Follow up

Source: Barbaree and Marshall (1998: 301)

Despite the positive political rhetoric in support of the SOTP, in practice the government made virtually no new resources available, significantly hindering early developments. Equally problematic was the long period before release post-treatment, which meant that prisoners could easily relapse into previous beliefs (Sampson 1994). In 1993, 284 sex offenders completed sex offender treatment programmes. This increased to over 600 by 1999 and in 2003 over 1000 sex offenders completed programmes. This is still short of demand, which is currently approximately 1400 prisoners per annum (Brown 2005).

Contemporary penal policy

In 2009 the SOTP ran in 27 prisons in England and Wales, with approximately 1000 men undertaking treatment that year.[8] Each prison is audited annually and treatment groups normally involve eight prisoners and three treatment staff, who may be psychologists or specially trained prison officers. Sessions are normally run three times a week. The Structured Assessment of Risk and Need (SARN) is used to assess sexual offenders' level of risk (low, medium, high), their perceived needs and progress in treatment. Approximately 80 per cent of participants are child sexual abusers, 15 per cent rapists and 5 per cent sexual murderers (Beech et al. 2005). There are currently six SOTPs operating in prisons in England and Wales.

The *core programme* is designed for medium to high risk offenders with IQs of 80 or above and takes eight months to complete (see Table 7.1). The core programme aims to challenge the offenders' thinking patterns; identify their own personal risk factors and triggers for abuse; develop an understanding of the victim's point of view; and encourage participants to adopt strategies so that they can be released without reoffending. The *rolling programme* is intended for lower risk offenders. It is highly flexible and allows prisoners to be 'rolled on' and 'rolled off' at short notice, and the average length of the course is four months. The *adapted programme* can be altered to meet the requirements of offenders with learning difficulties and those who cannot read and write. Its aims are similar to the core programme in terms of ability to recognize risk factors, modifying thinking patterns and generating new strategies to avoid offending and lasts for eight months. The *extended programme* is aimed at high risk offenders whose needs were not met by the core programme and takes six months to complete. Again the programme aims to help offenders to manage offence-related emotional states and sexual fantasies and to develop skills to manage these without recourse to offending.

The *Better Lives Booster Programme* aims to develop healthy lives for offenders and is delivered over a three month period towards the end of the sentence. The *Healthy Sexual Functioning Programme* is probably the most flexible course as it can be adapted to the specific needs of the offender, although it only comprises four modules. It is targeted at the highest risk offenders and aims to develop healthy sexualities by managing deviant arousal and learning how to avoid relapse (Brown 2005). Overall the sex offender treatment programmes aim to address (1) poor social skills, (2) cognitive distortions, (3) deficits in victim empathy, (4) deviant arousal and (5) to help develop skills around relapse prevention (Marshall et al. 1999). The difficulty is that these five interventions at 'sex offender school' are rooted in a number of flawed assumptions.

Table 7.1 Twenty core 2000 SOTP blocks

Block	Title	Number of Sessions
1	Establishing the group	3
2	Understanding distorted thinking	1
3	Coping strategies	2
4	My history	4
5	Active accounts	16
6	Fantasy	2
7	Patterns in my offending	8
Review	Coping strategies	1
8	Feedback and goal setting	1
9	Cost and gains of offending	1
10	Victim empathy	3
11	Victim perspective narratives	4
12	Victim perspective role-plays	8
13	Victim letters	1
Review	Coping strategies	1
14	Old me	3
15	Future me	3
16	Future me alternative to offending	8
17	Getting to future me	3
18	Setbacks	2
19	Future me role-plays	8
20	Feedback and goal setting	2

Source: Hudson (2005: 40)

Attempts to address *poor life skills* such as low self-esteem and self-confidence are predicated on the supposition that people who sexually offend are intellectually challenged socially incompetent misfits. In other words,

> [m]en who sexually abuse children often present with social difficulties, including social anxiety and avoidance, under-assertiveness, problems making conversation and difficulties in sustaining intimate relationships and resolving interpersonal conflicts.

> (Beckett 1994: 98)

The assumption of social inadequacy is, however, epistemologically flawed. In a well known study D.J. West (1987) found that convicted paedophiles often were people who were shy, insecure and socially isolated, yet when he looked at professional and high status people who had sexually offended a different picture emerged. These people were confident, assertive, socially integrated, well educated and in the main had managed to evade detection and prosecution.

Despite the continued enthusiasm shown by cognitive behaviour therapists for increasing the social skills of sexual offenders, there is no clear body of evidence confirming that they suffer from such deficits. For instance, while Segal and Marshall (1985) found some limited overall deficiencies in social functioning among incarcerated sexual offenders, no unique deficits were identified, and rapists, in particular, were found to function reasonably well.

(Marshall et al. 1999: 95)

Challenges to *cognitive distortions* are predicated on the assumption that people who sexually offend have culturally abnormal attitudes justifying the subjugation of women or children. This emphasis of male privilege allows people who sexually offend to deny the negative implications of their offence and deploy techniques of neutralization (Finkelhor 1986). In this sense offenders are able to rationalize away the injury or their responsibility for the act. This cognitive distortion allows the offender to continue their abuse while reducing any feeling of distress that their actions are harmful. Consequently challenging thinking distortions and facilitating more honest accounts of the sexual abuse are central to 'sex offender school' (see Boxes 7.2 and 7.3).

It is clear that many people who sexually offend persuade themselves that their victim enjoys the abuse and there needs to be an acknowledgement of the harm done before any progress can be made (Cohen 2001; Hudson 2005). Yet this recognition does not automatically imply significant differences between 'sex offenders' and 'non-sex offenders' exist. In a society which largely either glorifies, ignores or condones male violence, depending on the given circumstances and context of the act, people who sexually offend are perilously close to cultural norms while

---

Box 7.2 Handout: passive account of child abuse

1   I was just helping out my mates by looking after their kids.
2   The parents left me some beer.
3   There were three kids – the 4 and 6 year olds were going wild. I thought they would quieten down if I got them to bed.
4   I got all three into their night clothes – I had to help Samantha, the older one.
5   I got the younger two in bed by 9.30. It wouldn't have been right to send Samantha up too – the others were noisy and she wouldn't have been able to sleep.
6   She likes horror films – she asked if it was OK to watch it with me.
7   It was just great to sit quietly and drink my beer.
8   Samantha asked if she could sit by me as it was a scary film.
9   Samantha sat close to me. When Dracula was doing things to the girls in the film she came and sat on my knee.
10   Samantha was so scared she grabbed my prick. I'd forgotten to do up my trousers – because of the beer I think. Film turned me on – I got a hard on.
11   Samantha sat on my prick. I tried to stop her. I said 'What are you doing'. She said 'They've done it on the film – can't we?' We were both excited – she tried to force herself on to me, but she couldn't get it in.

Source: HMP Frankland (1998b: 27)

Box 7.3 Handout: active account of child abuse

---

1   I knew these people who had got kids – I thought they would let me baby-sit. I soon got what I wanted.

2   I asked for beer instead of payment.

3   I tried to get all three children excited. I wanted the younger ones to be tired and go to bed.

4   I made sure I undressed Samantha.

5   I got the younger ones in bed because I wanted to be alone with Samantha.

6   I chose a horror film video because I know she likes horror films and would want to see it with me. I knew it would turn me on – it wasn't an ordinary one (Dracula and the Seven Virgins).

7   I drank several cans because I know after a few drinks I become randy.

8   I moved closer to her and put my arm around her. The film got scary; I pulled her on my knee. I went to the toilet. When I came back I left my flies undone as I liked to feel her sitting on my prick.

9   I sat her on my knee. I had an erection.

10   I put her hand on my prick.

11   I lifted her nightie and said 'Shall we do what they're doing in the film?' She said nothing. She was frightened. I tried to force my prick into her. She screamed. That frightened me and I lost my erection, so I stopped.

Source: HMP Frankland (1998b: 28)

---

many 'sex offenders' engage in [hetero]sexual adult and consensual relationships (Hudson 2005).[9] Further, denial is universal: most people have cognitive distortions about something or other and utilize techniques of denial (Cohen 2001). The difficulty is that simply challenging individual denials leaves wider cultural norms unchecked, fundamentally undermining the effectiveness of any cognitive based form of therapy (Brown 2005). This is exacerbated by attempting to challenge denials in the prison place, which is more likely to foster denial than acknowledgement. Even here, the main tenets of the SOTP may be flawed. Levels of denial are not accurate predictors of subsequent sexual recidivism and in the words of some of the world's leading practitioners, 'there is no evidence that changing a denier's status to that of an admitter has any effect on subsequent recidivism' (Marshall et al. 1999: 72).

A further priority of 'sex offender school' is to address *deficits in victim empathy*. People who sexually offend are believed to have only limited understanding of other peoples' emotional states and specifically have no understanding of the feelings of those they abused (Marshall et al. 1999). At Frankland HMP, for example, prisoners on the SOTP in the late 1990s were shown a poem by a victim of sexual abuse to help engender their empathy (see Box 7.4). To develop a capacity to show emotional sensitivity, participants at 'sex offender school' must write a victim apology letter that accepts responsibility for the harm done and then re-enact their offence, only this time they are the victim (HMP Frankland 1998b).

Box 7.4 Victim empathy poem[10]

Geraldine

I remember the secret very well,
The one big secret I could not tell,
I remember the taps on the wall
I'd dread
At twelve years old,
I'd wish I was dead
'No one will believe you.'
You'd always say
'You'll be locked up – that's the price you'll pay.'
No one knew,
If they did they never cared
No one knew all my life I'd be scared
I was twenty years old when I got away
I've been running since, hiding
Thanking God for that day
You'll be locked up soon,
It's taken away
But that's the price you pay
For your dirty crime
Why did you do it? I need to know,
I was so young, I needed you so.
Why did you do it? My life has been so sad
I was your daughter,
You should have been my Dad.

Source: HMP Frankland (1998a)

Through tactical touching of the body the offender is made to feel vulnerable, with the expectation that the offender will grasp the consequences of their actions. This kind of intervention is ethically problematic as in practice it can be tantamount to a form of psychological rape. It may also be counter-productive as the re-enactment may merely make the prisoner feel like a victim and undermine any attempts to challenge the rationalizations of their offence.

The evidence from practitioners indicates that people who sexually offend can show empathy in other contexts, indicating that they merely neutralize their feelings for fellow human beings in relation to particular people or particular circumstances (Marshall et al. 1999). In other words they show the ability to deploy techniques of denial to neutralize the suffering of their specific victims.

We should not expect general empathy deficits in sexual offenders. While some sexual offenders, such as those who score high on measures of psychopathy, might reasonably be expected to demonstrate little empathy toward anyone, most sexual offenders . . . [are] empathetic in a variety of nonsexual offence-related situations.

(Marshall et al. 1999: 80)

Although empathy enhancement is practised in virtually all sexual offender treatment programmes there is no evidence that it leads to reduced recidivism.

> The inclusion of empathy-enhancing components in treatment is based on the belief that the attitudes of sexual offenders toward their victim will change if they understand how the victim feels, and the subsequent development of empathy will inhibit future sexual abuse. It is also believed that empathy will increase the offender's motivation to engage his relapse prevention plans. However, none of these rationales has yet been empirically validated.

(p. 80)

Sexual offending is assumed to be the outcome of *deviant sexual arousal* and treatments have aimed to decrease deviant arousal through aversion therapy (associating deviant arousal with unpleasant stimuli).[11] Electric aversion, foul odours and ammonia aversion therapy are fortunately now out of fashion and the main technique deployed today is satiation with orgasmic reconditioning, which aims to extinguish deviant arousal by breaking the link between masturbation and deviant fantasies.

> In this procedure, offenders were required to masturbate to ejaculation while verbalising aloud every variation of their deviant fantasy. Upon ejaculation, and throughout the refractory period, patients were instructed to continue to masturbate to the same fantasies, over several, hour long sessions.

(Barbaree and Marshall 1998: 305)

The first difficulty here involves identifying deviant arousal then attempting to assess the extent to which a person's sexual arousal is deviant. Sexual preferences are not fixed or permanent and there is little convincing evidence to support the notion that there is a biological or organic basis to sexual abuse. Measurement is difficult and an ethical minefield. There has been a marked failure to find evidence of sexual deviation during the 'laboratory testing' of people who sexually offend through showing visual images (videos, pictures) and audio tapes. One of the most well known controversial practices is the use of the penile plethysmograph. A central part of the SOTP in the early 1990s, this was gradually phased out over the following decade, but since 2005 has been introduced in more than ten prisons in the UK. The penile plethysmograph is a small, mercury filled loop placed over the prisoner's penis. The prisoner is then subjected to a number of pornographic images linked to the nature of their 'crime' and then their deviant arousal is measured by assessing the rush of blood to the penis. Prisoners, however, have learnt to manipulate the results by masturbating before being tested so as to give negative outcomes. In addition it can only measure that person's arousal to images rather than predict future offending (Sampson 1994).

Fundamental questions have also been raised about the relationship between deviant arousal and sexual offending. Sexual abuse is an expression of power, control, aggression and a desire to humiliate. Offenders do not have to have a deviant arousal to offend. Sex offenders are not necessarily sexually abnormal and 'many sexual offenders do not have primary arousal to deviant sexual stimuli' (Brown 2005: 136). For Bill Marshall and colleagues '[d]espite the continuing emphasis placed on sexual preferences, it is now apparent that most researchers do not expect all sexual offenders to display deviant preferences at phallometric assessment' (Marshall et al. 1999: 111).

A number of studies have confirmed this (Brown 2005). Marshall and Eccles (1991) found that only 50 per cent non-familial child sex offenders and less than 30 per cent of those who abused children in their own families had a deviant sexual arousal. Further, Marshall and Barbaree (1993, cited in Brown 2005: 136) found that less than one third of rapists had deviant arousal, while over one quarter of a group of non-offenders could also be considered to have a deviant sexual arousal. In addition many non-offenders may have deviant sexual arousal (Brown 2005).

Bill Marshall, one of the leading advocates of sex offender treatments, has also raised questions regarding whether CBT should focus upon changing sexual preferences.

[D]irectly targeting sexual preferences in the treatment of sexual offenders may be unnecessary. [Further] systematic research ... might suggest that deviant sexual preferences are an epiphenomenon, much as smoke is to fire. If equipping sexual offenders with the attitudes, perceptions, confidence and skills necessary to meet their needs in pro-social ways, indirectly eliminates deviant sexual preferences ... then deviant preferences can be construed as a way that some inadequate men have of fulfilling their needs.

(Marshall et al. 1999: 126)

It seems that, despite their limitations, challenging neutralizations and the deployment of effective strategies fostering empathy are much more fruitful.

A further key aim of 'sex offender school' is *relapse prevention*. Offending is understood not as a spontaneous action but the result of a pre-planned chain of events. Consequently prisoners are asked to identify their cycle of offending. Once their personal high risk factors have been identified they are taught new skills to help deal with future problematic circumstances (Marshall et al. 1999). There are, however, concerns about the self policing process of relapse prevention and how participation in the SOTP plays a significant part in 'making up' the identity of the 'sex offender'. Utilizing the insights of labelling theory, Lacombe (2008) points to the manner in which the prisoner is pathologized through the treatment process itself. Through 'sex offender school' the deviant master status of 'sex offender' is internalized. This leads to a negative one dimensional construction of the self which the labelled person actively resists in an attempt to re-align themselves with 'normal' people. Treatment becomes a dividing practice othering the offender by denying their 'ordinariness' and re-labelling them as 'consumed by sex'. As such 'by the end of treatment, the sex offender might not be cured, but he has become a *new self*' (p. 72).

Relapse prevention primarily targets sexual fantasies and is based on the assumption that such fantasies will be acted upon as offenders *engineer* future offending through imagining and rehearsing the offence.

Therapists specifically want to hear deviant fantasies and the offender's explanation as to why they are important. The script is easy to learn: deviant fantasies are those similar to an inmate's offence (a rapist fantasizes about rape; a sadist about inflicting pain; a paedophile about sex with children and youths); they are inappropriate because they increase the risk of reoffending.

(Lacombe 2008: 67)

Sex offenders learn a new language of 'thinking errors', 'triggers' and the 'planning' of offences and are told that '*once a sex offender, always a sex offender*'. The goal of treatment is not to cure but manage deviant sexuality. Consequently the SOTP looks for the offender to develop techniques of introspection and to internalize a prevention plan. Everything is sexualized and reduced to a sexual motive, but actual evidence of the link between 'crime' and fantasizing is relatively limited, with only 17 per cent of rapists in one study fantasizing about rape during the six months before the offence (Lacombe 2008). In a detailed empirical study of sex offender treatments in the UK Hudson (2005) found that most prisoners who signed up for the programme felt like they had to 'talk the talk' and comply with the theoretical assumptions of the SOTP, even though many of them did not display the assumed pathological characteristics.[12] In short the SOTP has proved to be very rigid and unable to recognize the different needs of offenders, making the facts fit the theory in an attempt to demonstrate how an individual offender fits the typical characteristics of their offence (Maden 2002).

Evaluations of the SOTP are patchy and have showed only limited impact on sexual offending. The definition of success is very important and, as treatment efficacy in terms of reduction in recidivism has proved elusive, other measures such as reduced frequency and severity of offence are deployed (Brown 2005). Very few now evaluate the SOTP on the assumption that it can lead to massive reductions in recidivism as Home Secretary Baker claimed back in 1991. If harm reduction can be demonstrated then the SOTP can be seen as effective, but as this is a subjective outcome that is difficult to measure, this could make positive outcomes inevitable. Successful treatment interventions are now largely understood as a 5 per cent reduction in offending by the treatment group compared to the control group (Brown 2005).

Positivistic claims of validity, reliability and objectivity provide a 'scientific' cloak of legitimacy but make it very difficult to actually deliver on these claims. The 'scientific' basis for the SOTP means that evaluations must adopt scientific methodologies and adhere to standards of scientific rigour. Measuring treatment efficacy has led to questions regarding the correct period to assess levels of recidivism (2, 5, or 10 years after treatment); the inclusion of treatment drop-outs (as opposed to outcomes for completers); and whether recidivism is measured by self report data, recorded data, or a combination of both.[13] There are also problems about the use of control groups.

Because of the nature of the offences these men commit, it has been argued that, in most clinical settings, a randomised, controlled, treatment-outcome study is ethically unacceptable; randomly assigning a dangerous offender, who might accept treatment, to a long term involvement in a no-treatment experimental condition seems difficult to justify . . . In withholding treatment from the sexual offender, potential victims are at risk who have not been informed and who have not given consent.

(Barbaree and Marshall 1998: 270)

Concerns have been raised that screening strategies have been used to exclude offenders deemed unsuitable for the intervention and highlighted how apparent treatment compliance may simply be an attempt to manipulate penal authorities (Lacombe 2008). In addition Brooks-Gordon et al. (2004) point out that because of the huge financial and political investment there is a great desire for CBT to be seen as effective, resulting in the suppression of negative findings.

There are three possible outcomes then of the SOTP: that it makes offenders worse; that it makes no difference at all; that it reduces future offending or the severity of any such offences. Very few studies have found that the SOTP increases offending, although a controversial study of 224 sexual offenders in the 1990s by Seto and Barbaree (1999) found that psychopaths undergoing CBT were more likely to reoffend than those who were not treated. Barbaree et al. (2006), however, undertook an extended follow-up of the same sample and found that the previous study had been based on partial data and when the complete data was examined there was 'no evidence in support of the notion that cognitive behavioural treatment causes psychopaths to re-offend at a higher rate than they would without treatment' (Barbaree et al. 2006: 170).

There are more claims that CBT has no effect in reducing sexual offences (Quinsey et al. 1993; Marques et al. 1994; Crighton 2006a). Many of the early studies of SOTP in the USA are now considered methodologically flawed, leading Furby et al. (1989: 25) to famously state that 'there is no evidence that treatment reduces sex offence recidivism'. In the UK Falshaw et al. (2003a) found no difference between the two-year reconviction rates for adult male prisoners on the SOTP and a control group of 'sex offenders'. In another widely cited study Friendship et al. (2003) found that the sexual re-conviction rate for both the treatment group of 647 adult male 'sex offenders' and control group of 1910 adult male 'sex offenders' was low over a two year period (2.6 per cent treatment group; 2.8 per cent control group). There are also studies which indicate that the SOTP has had some positive impact on reducing harm and victimization. In the UK Beech et al. (1998) found that 67 per cent of their sample (53 of 77 male child abusers) made significant changes as a result of the SOTP. Similarly McGrath et al. (2003), in a six year follow-up study, found that of 195 adult male 'sex offenders' the sexual re-offence rate for treatment completers (56 prisoners) was as low as 5.4 per cent while the rate for those who had dropped out (49 prisoners) or refused treatment (90 prisoners) was over 30 per cent.

Sex offender treatment programmes in prison appear in the main to be ineffective in reducing recidivism, especially for high risk offenders (Lewis and Perkins 1996).

Low risk offenders are more likely to respond to treatment, but the efficacy of the programme is cast into doubt because these people were probably likely to desist anyway (Brown 2005). Advocates of the SOTP argue that while there is still some possibility that treatment may work it should not be abandoned and that joining the SOTP may be the only way that a familial abuser can demonstrate to their victim and other family members that they are trying to change (Perkins 1991). These grounds, however, hardly present a strong case for the prison place to be considered a desirable option. It seems unlikely that the SOTP makes offenders more likely to offend, but 'sex offender school' is not as helpful as advocates hope.

Legitimacy

A critical deconstruction of the 'sex offender' label demonstrates that assumptions around the pathologized other are completely inaccurate. The focus on a small number of sexually deviant men (sic) is counter-productive because not only does it scapegoat those who are actually processed by the CJS, but it leaves 'invisible' the harms perpetrated by the un-convicted 'other'. Society is lulled into a false sense of security, under the pretence that something is being done and that society is 'safer' because of current penal policies. The key question is whether the incarceration of people who sexually offend reduces or escalates harm for either the actual victim or perpetrator. The argument presented here is that the prison place is likely to make the situation worse. Its negative environment becomes a breeding ground for a misogynist counter-culture, fatally undermining therapeutic endeavours. It may be that some people who sexually offend do benefit from the SOTP, but the evidence is not strong enough to justify incarceration on efficacy of treatment alone.

Penalization and criminalization hinder the resolution of interpersonal conflicts. Because there is very little 'distance' between perpetrators and victims/survivors solutions rooted in the penal law may be unattractive to people who have been sexually violated. Survivors want to know why the perpetrator harmed them; to know they are now safe; to have acknowledgement of the harm done; and hope that there will not be other people harmed by the perpetrator (Renvoize 1993). These harm reduction objectives are more likely to be achieved through social rather than penal policy (Brown 2005). Social policy interventions can provide help without monstering and are more likely to be adopted by those who have done wrong.

Voluntary community interventions are not only located in the perpetrator's natural environment, but evidence seems to demonstrate that such programmes are just as effective or more effective than those based in an institutional setting (Perkins 1991; Barker and Morgan 1993; Hedderman and Sugg 1996; Polizzi et al. 1999; Hanson et al. 2002; Brown 2005). There should be recognition that people who sexually offend can be helped, but this seems most effective in voluntary and non-custodial treatments, such as those that prospered at the Gracewell Institute in the early 1990s.[14] Other strategies that should be promoted alongside this include moral education campaigns on sexual abuse; easily accessible information, guidance and confidential support for those who have been harmed; and government funded support networks, refuges and confidential help-lines that can help rebuilding the lives of those harmed. All this requires moving beyond the 'sex offender' master status. It is important to point to the normality, not the pathology, of people who sexually offend. This is the first step on the path to taking sexualized harms seriously. The true nature and impact of sexual harms must be acknowledged alongside recognition of just how deeply ingrained this problem is in contemporary culture. Feminists have understood sexual violence as an abuse of (mainly male) power and privilege and hierarchies of male power (Jagger 1983).

> Masculine sexual identity is established through feeling superior to women we are close to and through establishing our sense of identity in a masculine competitive world. It is as if we only know how to feel good about ourselves if we put others down.
>
> (Seidler 1985, cited in Glaser and Frosh 1993: 31)

It is crucial that structural and political contexts of sexually abusive behaviours are engaged and,

> it is of paramount importance that distorted ideas and images of women and children are not seen as the unique, pathological, property of the convicted 'sex offender' alone. There needs to be an exploration of sexism at a societal, systems and personal level, questioning the attitudes which inform professional ideology and practice.
>
> (Mercer 1998: 121)

Current understandings are skewered through individualized pathologies and the incapacitation of a small number of (unrespectable and low status) abusers. These are simply those people who sexually offend who have been caught, while the vast majority of people who perpetrate sexual abuse continue to evade the system. Society must find a means to effectively demonstrate that the abuse of women and children is simply not acceptable. To do this requires first and foremost the acknowledgement of the social contexts that perpetuate and normalize the degradation of women and children. It is not just individuals that need to change; it is not just the scapegoated offender who is caught that needs to acknowledge the problem; we need to take sexual abuse seriously at the societal level and be prepared to make profound social changes.

Further reading

Brown, S. (2005) *Treating Sex Offenders: An Introduction to Sex Offender Treatment Programmes.* Devon: Willan.

Cohen, S. (2001) *States of Denial: Knowing about Atrocities and Suffering.* Cambridge: Polity Press.

Hudson, K. (2005) *Offending Identities: Sex Offenders' Perspectives on their Treatment and Management.* Devon: Willan.

Marshall, W.L., Anderson, D. and Fernandez, Y. (1999) *Cognitive Behavioural Treatments of Sexual Offenders.* Chichester: John Wiley.

Sampson, A. (1994) *Acts of Abuse: Sex Offenders and the Criminal Justice System.* London: Routledge.

Sim, J. (1990) *Medical Power in Prisons: The Prison Medical Service in England 1774–1989.* Milton Keynes: Open University Press.

We also recommend that students look up the latest debates in specialist journals such as *Criminal Justice and Behaviour; Journal of Sexual Aggression; Psychology, Crime and Law;* and *Sexual Abuse: A Journal of Research and Treatment.*

8

Drug taking

Two of the most painful harms of imprisonment are the conscious experience of time and the loss of personal autonomy (Medlicott 2001). It is well documented that prison life is profoundly contradictory for it is both highly controlled yet filled with emptiness (Cohen and Taylor 1972). The numbing monotony of penal regimes determining the time a person wakes, works and eats must be contrasted with sudden and unexpected changes in daily routines (Malloch 2000). Prison is a 'paradox as it can be both routined and non-routined, certain and uncertain' (Cope 2003: 162). Time consciousness is painful because it exposes those deprived of their liberty to the cruel fact that their life is simply wasting away. Not surprisingly many prisoners attempt to suspend time and find ways to manage life on the edge of this meaningless abyss. Illicit (illegal) drugs, especially cannabis, can be a means of controlling unstructured time by inducing sleep, thus making time experienced consciously 'become unconscious again' (Cope 2003: 172).

Taking drugs can provide sanctuary for prisoners overwhelmed by the prison place and can also be a means of self-medication and self-help (Swann and James 1998; Bullock 2003). Drugs can help mask the harsh realities of penal regimes and ease the consequences of being exposed to low levels of mental and physical stimulation (Wheatley 2007). This indicates that drug taking is a direct consequence of the processes of confinement and could be an important survival strategy (see Box 8.1 and Table 8.1). Yet the nature, form and extent of drug taking in prison must be also understood as a means of creating conflict as well as pacification (Swann and James 1998). Drug taking can lead to transgressions of the 'prisoner code', and heroin in particular is seen as having a corrosive effect upon collective prisoner values such as solidarity, trust and goodwill (Crewe 2005). Prisoners whose heroin habits are out of control are regarded as weak outsiders and referred to as ' "smackheads", "smack-rats" or "bagrats" who may be manipulative, ruthless or violent in order to obtain their fix' (Crewe 2005: 468).[1]

Taking drugs can cause other problems within prisons. As substances inside prison are likely to be less pure than those available on the outside, users are likely to face intermittent intoxication and an increased risk of overdose on release due to reduced opioid tolerance (Farrell and Marsden 2005). Injected drug taking is often

---

Box 8.1 *Models of drug use*

1   *Time-management model:*
    helps pass the time in prison
2   *Self-medication model:*
    a way of responding to isolation, loss of autonomy and boredom
3   *Social network model:*
    a way of helping people make social connections and friendships in prison
4   *Status model:*
    promotes status and elevates individual up the prison hierarchy
5   *Economic model:*
    fuels the prisoner economy

Table 8.1 Reasons for use of the three main drugs of choice in prison

	Cannabis	*Heroin*	*Tranquillizers*
Relaxation	54	28	38
To relieve boredom	43	40	27
Calming effects	27	19	19
Easily available	19	26	22
Enjoyment	29	19	17
To block out current situation	22	28	18
Depression	12	12	4
Less chance of detection	2	10	1

Source: Wheatley (2007); Bullock (2003: 32)
Note: Figures reflect the percentage of users of the specific drug

impromptu and unplanned, and so less attention is paid to the risk of transmitting blood borne viruses through the sharing of needles and syringes (Turnbull 2000). Prisoners in withdrawal can be unpredictable, have violent mood swings, develop suicidal ideation or experience exacerbated mental health problems (Forum for Preventing Deaths in Custody 2007). Drugs can also feed a black market leading to intimidation, corruption, and violence as well as increasing tensions between prisoners and staff (Keene 1997a).[2] Drug taking can result in a prisoner amassing huge debts, with non-payment seeing them placed under pressure to bring in drugs when on home leave or to force their partners and family members to smuggle when visiting (Penal Affairs Consortium 1996).

This chapter critically reflects upon the main definitions and interpretive frames concerning the definition of illicit drug taking. It then proceeds to discuss the data on both pre-prison and prison drug usage. The historical constructions of drug takers in prison are then explored and this is followed by a critical overview of contemporary Prison Service policies. The chapter concludes with a consideration of the legitimacy of the current penalization of drug takers and possible alternative means of controlling usage.

Thinking critically about illicit drug taking

A drug can be broadly defined as a chemical substance that has the ability to modify an individual's emotions, behaviour or body functions (Bennett and Holloway 2005). Drugs include substances such as LSD, cocaine, alcohol, heroin, tobacco, cannabis, barbiturates, XTC, methadone, solvents, and caffeine (see Table 8.2).

Drug taking is almost universal in human society and so the key question becomes which substances are seen as problematic at a given time and why. Deciding which drugs to control and whether the consequences of its usage are harmful or beneficial are not necessarily linked to the substance, but to the social, legal and personal problems created through their use. In this sense, illicit drug taking refers to morally and legally disapproved drugs or socially disapproved usage (Griffiths and Pearson 1988).[3] When understood in a historical perspective it is clear that there is a distinction between the drug usage of the unrespectable poor, who have been understood as weak, inadequate and immoral and susceptible to vice, and drug usage by the respectable, professional and middle class, who are more likely to be understood as suffering from a disease (Berridge 1999). Negative stereotyping then is linked as much to who takes drugs as much as the substance being taken (Newcombe 1992). For example, cannabis accounts for four-fifths of all convictions but only about one in 50 people who use the drug are sentenced (Keene 1997a).[4]

There are three main responses to illicit drug taking: treatment; abstinence; and harm reduction. Treatment perspectives derive from the psycho-medical model which conceives drug usage as an illness. The psycho-medical model understands the 'drug problem' as an individual pathology and a public health issue (Berridge 1999). As such wider social contexts are obscured through the medical lens and dividing practices are utilized to categorize those offenders who should be deemed suitable for treatment and those that should be merely contained (Sim 1990). From a somatic

Table 8.2 Pharmacological classification of substances

Classification	Effects	Examples of drugs
Stimulants	Activate the central nervous system and increase physical activity and may induce a feeling of euphoria	Cocaine, crack and amphetamines
Depressants	Depress the activity of the central nervous system and induce sleep and may reduce stress	Benzodiazepines and barbiturates
Analgesics	Used to relieve pain	Opium, morphine and heroin
Hallucinogens	Can change perceptions, sensations, thinking and emotions	LSD, magic mushrooms and ecstasy [XTC]

Source: Bennett and Holloway (2005)

(biological) perspective the user is seen as physically addicted to a given substance and who will suffer unpleasant withdrawal symptoms. From a psychological perspective the user only believes they are dependent (Bean 2002). Drug taking is a choice that may be experienced as pleasurable and the aim of CBT is to persuade the offender to desist (Keene 1997a).

Abstinence is predicated on the assumption that drugs are harmful because they are illegal and is rooted within the moral and disease models (Pearson 1992). The moral model locates drug taking within an individual's moral weakness and users are constructed as undeserving, unworthy and less eligible subjects who need to be controlled (Keene 1997b). The disease model understands the user as suffering from a physical or spiritual disease. The 'addict' is pathologized and regarded as having an 'addictive personality'. The only response is total abstinence (Berridge 1999). An 'addict' is considered dependent if they have (1) increased tolerance to a given substance, (2) are physically or psychologically reliant, and (3) experience withdrawal symptoms following cessation of usage (Bullock 2003; Bennett and Holloway 2005). Drug dependency is believed to be a chronic long term and relapsing condition although there is considerable difference of opinion between practitioners and users regarding what the phenomena actually entails (Bean 2002). Indeed there is now considerable weight behind the opinion that most people who use drugs are not dependent (Keene 1997a).

Doubt regarding the understanding of substance usage has not prevented the deployment of dividing practices categorizing drug takers into classifications of 'non-problematic' and 'problematic drug users' (PDU) in the official literature.[5] In short PDUs take 'cannabis more than once a day or any other drug four times per week or more' (Ramsay et al. 2005: 273).

> The term 'problematic drug use' is imprecise, but . . . we are using it to mean drug use whose features include dependence, regular excessive use and serious health and social consequences. It will typically involve the use of opiates, particularly heroin, and stimulants, particularly crack cocaine, often as part of a pattern of polydrug use.
>
> (UK Drug Policy Commission 2008: 17)

There is, however, an alternative abolitionist approach that does not negatively categorize and pathologize drug taking. This harm reductionist perspective accepts that drug taking occurs without moralizing about the act and strives instead where possible to mitigate harm and reduce health risks (Fuhrer and Nelles 1997). Harm reduction initiatives range from opiate maintenance and needle exchange schemes to the provision of factual information and moral education aimed at preventing future harms (Fromberg 1992). Drug takers are recognized as rational beings needing information and support rather than 'victims' whose abuse is out of control. In this chapter we advocate harm reductionism as the most appropriate way to respond to illicit drug taking.

Problematizing data on illicit drug taking

There are estimated to be more than 400,000 illegal drug users in the United Kingdom (Seddon 2006). As many as 250,000 drug takers have been defined as PDUs. It is estimated that about 75,000 PDUs pass through the prison system annually and that around 45,000 PDUs are in prison at any one time (NOMS 2005; UKDPC 2008). Somewhere between 60 and 85 per cent of prisoners report some drug misuse prior to imprisonment, 66 per cent within one month of incarceration, and 55 per cent report a severe drug problem (Wilkinson et al. 2003; Singleton et al. 2005). Cannabis is the most common drug used by prisoners in the twelve months prior to custody, followed by heroin, cocaine (powder) and crack cocaine (Ramsay et al. 2005). There is also evidence that large numbers of men (63 per cent) and women (39 per cent) have hazardous alcohol consumption levels in the year prior to prison (Singleton et al. 1999).

The official data appears to indicate that prison may reduce the prevalence of drug taking (Turnbull 2000). Bullock (2003) found that 81 per cent of prisoners decreased usage, largely because of the relative lack of availability, prohibitive costs and personal efforts to come off drugs. According to Random Mandatory Drug Tests (RMDTs) drug taking has been on the decrease since the mid-1990s. In 1995 38 per cent of prisoners tested positive. This decreased to 24 per cent in 1997, 12 per cent in 2003 and as low as 9 per cent in 2007. As a means of accurately estimating the level of drug taking in prison, however, the RMDT is fundamentally flawed. Long term comparisons can be misleading as there have been changes to equipment and interpretations of results, as well as in the number of people tested. The testing process can also prove to be unreliable, leading to problems around false positives and false negatives. It may have an impact on the drugs being taken, is expensive and potentially counterproductive (Penal Affairs Consortium 1996). There are also ways of subverting tests such as drinking large amounts of liquid to dilute samples ('flushing'), taking other substances to cloak a drug, or using (clean) substitute urine samples (Home Affairs Committee 1999: xxx).[6]

Much of the evidence from other sources indicates that prisoners' drug taking is much higher than the official rates (Singleton et al. 2005). According to one study 70 per cent of prisoners used drugs at some point during their current sentence (Wilkinson et al. 2003). In a major independent study Hucklesby and Wilkinson (2001) also found that 70 per cent of the 240 prisoners in their sample misused drugs at some point during their current sentence, and that the drug of choice of around half (54 per cent) was cannabis.[7] This is similar to the earlier findings by Edgar and O'Donnell (1998) who found that 76 per cent of prisoners used drugs at some time during their sentence. Drug taking in prison appears to be closely related to prior drug use and an accurate picture of its extent must distinguish between daily, weekly or monthly usage and the substance used. Wilkinson et al. (2003) found that of prisoners who only used cannabis, 49 per cent used it daily, 29 per cent used it weekly and 22 per cent used it less than every week. For those prisoners who used drugs other than cannabis, 70 per cent reported daily use, 22 per cent reported weekly use and 11 per cent used it less than every week (Wilkinson et al. 2003: 134–5). Another major study found that while 40 per cent of prisoners used drugs during their current sentence only 25 per cent had taken drugs within the last month and this fell to 16 per cent for the previous week (Singleton et al. 2005). Thus while usage does appear to decrease for some substances in prison compared to use on the outside, the vast majority of studies indicate that the prevalence of cannabis remains high in prison. The high frequency of daily and weekly usage for this particular drug must consequently be contextualized within its role in coping with the daily degradations of prison life.

The archetypal drug taker in prison is around 23 years of age (HM Prison Service 1998a). BME prisoners have similar levels of cannabis use to 'white' prisoners, but are less likely to use drugs such as heroin (Borrill et al. 2003). From 2003 to 2005 86 per cent of drug treatment prisoner assessments where white, compared with 7 per cent 'Black', 3 per cent 'Asian', 4 per cent mixed ethnicity and 1 per cent other (Wheatley 2007). Younger prisoners are much more likely to have used cannabis and in one recent study 80 per cent of prisoners aged 17–24 used cannabis compared to 54 per cent of those prisoners aged 25–59 (Liriano and Ramsay 2003).

There are also significant differences between men and women prisoners. It is estimated that 70 per cent of women prisoners require clinical detoxification compared with 50 per cent of men (Corston 2007a). Borrill et al. (2003) found that over 79 per cent of women in custody used illicit drugs in the month prior to imprisonment, and that almost 50 per cent were dependent on at least one drug. Women in custody are more likely to be dependent upon opiates, with 41 per cent of remand and 23 per cent of sentenced women prisoners defined as 'dependent', compared with 26 per cent of remand and 18 per cent of sentenced male prisoners (Kesteven 2002; Borrill et al. 2003). It is also believed that around 40 per cent of women prisoners have a serious alcohol problem (Corston 2007a).

Women drug users and alcoholics face three layers of stigma as they have transgressed the law, moral respectability and norms about being a good woman (Broom and Stevens 1991). Feminists, such as Gloria Steinem (1979, cited in Broom and Stevens 1991), have argued that women are expected to demonstrate legitimate dependency (on men) and so women who take drugs in effect demonstrate a socially disapproved form of dependence. Women are also more likely to take drugs to self-medicate and alleviate physical or emotional pain. Drugs and alcohol are likely to be 'chemical comforts' to deal with isolation, alienation and stress rather than hedonism (Ettorre 1992). Imprisonment is highly stressful for women and thus drugs become a crucial 'coping mechanism' (Borrill et al. 2003: 19).

Historical context

The socio-historical construction of problematic drug taking is closely associated with notions of respectability. Drug taking in the nineteenth century, such as opium use, 'by the working class was much more likely to be considered problematic than use of the drug in any other class' (Berridge 1999: xxx). Dependency was believed to be caused by the poor's inferior moral backbone rather than by any particular qualities of the drug (Conrad and Schneider 1992). The regulation of drug taking was, however, closely tied with the ascendancy of the medical and pharmaceutical professions and the medicalization of social problems. Consequently the penal law and the use of imprisonment were initially a relatively marginal means of controlling illicit drug taking.

Prison appears to have been in reality a very minor way of dealing with addicts. In 1896, for instance, the Scottish prison commissioners reported two cases treated in prison in Glasgow for the morphia habit. Many addicts could have been sent to prison for offences unconnected with their condition. The absence of published medical comment on the incidence of prison confinement of addicts was an indication possibly of its relative rarity and, too, of lack of medical interest in the non-professional side of the question. It was mostly the working-class addicts who went to prison.

(Berridge 1999: 168)

Although it was acknowledged that there were artistic, medical and higher-class drug takers, when the penal law was deployed under the 1916 and 1920 *Dangerous Drugs Acts* it focused almost exclusively on the regulation of 'unrespectable' lower class users (Berridge 1984, 1999). The highly influential humanitarian Rolleston Committee 1924–26, which was comprised of people largely from the medical profession, defined 'drug addiction' as a disease requiring treatment rather than a 'crime' requiring punishment (Berridge 1984). This approach was widely shared in the medical profession, although the Prison Medical Service rejected the disease model, promoting punishment rather than treatment. Prison doctors advocated policies including compulsory institutional confinement and immediate withdrawal for their lesser eligible clients. As Berridge (1999: 274) points out, 'prison doctors formed a distinct group who always favoured harsher methods, in particular the abrupt withdrawal from methods of treatment; their addiction clientele was distinctly different'.

For the following forty years the medical profession used its clinical judgement to determine the treatment of 'drug addicts'. One main reason for the ascendancy of the psycho-medical model was that the number of known addicts remained small, with numbers falling as low as 300 in the 1950s (Conrad and Schneider 1992). By the 1960s, however, there appeared to be a major increase in the extent of drug taking by young people from the lower classes and the first modest moves away from diversion came with the Brain Report of 1965. Although Brain continued to argue that 'the addict should be regarded as a sick person, he should be treated as such and not as a criminal, provided he does not resort to criminal acts' (1965, cited in Conrad and Schneider 1992: 133), greater emphasis was now placed on public health and tighter controls were imposed on drug prescriptions. For those 'addicts' who did 'resort to criminal acts' the prison was seen as a place where the drug offender could be sent to come off drugs and 'assume or resume a normal social life' (Home Office 1968: 3). Further, addicts in prison 'are withdrawn from drugs in much the same way as they would be in hospital. These circumstances therefore give rise to possibilities of rehabilitation and the opportunity should not be allowed to pass' (p. 15).

By the early 1970s, most notably through the 1971 *Misuse of Drugs Act*, diversion of drug takers via medical treatment was gradually replaced by their punishment.[8] While numbers of 'addicted' prisoners in the 1970s remained relatively stable at around 1100 per annum (Advisory Council on the Misuse of Drugs [ACMD] 1979: 1), there was increasing emphasis on providing treatment. In 1972 the Holloway Therapeutic Unit was established to cater for up to 20 women 'addicts' while the therapeutic community annexe at Wormwood Scrubs was able to cater for 40 male prisoners (ACMD 1979: 5). In 1976 HMP Pentonville had 87 prisoners undergoing 'withdrawal treatment' while there were 30 drug dependants at HMP Grendon in the late 1970s (ACMD 1979: 6). The ACMD (1979: 1) report *Drug Dependants within the Prison System in England and Wales* once again maintained that imprisonment 'presents an important opportunity' for drug treatment and rehabilitation.

> The opportunity provided by abstinence in the course of a prison sentence ought to be used, wherever possible, to help a drug dependant towards better relationships and the possibility of improved functioning on release. In theory treatment is offered to whoever wants it for the personality disorders of which, in the view of the Prison Service, drug dependence is only one symptom.
>
> (ACMD 1979: 4)

Although the report made clear connections between drug dependency, 'personality disorder' and mental health problems, the ACMD (1979) also raised concerns regarding the austere withdrawal programmes that existed in prison. While official reports up to the 1970s had reproduced the medical language adopted in the Rolleston Report, in an important and symbolic move the ACMD (1982) report *Treatment and Rehabilitation* replaced the term 'drug addict' with 'problem drug taker'. This user was,

> any person who experiences social, psychological, physical or legal problems related to intoxication and/or regular excessive consumption and/or dependence as a consequence of his own use of drugs or other chemical substances (excluding alcohol or tobacco).
>
> (ACMD 1982: 34)

While there were no explicit statements of policy on drugs in prison, by the early 1980s it was clear that the Home Office advocated abstinence. Prison was an opportunity for desistance and there was little official recognition that drug taking could actually occur in prison (Duke 2003). This invisibility was gradually challenged by knowledge seeping into the public domain, such as the 1984 Prison Officers Association survey which suggested that more than 80 per cent of the prisoners had a serious drug problem (*Guardian*, 3 October 1984, cited in Malloch 2000: 102).

As the 1980s progressed it was becoming apparent that not only were an increasingly large number of drug users being sent to prison but that intravenous (injecting) drug use could create significant problems for prison administrators and the wider general public. Drugs could lead to internal discipline problems but most significantly of all it became clear that 'risky' behaviours by prisoners could facilitate the spread of Human Immunodeficiency Virus (HIV). Prison was seen as a possible bridgehead for the disease into the outside community of 'law-abiding' and respectable heterosexuals. Initially there were concerns that large numbers of prisoners were being infected with HIV in prison each year, which reflected wider concerns in the mid-1980s that HIV was spreading at an alarmingly fast rate (Berridge 1996). At the time it was believed that more than one prisoner a week was being infected and that as many as 5 per cent of the prison population had HIV (Dolan 1997). While this data later proved false, the belief that prison was a hot bed for HIV transmission significantly influenced prison policy makers.[9]

The concerns about the spread of HIV saw a new emphasis on treatment and harm reduction and in 1987 the Prison Service published its *Policy Statement on Throughcare of Drug Misusers in the Prison System*, which focused on the treatment and care of offenders.[10] In 1988 the ACMD reported that the transmission of HIV was a 'greater threat to the public and individual health than drug misuse' (ACMD 1988, cited in Berridge 1996: 224). Three years later, and in conjunction with the Advisory Group for Drug Education, the Prison Service published *Caring for Drug Users: A Multi-disciplinary Resource for People Working with Prisoners*, which aimed to deal with both the supply *and* demand of drugs in prison. Even at this high tide of harm reductionism abstinence remained important. In the words of the Prison Service (1991: 2) prisoners should 'make the most of the opportunity presented by imprisonment' to help them 'break or modify their habit', while methadone (physeptone linctus) was offered in prison on an accelerated seven day period only, which was much quicker than on the outside.

The mid-1990s witnessed the end of the HIV moral panic and the normalization of the disease (Berridge 1996). Emphasis was once again placed on the apparent relationship between drugs and 'crime' and the marginalization and criminalization of users (Malloch 2000). The government white paper *Tackling Drugs Together* published in May 1995 and the Prison Service strategic framework document entitled *Drug Misuse in Prison: Policy and Strategy* (HM Prison Service 1995) set the new agenda. Drug taking was now seen as a destabilizing influence that created conflict and needed to be firmly controlled (Duke 2003). Consequently the 'Prison Service will not tolerate the presence and use of illicit drugs in its establishments' (HMPS 1995: 2). The aim of the 1995 policy was to reduce supply and demand for drugs and rehabilitate users. Strategies included the use of sniffer dogs; searching of prisoners, staff and visitors; closed circuit television during visits; and closed visits for prisoners who had been caught smuggling drugs into prison. The other key reform of the 1995 policy was the introduction of RMDT, which had first been revealed in the then Home Secretary Michael Howard's infamous 'Prison Works' speech in 1993. According to the Prison Service (1995) drug testing would act as deterrent, improve surveillance and identify people needing help, although in practice RMDT was seen as a means of discipline and punishment (Duke 2003).

Originally introduced in eight prisons, by March 1996 RMDT had been rolled out to all prison establishments. It seems likely that RMDT had some limited impact in discouraging cannabis usage[11] but had virtually no impact on other drugs, such as heroin. Indeed, according to one recent survey, 'while heroin use on aggregate has not increased in prisons, heroin use as a proportion of all drug use in prison has increased substantially due to the reduction in cannabis usage' (Singleton et al. 2005: xix–xx), though as discussed above, cannabis remains the drug of choice. There are a number of other problems associated with RMDT. Tests themselves are intrusive and can be experienced as humiliating. In addition RMDT could discourage openness about a drug problem and create a currency in drug free urine (Duke 2003).

Although punishment, abstinence and supply control were now firmly in the ascendancy, lip service was still paid to treatment and harm reduction strategies.

From 1995 to 1997 there were 21 drug treatment and rehabilitation programmes piloted in nineteen prisons and influential bodies such as the ACMD (1996) continued to maintain that considerable progress could be made in reducing the harm created by drug taking. In April 1998, the government introduced a new White Paper *Tackling Drugs to Build a Better Britain* and in response on 12 May 1998 the Prison Service introduced a revised 10 year strategy entitled *Tackling Drugs in Prison*. The 1998 initiatives were backed by an unprecedented investment in treatment and aftercare services for prisoners. From 1999–2002 over £76 million was made available by the government to fund initiatives, such as introduction of the Counselling, Assessment, Referral, Advice and Throughcare (CARAT) Services. Although *Tackling Drugs in Prison* aimed to increase treatment referrals and treatment completions, concerns were raised that as its emphasis was on deterring and detecting drugs 'the importance of reducing the supply of drugs in prison continues to be elevated above reducing demand' and that there was no evidence that this actually worked (Hucklesby and Wilkinson 2001: 351). Drugs policy was, however, intended to be fully integrated with the wider improved management of the Prison Service and the delivery of 'the necessary conditions and healthy atmosphere in which attempts at rehabilitation can prosper' (Home Affairs Committee 1999: xvi).

Contemporary penal policy

The 1998 Prison Service drugs strategy was updated in 2003 (HM Prison Service 2003). This was further augmented in 2005 when NOMS published its *Strategy for the Management and Treatment of Drug Users Within the Correctional Services* which itself was updated towards the end of 2008 (NOMS 2008b) with a new three year strategy. In each of these documents drug taking continues to be represented as a major public health problem closely associated with the perpetration of 'crime'. There are three main strands to contemporary Prison Service policy: supply reduction, treatment and harm reduction. Let us consider these three approaches in turn.

The government remains committed to challenging the supply of drugs.[12] Drugs are brought into prison through visits, prison officers, administrators, teachers, the delivery of supplies by outside contractors, mail, and 'drops' over the fence (ACMD 1996). In one well-known case a drug dealer used a ladder to break into HMP Everthorpe to sell drugs to prisoners through their cell windows (Doward 2008a). Prisoners cited in research by Ben Crewe (2006: 356) claimed that the 'most fruitful' method bringing in large amounts of drugs was by members of uniformed and civilian staff, followed by drugs being thrown over the prison fence and, third, through prison visits.

> [D]rugs may be held in a visitor's mouth and passed to the prisoner via a kiss; anal or vaginal concealment of drugs which are removed during a trip to the toilets or by other discrete methods and then swallowed or plugged by the inmate; and the hiding of packages in children's clothing and babies' nappies. Other methods include packages thrown over the perimeter fence or wall, sometimes in tennis balls; in deliveries of goods; by prisoners who have been to the court (particularly those who have been on bail) or temporarily released; under postage stamps on incoming letters; and via prison personnel and civilian workers.
>
> (Health Advisory Committee for the Prison Service (HAC) 1999: xix)

The three key principles that underlie supply reduction in prisons are *detection,*
deterrence and *disruption* (see Table 8.3). To help detect drug smuggling the Prison
Service has 250 'passive search dogs', which indicate the presence of drugs on individuals, and 250 active search dogs which are trained to seek and find drugs across the
prison, such as in cells and incoming vehicles (Gravett 2000). Targeted cell searches
also attempt to control prescribed medication for prisoners, such as methadone, that
may be sold to other prisoners for non-medical use. Visiting areas are controlled by
CCTV surveillance, low-level fixed furniture and bans on visitors handing property
such as clothes to prisoners. From March 2009 the BOSS (Body Orifice Security
Scanner) chair was introduced across the prison estate. The person under suspicion
sits on the BOSS chair which then scans their posterior for internally concealed
items. Searches of prisoners and visitors have three levels: (1) the rub down search,
(2) the full (strip) search and (3) the intimate search, which involves 'the searching
by a medical practitioner of the mouth, the vagina and/or the anus'. Clearly infringing
bodily integrity, it is officially acknowledged that this should be used rarely as it may
be 'counter-productive' (Blakey 2008: 22).[13]

To deter potential smugglers leaflets and posters advertise the serious penalties
for those caught. Under *The Offender Management Act* 2007 people who smuggle
phones or drugs into prison can be sentenced to up to 10 years in prison. Prisoners
caught with drugs can be placed on 'closed visits' preventing physical contact with
families and partners. The Prison Service aims to disrupt the supply of drugs through
the monitoring of telephone conversations and the targeting of outside suppliers
of drugs via liaison with the police. Prisoners can also be removed at short notice
to another prison while the anti-corruption and Professional Standards Unit (PSU)
aims to identify corrupt staff. Focus on supply reduction may in reality only lead to
an escalation of risky behaviours and more covert strategies from prisoners. While the
strategies of disruption, deterrence and detection have a certain philosophical con-
gruence with current Prison Service priorities of security and control as yet they have
proved relatively ineffective in impacting on drug taking in prison (Malloch 2000).

Table 8.3 Supply reduction strategies

Detection	Interception of drugs coming into and circulating around the establishment	• Searches of staff and visitors • trained drug dogs • searches of prisoners' cells surveillance and CCTV
Deterrence	Discourage people from bringing drugs into the prison or stifling circulation	• use of leaflets or posters • perimeter patrols • criminal prosecution • banning or restricting contact during visits
Disruption	Disorganize and disturb supply	• prisoner transfers • police operations • phone-conversation monitoring

Source: Derived from Wheatley (2007: 410)

The second main approach is treatment. Despite concerns about its effectiveness, approximately 60 per cent of the drug strategy budget is spent on treatment (Ramsay et al. 2005). It is believed that the average male problem drug user 'costs' society £827,000 in government interventions over their lifetime and that for every £1 spent on treatment, between £9.50 and £18 is saved on costs associated with drug taking (UKDPC 2008). Drug rehabilitation programmes are currently provided in 117 prisons. The main treatment initiative is the CARAT service, which was introduced in 1999. CARAT provides low-level interventions and assessments for all adult prisoners, producing care plans, counselling, group work, and support. CARAT services manage non-clinical treatment and act as a gatekeeper to further support. In recent years CARAT services have been supplemented by the Drug Intervention Programme (DIP), established in April 2003, to engage with 'problematic drug users' and the Integrated Drug Treatment System (IDTS), which had been rolled out across 53 prisons by 2009. IDTS was established in 2008 to boost CARAT services for prisoners in the first 28 days of custody and provide greater continuity of care between community and prison treatment services.

IDTS also aims to improve clinical services, such as detoxification programmes. Detoxification is undertaken in the prison healthcare centre and entails the medically supervised removal of believed poisonous substances (toxins) from the body. Detoxification and maintenance prescribing programmes involve the gradual reduction of illicit drugs, such as opiates, through the use of licensed medication such as physeptone linctus (methadone) over a seven day period to help ease the withdrawal symptoms (Wheatley 2007). Numbers on maintenance-prescribing or detoxification programmes in prison in England and Wales rose from 14,000 in 1996/97 to over 51,500 in 2006/07. Abstinence is also supported through Voluntary Drug Testing (VDT) and Voluntary Testing Units (VTU), which are drug free wings where prisoners agree to undertake extra tests. Each year there are around 60,000 random and 40,000 targeted VDTs and there currently are more than 4000 places on VTUs.[14] There is though some debate as to whether there really are any drug free wings: 'There is anecdotal evidence that drug dealers can find it helpful to operate from the VTU; it is recognised that the dealers may neither be users themselves nor need to store the drugs in which they are dealing' (HAC 1999: lii).

There are a number of treatment initiatives accredited by the Prison Service (see Table 8.4). The 12 Step programme is based on the disease approach developed by Alcoholics Anonymous and has been deployed by the Rehabilitation of Addicted Prisoners Trust (RAPt) in prison. Revealingly, this group was previously known as the Addicted Disease Trust and philosophically RAPt interventions are grounded in the assumptions that 'addiction' is a chronic and incurable illness. The aim of 12 steps programmes are to manage rather than cure their addiction through abstinence from all drug taking (Martin and Player 2000).

The RAPt programme aims to challenge denial, motivate change, and identify the prisoner's personal strengths and weaknesses to facilitate an effective recovery plan. The first interventions by RAPt were at HMP Downview in 1992 and by 2008 RAPt's 12 Steps treatment programme was being delivered in nine prisons. In a major review of RAPt Martin and Player (2000) undertook a study of 200 male prisoners in four male prisons in England and Wales. The study found that RAPt graduates were more

Table 8.4 Main types of prison-based provision

Type of Provision	Numbers
CARAT (Counselling, Assessment, Referral, Advice and Throughcare) teams undertake assessments of need for drug services and provide one-to-one motivational support and group work for problem drug users. They also undertake a case management role facilitating access to a wider range of services both in custody and upon initial release.	77,860 initial CARAT assessments in 2006/07
DIP (Drug Intervention Programme) which aims to break the relationship between drugs and crime for problematic drug users.	2008 45,000 PDUs
The **Integrated Drug Treatment System (IDTS)** aims to expand and improve drug treatment in prison through enhanced clinical services, psychosocial support and improved coordination and continuity of care.	In 2008, 29 prisons have a full IDTS and 24 have enhanced clinical services
Detoxification for drug-dependent prisoners on reception. **Maintenance prescribing** is becoming increasingly used for short term prisoners who were receiving this prior to imprisonment.	51,520 detoxification or maintenance prescribing in 2006/07
Drug-free voluntary testing units and **voluntary drug testing programmes** aim to help prisoners remain abstinent from drugs while in prison.	More than 4,000 places in 2005/06
12 step treatment models such as those provided by RAPt (Rehabilitation of Addicted Prisoners Trust).	930 in 2006/07
Cognitive behavioural therapy (CBT) high intensity programmes (FOCUS or STOP).	360 in 2006/07
Short Duration Programmes (SDPs) are 4-week programmes based on CBT and harm minimization approach for short term prisoners.	5,760 in 2006/07
P-ASRO (Prison-Addressing Substance Related Offending) is an offending behaviour programme of low to medium intensity.	3,780 in 2006/07
Therapeutic communities (TC) provide treatment based on a social-learning approach and peer support.	300 in 2006/07

Source: Derived from UK Drug Policy Commission (2008: 10)

likely than non-graduates to abstain from drugs and that completers of the programme were less likely to be reconvicted within a year of release. A further subsample of 75 prisoners were followed up and again it was found that graduate reconviction rates were lower than the comparison group. It should, however, be noted that there were a number of methodological limitations with this study, most notably regarding the selection of candidates with strong family and social ties (i.e. most likely to succeed) in the later study. On a wider level this abstentionist approach can be criticized for promoting self-policing, embedding dividing practices, and being predicated on theoretical assumptions that contradict prisoners' experiences of drug usage.

A number of other drug treatment programmes follow the principles of CBT. CBT is rooted in the assumption that drug usage is the product of distorted thinking processes and treatment is primarily targeted at altering the user's thought patterns as a means of overcoming dependency (Bullock 2003). CBT is most commonly used as part of the Short Duration Programme, which is designed for prisoners with short custodial sentences and is available at 35 penal establishments (HM Government 2005). A further initiative introduced in 2002 is the P-ASRO course (see Box 8.2). The aim of P-ASRO is to target prisoners dependent on more than one illicit substance and whose usage is likely to be related to the risk of reoffending. The aim of P-ASRO is abstinence and courses normally involve 12 prisoners undertaking 20 sessions, with each session two and a half hours in duration (HMP Risley 2005).

There are a number of significant flaws with drug rehabilitation in prison. Drug taking can be episodic and may be a 'chronic relapsing condition' (Wheatley 2007). More broadly it is also highly unlikely that the prison place can be conducive to recovery (Townsend 2008). Indeed it may be the opposite. In terms of the actual treatment programmes themselves evaluations have found that 'the evidence about the effectiveness of different interventions is seriously weak or absent' (UKDPC 2008: 12). Not only this, but prison drug services were 'patchy', 'poorly coordinated'

Box 8.2 P-ASRO

Section 1:

Sessions 1–4, Motivating Offenders to Change
(enhancing participants' motivation)

Section 2:

Sessions 5–10, The Personal Scientist
(model of behavioural control, maintaining abstinence)

Section 3:

Sessions 11–16, Relapse Prevention
(identify skills needed to cope with high risk situations)

Section 4:

Sessions 17–20, Lifestyle Modification
(A holistic approach facilitating the development of a reinforcing non substance non criminal lifestyle by:

- identifying what is being met by an anti-social lifestyle
- selecting substitute activities which will satisfy those needs
- encourage a commitment to a new lifestyle by reviewing the decision to change, enhancing social support and abandoning the 'addict' or 'criminal' identity)

Source: HMP Risley (2005: 6)

---

and 'frequently fall short of even minimum standards' (pp. 50 and 64). Across the penal estate there is widespread 'variation in the volume and type of service' and a 'lack of continuity and consistency of care' (PricewaterhouseCoopers 2008: 3–4). Further, while 61 per cent of prisoners with pre-prison drug problems do receive some form of help and support, the vast majority are through CARAT assessments and detoxification (Ramsey et al. 2005; UKDPC 2008). Indeed it is believed that as few as one in ten prisoners with pre-prison drug problems currently participate in rehabilitation programmes (Ramsay et al. 2005). Even then, there are serious concerns that though 12 steps and cognitive behavioural programmes may be able to demonstrate some short term impact 'the effects are not long-lasting' (Keene 1997a: 217).

For prisoners who do reduce their intake or abstain from drug usage in prison, treatment programmes are not a major contributing factor. A recent study by Ramsay et al. (2005) found that 33 per cent of respondents claimed their own will power was the most important factor in decreasing their drug use, while 21 per cent of prisoners with a drug problem prior to incarceration said that 'nothing' about their time in prison had helped with their substance usage. Imprisonment is more likely to do harm than facilitate positive changes for people whose drug usage has become out of control.

Prisons are designed to contain, punish and deliver blame through pain rather than facilitate the care or positive transformation of individuals. The notion of effective care within a regime rooted in discipline, categorization and regulation is inherently contradictory (Sim 1990; Malloch 2000). The emphasis on rehabilitation leads to scapegoating and the prisoner is perceived as directly responsible for not only their drug usage, but also for making the most of the rehabilitative opportunities in prison. Indeed 'those who do not comply become redefined as "dangerous"' (Malloch 2000: 48). Treatment may provide a cloak of legitimacy for penal practices but does nothing to fundamentally change the wider social inequities that impacted upon confinement in the first instance. Focusing in individualized treatments obfuscates structural problems and helps ensure that socio-economic contexts remain marginal to the debate.

The Prison Service has been much more reluctant to implement the third strategy in response to drug taking – harm reductionism. The two harm reduction initiatives that have been widely debated are disinfectant tablet and needle exchange dispensers. After an unsuccessful short trial in 1995, 11 prisons piloted the use of tablets to disinfect shared needles and syringes in 1998. Since October 2007 all adult prisoners have had 'easy and anonymous' access to wall-mounted dispensers of disinfectant tablets alongside guidance on cleaning techniques (Offender Health 2008: 1). The introduction of needle exchanges in prison, however, has been consistently ruled out. The Prison Service believes needle exchanges would 'give confusing messages to staff and prisoners about the acceptability of injecting in prisons' and could 'be used as offensive weapons' (HM Government 2005: 31). In November 2004 a Judicial Review supported the government's decision not to introduce needle exchanges even though successful needle exchange programmes have been introduced into prisons across Europe, most notably in Switzerland, which began the distribution of sterile injection equipment at Obershongrun in 1993 and Hindlebank institution for women in June 1994. It is clear from studies of these exchange programmes that they can be introduced quickly, easily and at relatively low costs; are quickly accepted by both prisoners and staff; do not increase intravenous drug use; and significantly reduce the reduce the risk of spreading diseases such as HIV (Nelles et al. 2000).

Legitimacy

Problematic drug taking must be understood as a social and historical construction reflecting the given moral and social order. Drug-taking prisoners come largely from socially excluded backgrounds and the main drug taken in prison, cannabis, is often used as a means to combat the inherent pains of imprisonment, most specifically the consciousness of unstructured time. In the words of Margaret Malloch (2000: 100) the 'boredom of prison routines, particularly the unstructured regimes for remand prisoners, combined with the stress of life inside and problems prisoners had left outside, meant that many prisoners were willing to take any possible measures to escape from their surroundings or to pass the time.'

The very processes of the prison place operate directly against abstinence and treatment initiatives, and the idea that the prison place can provide rehabilitation for drug takers is widely considered to be 'fundamentally flawed' (Malloch 2000: 111). Extensive evidence suggests that treatments of drug takers are more likely to be successful in the community than through criminal justice interventions (Bennett and Holloway 2005). This implies that if treatment is a genuine aspiration then it would be more sensible to divert drug takers from custody. Users should be given support and where necessary access to structured voluntary treatments in the community rather than punishment. Drug takers should also have access to social supports; drug free substitutes and counselling; options to participate in leisure activities; improved work opportunities and living conditions; and the option to participate in pharmaco-logical and psychosocial relapse prevention programmes (Uchtenhagen 1997). As such there is a strong case for the selective abolition of imprisonment for substance users. Yet crucial to the debate is the acknowledgement of the sameness of drug takers and the universality of drug usage in some form or other. All the evidence indicates that dividing practices othering people as 'problematic drug users' have proved to be counter-productive and have done little to address individual or social harm while prison is only likely to escalate usage.

Criminalization and penalization lead only to the concealment of drug taking rather than encouraging people who do have a problem to seek help, thus inhibiting the development of safe drug usage (McDermott 1992). We should be sceptical of the application of the penal law to this problem and advocate rather social policies integrating and assimilating drug users into society. The way to address illicit drug taking is through advocating harm reduction strategies which challenge the reliance on coercive controls and promote informal restrictions similar to those used in the regulation of alcohol use. Harm reduction and de-criminalization strategies can involve detailed and comprehensive information about the harms related to intraven-ous drug use, the spread of blood borne diseases and the cultivation of safe practices for users (Keene 1997a). This does not mean that nothing should be done to deal with those drug takers who do wrong. Other means of redress should be put in place to resolve conflicts and problematic behaviours and foster the principles of social justice (de Haan 1990). The proposed removal of the penal law should be replaced by moral education campaigns on the realities and potential dangers of certain drug usage, and the introduction of un-coerced treatments for users in the community. If the government continues, however, with its current reliance on penal sanctions, we anticipate that drug taking will remain a central part of prison life, with all the positive and negative consequences that entails.

Further reading

Berridge, V. (1999) *Opium and the People*, 2nd edn. London: Free Association Books.

Duke, K. (2003) *Drugs, Prisons and Policy-Making*. London: Palgrave.

Keene, J. (1997a) *Drug Misuse: Prevention, Harm Minimisation and Treatment*. Cheltenham: Nelson Thornes.

Malloch, M. (2000) *Women, Drugs and Custody*. Winchester: Waterside Press.

Shewan, D. and Davies, J.B. (eds) (2000) *Drug Use and Prisons: An International Perspective*. Amsterdam: Harwood Academic Publishers.

Sim, J. (1990) *Medical Power in Prisons: The Prison Medical Service in England 1774–1989*. Milton Keynes: Open University Press.

Alongside other general criminal justice internet resources we recommend that students keep up to date with organizations such as RAPt, SCODA, Addaction and Cranstoun.

9

Prisoners and their families

One of the most controversial aspects of imprisonment is the impact of incarceration on prisoners' families.[1] Despite over 40 years of research in the United Kingdom (Morris 1965), families of prisoners continue to often go unnoticed and un-discussed in media and public debates about 'crime' and punishment. Fundamentally important questions are raised, however, by a number of aspects of prisoners' relationships with their families and the interaction between penal policies and practices. Although strong family ties have been linked to a decreased risk of suicide and self-harm and to an increased likelihood of successful community re-entry and desistance from offending, for many families maintaining relationships with prisoners is not easy (Codd 1998; Social Exclusion Unit 2002; Mills and Codd 2007).

Wherever and whenever prison exists, there are, and always have been, prisoners' families. Despite this constant presence, prisoners' family members have been simultaneously visible and invisible in policy terms, with recent government policy recognizing their role in resettlement but at the same time continuing to send high numbers of people to prison and, despite the social, financial and other costs, justifying this on grounds of reducing 'crime' and public protection. Recent research on prisoners' families has considered how family members are themselves being co-opted into the management and surveillance of released offenders, and similarly critical research has assessed how the experience of prisoners' family members is gendered (Codd 2008). It is usually but not always men who go to prison, but it is women who cope with the burdens of caring from the outside (Girshick 1996).

Separation from, and limited and regulated contact with, family and friends is one of the most significant 'pains of imprisonment' and a prominent source of stress, worry and anxiety for many prisoners. These pains are felt particularly acutely by imprisoned mothers who are separated from their children. Research has demonstrated that for a high proportion of prisoners their relationship with their partner or spouse does not survive the period of incarceration (Salmon 2007). We do not know, unfortunately, how many relationships survive the prison sentence but returning home can raise as many difficulties and challenges in adaptation as invoked by the initial incarceration.

For prisoners, strong and supportive family ties have been linked to a greater chance of having housing on release and ultimately a decreased risk of reoffending. Qualitative data indicates how much prisoner time and energy is put into thinking about family relationships, and disruption in, or denial of, visits can be a key trigger for acts of aggression, violence and disorder (Mills 2005). That said, not all prisoners want their families to see them in the prison setting and some choose to 'do hard time' and sever or limit contact with their families during the sentence. Contact between prisoners and their families has been viewed positively but it is important to note that strong links to the outside may lead to increased levels of disciplinary infractions. Effectively, some prisoners become more frustrated, more 'pained' if they are constantly aware of the relationships which are being denied to them (Wolff and Draine 2004).

Despite the challenges, imprisonment may strengthen family ties due to the period of enforced separation, which allows the inmate to reflect on his or her behaviour but which may also prompt renewed expressions of love and courtship. Visits are prepared for by partners as if they are 'dates', and prisoners may write love letters and spend time planning and daydreaming about the future. Of course, many of these dreams do not come to fruition in the cold light of the post-release period, but the break in the pattern of the existing relationship can prompt renewed commitment to the relationship. Overcoming the challenges of imprisonment can add a renewed element of romance and prompt new expressions of 'togetherness' (Fishman 1990).

Partners and children of prisoners may experience social stigma and feared or actual hostility (Coulter 1997). Some family members move house and change their names in order to conceal their identity, especially in relation to 'crimes' which have attracted widespread social disapproval. In her significant study of families of serious offenders, Condry (2007) documented how family members negotiate and respond to these questions of identity. Family members, especially mothers and female partners of male prisoners, may find themselves blamed for the offending and it is often assumed in everyday life and the media that 'she must have known'. Sometimes the partner becomes the target of social disapproval, violence and hostility, as was experienced by Sonia Sutcliffe, the wife of the so-called 'Yorkshire Ripper', and more recently by Maxine Carr, the partner of Ian Huntley. Although Maxine Carr's offence was one of giving a false alibi to her partner, media and public responses at the time of her trial and subsequent release have portrayed her as Huntley's willing accomplice when he murdered two young girls. This blanket blaming of families in some countries leads to actual detention or punishment of family members, as happened in the Nazi era in Germany when the doctrine of *Sippenhaft* (kin punishment) allowed for the detention of members of families of political opponents of the regime. In some countries family members, especially of political prisoners, are routinely held, and sometimes tortured, in order to secure their testimony against their family members or in order to send a message to other potential offenders and their families.[2] The stigmatization of family members may also indirectly lead to greater criminal justice involvement: children whose parents are well-known offenders may find that as they grow up they are assumed to be as similarly oriented towards 'crime' as their parents.

It is important not to be naïve and over-romanticize family life. Some prisoners might have been incarcerated for physically or sexually harming members of their own families while many offenders have found accomplices among their kin, encouraging children to co-offend with adults as they grow up. That said, a child's future chances in life should not be blighted because of who their family members are. This is one of the main problems with policies aiming to identify children of prisoners from an early age as interventions may result in the negative labelling and stigmatization of the children involved.

The impact of high levels of imprisonment on some, mainly urban, communities has been well documented (Braman and Wood 2003). Da Cunha (2008), for example, points out that the separation between the prison and the community, and the idea that imprisonment involves offenders being cut off from family members, is being challenged as the 'imprisonment binge' has led to multiple generations of family members from the same family being incarcerated, sometimes in the same institutions at the same time. Thus family relationships continue, but in a different location. Being imprisoned at the same time as kin can offset loneliness, and offer protection and support especially to new prisoners. One of the consequences of this, however, is that if multiple relatives are imprisoned at the same time then there may not be additional kin outside the prison walls who are able to visit and supply extra items. Consequently it must be recognized that the significance of strong family ties goes beyond traditional assumptions restricted to visits, letters and supply of external goods.

This chapter considers the importance of family relationships for prisoners in the context of the many difficulties experienced by prisoners' partners and children in maintaining contact and promoting positive family relationships. It problematizes the model of the 'prisoners' family' which dominates the literature and explores the diversity of prisoners' family and kin relationships. The chapter then explores particular concerns such as the gendered nature of the responsibilities for caring for prisoners and controversies surrounding the housing of mothers and babies in the prison setting. It concludes with an assessment of the different roles played by campaigning and support groups of families who have members in custody. Interspersed throughout this chapter are case studies detailing three pertinent penal controversies.

Thinking critically about prisoners' families

The first question we must consider is 'what do we mean by "prisoner's family"'? The traditional view has always linked this to the nuclear family, usually involving an imprisoned male leaving a female partner with children to cope (Paylor and Smith 1994). Within this formulation of the stereotypical family, the children are usually young, the parents are not elderly, and the relationship is heterosexual. Family life, however, is much more complex than this. Indeed sometimes de facto parenting is more significant than biological parenting, such as when 'mum's boyfriend', for example, is more of a day-to-day father than a child's biological father. Also, the impact on parents, siblings and significant friendships beyond traditional bonds of kin and family of those imprisoned are often neglected (Meek 2008). Prisoners have multiple significant relationships across a web of connections and while family forms part of this, other relationships may be equally or more important.

There is a great deal written about the children of prisoners, although there are still debates as to the precise nature of the linkage between familial imprisonment and later incarceration of children. The impacts of imprisonment on families can be obvious but also operate in subtle and sometimes invisible ways. For example, the imprisonment of a man may mean the loss of the main family income, even if that income was gained by illegal means. Although assisted prison visits are available to those on low incomes, the scheme does not allow for the additional costs of travelling long distances, often with children, and paying for food and drinks during the journey and also during the visits. In addition, family members provide clothes, toiletries and other items for prisoners.[3]

The emotional impact of imprisonment of a family member can be great and lead to ill health. As well as documenting the many aspects of poverty and disadvantage experienced by members of prisoners' families, Smith et al. (2007) examined the social welfare costs of imprisonment, providing a more complete summary of the costs of imprisonment beyond the 'bed and breakfast' price of detention. Where, for example, the imprisonment of a man leads to depression and anxiety in his partner, exacerbated by stigma and actual or feared victimization, this can lead to healthcare costs including time spent with a GP, medication and counselling. If a child develops emotional or behavioural disturbances then there may be costs due to exclusion from school or the need for psychological help. If children themselves go on to offend, the extent of which is currently a matter for debate and discussion, then the long-term costs can be high.

For some families the imprisonment of a family member can be welcome, as when the offending is intra-familial or where the individual concerned has led a chaotic lifestyle due to drug taking or mental health problems. In these situations the chaotic family member in effect brings the life of the street into the home, often leading to disruption, unpredictability, lack of stability and sometimes neglect of familial responsibilities. Imprisonment of a family member may be the only means by which a prisoner's partner can regain control of family finances which had previously been spent on alcohol, drugs or other non-essential items. In these situations families can benefit from imprisonment as a period of respite. Comfort (2007), who studied the female partners of male prisoners at San Quentin in the US, points out that for many women in relationships with offending men, in an era of swingeing welfare cuts, the prison was the one resource which was consistently available to them.

The prison place changes not only the behaviour of incarcerated prisoners but of their female partners, who experience 'secondary prisonisation' as a consequence (Comfort 2007). Thus the usual rituals of a relationship, such as eating meals together, getting married and spending the night together, are relocated and reshaped in the context of the prison. Imprisonment can also render men romantic, emotionally attuned and highly communicative. As Megan Comfort (2007: 126) puts it, 'women decide to continue their relationships because romance within the penitentiary's grasp is in some way more promising or more rewarding than alternative associations have been or are anticipated to be'. For the women Comfort (2007) interviewed the difficulties of communicating with and visiting prisoners were preferable to the troubles caused to them by the previous men with whom they had had relationships.

It is interesting to note that for *men* a stable relationship with a female partner plays a significant role in the process of successful release and community and re-entry. Leverentz (2006), however, found that for *women* their pathway into prison often involved negative implications in relation to men, such as co-offending with men. Consequently although for men a stable relationship can be of value, women may choose not to be in a relationship, or have same-sex relationships during their time of what could be called 'recovery' from 'crime'.

Prisoners' children often react badly to parental imprisonment. Different explanations have been offered, but in relation to young children, are often linked to maternal separation (Bowlby 1946). Children may witness the arrest of their parent and may also have to witness their parents in court and then later in custody. Although for some children this is a relief and a respite, for others it is profoundly traumatic. Of course, for some children the parent is simply absent without any explanation being offered. For others, they are lied to, often with ostensibly benevolent intentions, and the true location of their missing parent is concealed. In some cases, especially where children are well-informed and able to read, they may realize where the parent is or other children or adults may tell them but they then have to bear the burden of keeping the secret, or not telling their parent what they know for fear of upsetting them. Some children display externalized problematic behaviours, such as trouble-making in school, whereas others may develop enuresis, eating disorders, anxiety and depression. Boys tend to 'act out' whereas girls tend to 'act in', and this can cause extra pressure for families as they may then have to cope with consequences of their child's poor behaviour, such as school exclusion and sometimes involvement in antisocial and criminal behaviour.

A particular concern has been to assess whether parental imprisonment leads to an increased likelihood of young people going on to be offenders themselves. A large number of studies have documented the intergenerational effect of criminality, although there is little research into the process by which this takes place. Recent psychological research has been carried out by Murray and Farrington (2005), who have drawn on the Cambridge longitudinal Study in Delinquent Development to assess several aspects of the psychological impact of imprisonment on prisoners' children. As they themselves recognize, however, their quantitative data only relates to boys and more needs to be explored as to the impact of the gender of the imprisoned parent. A particular issue is that of separating out the effects of criminality and imprisonment on children from other socio-economic and individual difficulties which seem to permeate the lives of prisoners' children. Parental imprisonment is often 'one more problem' for children who are already experiencing multiple difficulties and social exclusion (Golden 2005). The Children, Schools and Families Department and Ministry of Justice (2007) has considered how outcomes can be improved for children in schools, but it is unclear how the imprisonment of a parent translates into criminal behaviour by the child, either as a child or later as an adult (Johnston 2006). In addition, schools may not know a great deal about the experiences or needs of children who have a parent in prison, although the Ormiston Trust has published a guide and Gloucestershire now has a county-wide policy (Pugh 2007).

It is often stated that prisoners' children are six times more likely than their peers to be imprisoned themselves, but there appears to be no documented evidence in support of this claim (Murray and Farrington 2005). Murray and Farrington (2005) suggest that parental imprisonment appears to affect children over and above factors linked to separation and associated risks. Their work draws on prospective longitudinal

Table 9.1 Four approaches to thinking about prisoners and their families

	Central concern	Key principle	Solution	Weakness
Common sense	Attribute blame and/or responsibility of the offending to family members	Lack of support and services for families in need Hostility and stigmatization	Programmes that challenge children of prisoners at a young age	Limited knowledge base and problem of labelling and stigmatizing children
Psycho-medical	Focus on psychological consequences of imprisonment of a family member, especially for prisoners' children	Utilizing positivistic methodology and assumptions about maternal deprivation children are understood to be more likely to offend if parents are 'criminals'	Emphasis on individual intervention and identification programmes	Interventions can lead to 'false positives' as we do not have the ability to 'scientifically' predict future behaviour
Legalism	Establishment of legal rules and judicialization of relations concerning family members of prisoners	Application of the law to various aspects of prison life and its impact on the lives of family members	Common law and human rights jurisprudence as a means of providing legal guarantees for prisoners' families for issues ranging from mother and baby units to the right of access to prisoners' sperm	Legal rules cannot always adequately address the subtle complexity of family life and cannot account for the consequences of bad law
Abolitionism	The negative social and personal consequences of imprisonment for family members	Interventions to help families, especially bereaved families, and calls for greater visibility of prisoners' families	Challenge collateral consequences of penalization and alternative redress rooted in the principles of social justice and human rights	Requires radical social, economic and political change to fully implement aims

data from the Cambridge Study in delinquent development (CSDD), which includes data on 411 Inner London males and their parents. Murray and Farrington (2005) are dismissive of other studies of prisoners' families, viewing many as small scale and methodologically flawed. That said, they recognize consistency between previous studies, identifying depression, hyperactivity, aggression, withdrawal, clinging behaviour, sleep problems, eating problems, truancy and school refusal, running away, poor grades and delinquency. They found that separation due to parental imprisonment was a strong predictor of all the antisocial and delinquent outcomes in the study, even up to the age of 40. This quantitative research, however, can be criticized on a number of grounds. It focuses on the individual psychological impact of parental imprisonment rather than exploring socio-economic and cultural issues and does not consider the experiences and explanations of children of offenders themselves. Interestingly, this kind of research continues to attract funding, which reiterates the dominance of individualized psycho-medical explanations of harm suffered, diminishing the focus on sentencing and the prison system.

There is relatively little research on the experiences of prisoners' children in school. Anecdotal evidence suggests a wide variation in teachers' knowledge of the issues affecting children whose parents are in prison or who have been in prison. For teenagers, school disciplinary problems, sometimes including exclusion, have been recognized in children of prisoners.[4] The needs of prisoners' children in school are difficult to assess and meet because parents may not wish the school to know about the situation, either because of shame, stigma or fear that the child will be victimized or identified as a potential 'troublemaker'. Sometimes a school only becomes aware of the imprisonment of a parent when the child is not collected at the end of the school day because the parent has gone to court and has not made arrangements for the child to be collected in the event of a custodial sentence. There are a number of possibilities which could be developed by schools in order to make questions of criminal justice and imprisonment much more visible topics; at present it seems that schools are open and aware of the impact on children of parental illness, relationship breakdown and divorce, and physical and sexual abuse, but when a child's behaviour, demeanour and attitude changes dramatically the school may not think of family criminal justice involvement as a possible cause or trigger, whereas they might think of these other familial difficulties.

Problematizing the data about prisoners' families

In terms of the official data available, its comprehensiveness and its accuracy, the issue of prisoners' families constitutes one of the most challenging and unsatisfactory case studies in this book. It is difficult to ascertain exactly how many families and relationships are affected but, for example, the majority of imprisoned women are mothers who have children under 16 living with them at the time of the sentence.

The figures in Box 9.1 are important but do not include the children who are affected by the imprisonment of other family members and kin, such as siblings, grandparents, aunts, uncles and close family friends. It is also important to consider the effects of imprisonment on prisoners' parents, who may blame themselves for their child's offending and, particularly in the case of mothers, who continue to support

---

Box 9.1 Data about prisoners' families

- 160,000 children are affected by imprisonment per year.
- Over 17,700 children each year are separated from their mother.
- 66% of women and 59% of men in prison have dependents under age of 18.
- Of the women, 34% had children under 5 and another 40% had children aged 5–10.

Source: Prison Reform Trust (2009)

---

and visit their child once other people, such as partners, have moved on with their lives and ended their relationship with the prisoner.

Historical context

Wherever and whenever there are prisons, there are prisoners' families. In historical documents, we see family members at public executions, pulling on the feet of the person undergoing execution in order to hasten death and save them from the prolonged agonies of death by strangulation. Prisoners' families are omnipresent despite time, geography and variation in prison regimes. Thus throughout the history of the prison, we see family members bringing in food and clothing for prisoners. We see family members at the foot of the scaffold, following the prison van or simply waiting outside the gates of the prison. The twentieth century, with the development of social work and the Probation Service, meant that some attention was paid to families, such as the research by Pauline Morris (1965), though the modern reader might wince at some of her descriptions and judgements of the prisoners' wives, especially in terms of their housekeeping skills.

Case Study 9.1 Support groups for families of prisoners

There is no single statutory organization with responsibility for prisoners' families. A number of non-statutory, voluntary self-help and support groups have developed in the UK. The most significant national body is APF (Action for Prisoners' Families), which developed from its previous incarnation as the Federation of Prisoners' Families Support Groups, which was established in 1990. APF runs a national helpline, publishes a magazine and e-news bulletin, organizes events and works with the media to raise awareness of issues relevant to prisoners' families. Some self-help groups run visitors' centres in prisons, such as those run by POPS (Partners of Prisoners) based in Manchester. Advice is also provided to bereaved families of those who die in prison by the London based penal pressure group INQUEST. This organization provides information about the role of coroners and helps families gain legal representation. For prisoners who have no family, have been rejected by their kin, or for whom it is simply too difficult for family members to visit due to mobility problems or physical distance, such as in the case of foreign nationals, prisoners can be befriended by 'Voluntary Associates' working for New Bridge. New Bridge is a charity established by Lord Longford in the 1960s and is run in conjunction with the National Probation Service. It has branches in regions across the UK.

Through the 1970s, 80s and early 90s there was a steady trickle of UK-based research on prisoners' families, mainly by writers such as Roy Light (1992, 1993, 1995) and Gwyneth Boswell (2002: see Boswell and Wedge 2001). The most significant recent impetus for discussion of prisoners' families has come as a consequence of the report by the Social Exclusion Unit (2002) on preventing reoffending by ex-prisoners, which reiterated the role played by strong family ties in prisoner resettlement. Although the era of social work specifically aimed at prisoners' families has gone, families have found themselves with a new role to play, worthy of notice and attention from government as a consequence of their value in promoting ex-prisoner resettlement and desistance. Rather than being viewed as people affected by imprisonment and in need of support, they have become part of the penal machinery, co-opted as tools within the new emphasis on preventing reoffending. Thus, for the first time, APF has received funding from NOMS, a significant indication that the government recognizes the significance of family relationships for prisoners. Similarly, the commitment towards improving outcomes for prisoners' children detailed in the report by the Children, Schools and Families Department and Ministry of Justice (2007) could be argued to amount to recognition of the negative impacts of parental imprisonment on children and of the need to do something to counter this.[5]

Contemporary penal policy

Prisoners with strong, supportive family ties have been shown to have a decreased likelihood of reoffending after release. This recognition of the importance of family ties has provided the impetus and justification for renewed interest in prisoners' families on the part of government agencies. Families, however, can be dysfunctional, abusive, criminal and crime-supportive. Family members may indeed encourage desistance, but family networks can also provide opportunities and criminal partners. It is interesting to note the paradox that imprisonment of a parent is a key indicator in the likelihood of a young person going on to offend themselves, yet when governmental documents discuss families in terms of resettlement there is little mention of such a potentially criminogenic role: suddenly families become a perfect institution with an interest in, and commitment to, preventing recidivism. This is at best naïve, but also renders attempts to co-opt family members as unpaid informal law enforcement personnel doomed to failure. A cynic might argue that in ten years' time when supporting families will be shown not to have 'worked' in reducing recidivism the financial support given to the APF and others will be withdrawn. Of course, supporting prisoners' families for welfarist or humanistic reasons is a different issue, but if we support families in relation to resettlement then we need to avoid idealizing the family.

It is important to recognize that without the support of families many prisoners' experiences of imprisonment would be worse, as family members provide clothes, leisure items, pay for phone calls and generally try to ameliorate poor prison conditions. Provision of these items has been identified as difficult for some families, but some writers have argued that the idea of prisoners pressuring family members to provide goods, and the stresses of doing so, serve to obscure the real injustices and indignities meted out to family members (No More Prison 2006a and 2006b).

The policies and practices of the Prison Service have a central role to play in relation to the experiences of prisoners' families, especially in facilitating contact between the family and the prisoner. Visits are the lynchpin of continued contact between prisoners and their families. They are stressful and time-consuming events, involving as they often do arranging time off work or school for children, long journeys, coping with the increasing levels of prison security, and a fear of either not being allowed in or not having a 'good' visit. Both family members and prisoners may attempt to 'put a brave face' on things and present a positive front to their visitor, neither wanting to cause worry or concern to the other. Visits facilities and regimes vary widely between prisons, some allowing visitors to hug and kiss prisoners, others not for fear of contraband being transmitted and some insisting on closed visits.

Some prisons run extended all-day or 'family' visits but these are not usually available to all prisoners. That said where they are permitted the experiences of all concerned seem highly positive. Visits, however, are a problem for foreign national prisoners and this disproportionately affects women who have been detained as a consequence of attempting to smuggle drugs. The distance between the homes of many women prisoners and the prisons in which they are held has long been a matter of concern and of course this is even more extreme when women, whose offending may be motivated by poverty in the first place, are detained outside their own country. Even for UK national women, many family members have to travel long distances to visit.

Conjugal or private visits are not permitted in the UK, in contrast with some other jurisdictions.[6] On an international level, there is a great deal of variation in how such visits are allowed and managed: in some countries the emphasis of the visit is very much on sexual contact, with the visits taking place in a small room or cubicle containing a bed. In other jurisdictions prisoners may be allowed access to houses, flats or trailers where, except for roll-call, they have a certain amount of privacy. The experience of being allowed a marital visit can be welcome but also stressful and expensive in that visitors have to supply food (Bandele 1999). For family members sexual activity seems less important than the opportunity to eat, spend time and talk together. Indeed, such visits allow for a kind of relaxed intimacy which is not possible under the constant surveillance of officers in the visits room, where couples have to play out their relationships under the scrutiny of the officers. The rules on such visits vary between institutions and states in the US, but in many the couple must be married. This is not the same in all countries; for example, in Mexico same-sex partners can apply for conjugal visits and in Brazil men can have conjugal visits but for women these are tightly controlled.

There is a great deal of variation in the conditions and experience of visits between prisons in the UK. Most share commonalities of experience in terms of security, the security regime being even tighter in the 'dispersal' high-security prisons. Families often experience a feeling that they are being treated by prison staff as if they are themselves offenders, and this is echoed in Comfort's (2007) work in the US, based on long periods of observation and interviewing around the women visiting San Quentin. She documents how prisoners' partners undergo 'secondary prisonization'. This courtesy stigma of offending extends to family members even though they have not themselves been convicted of offences. It could be argued that prisoners' partners take on the status of their imprisoned men; thus the partners of those 'high up' in the prison criminal hierarchy, such as the partners of bank robbers, may not experience the same hostility and difficulties as, for example, the wives of sex offenders, who may experience hostility from other visitors. Prisoners may decide not to allow family members to visit, either because, for example, they may not want children to know where they are, or because they do not want their family to see them in such surroundings or experience the stress of the prison environment. It is interesting to note that at the time of a rapidly rising prison population the number of visits is falling (Brooks-Gordon and Bainham 2004).

That said some prisons have developed innovative and successful programmes to encourage family relationships, many involving non-statutory bodies such as charities. Some have whole-day family visits, which are more informal than ordinary visits.[7] Others have developed programmes which work to maintain and promote family relationships, such as parenting programmes (Jarvis and Graham 2004). These have been particularly developed for young male offenders, many of whom are fathers who may have experienced poor parenting as children themselves. For example in the study by Jarvis and Graham (2004) the young men explained that they had not really been played with as children and knew little about age-appropriate activities for children or the developmental stages gone through by children. The 'Storybook Dad' and 'Storybook Mum' scheme, initially begun at HMP Dartmoor, has expanded into a number of institutions and helps parents to maintain links with their children, with the associated benefits of promoting and developing adult literacy and, at Dartmoor, allowing for training in sound engineering and editing techniques as the tapes from other establishments are processed, edited and finished at Dartmoor. Good practice in prison working with families is highlighted every year by Action for Prisoners' Families, the main charity for families of prisoners, in their 'Daisy and Tom' awards, and also by POPS with their Crystal Hearts award scheme.

Case Study 9.2 Mothers and babies in prison

In the UK there is no prohibition on pregnant women being sent to prison and some women may not realize they are pregnant until they have begun their sentence. Concerns have long been expressed about the adequacy of antenatal care for pregnant women in prison. When women are about to give birth the stated Prison Service policy is that they are taken to an outside hospital so that the baby does not have the prison as place of birth on the birth certificate, but sometimes this is not possible and has not been done. Indeed in 1994 there was a huge media furore over the handcuffing of women prisoners while in labour, although the Prison Service claims that this practice has now ceased.

After the baby is born, if there is a place in a mother and baby unit (MBU) and it is in the best interests of the child then the baby and the mother can live together up until the set age at which the child must leave the prison. Currently eight mother and baby units provide places for up to 75 mothers and babies at a time. At Holloway and New Hall babies can stay with their mothers until they are nine months old; at the others the upper limit is eighteen months. After this point the child is, if possible, cared for outside by other family members or friends. If this is not possible then the child is taken into the care of the local authority. The MBUs have strict rules about drug use and drug testing and also disciplinary issues which mean that some women may not be eligible. In addition, women can be removed from MBUs if they fail to comply with the rules.[8]

Concerns have been raised about the legitimacy of MBUs and abolitionists have argued that the best solution is to re-think sentencing options for women lawbreakers.

Source: Codd (2008)

There are a number of important debates about the question of whether mothers and small children should be imprisoned together. The arguments in favour, especially of keeping babies with their mothers in their early years, rely on the psychological importance of mother-child bonding and also the importance of breastfeeding by mothers in terms of the child's health and future wellbeing. As became clear in the case of *P and Q* in 2001, however, prison is not an ideal environment for a developing child. Although in Holloway, for example, mothers and babies can go out on the roof garden, and volunteer 'pram-walkers' take the babies out at weekends, babies do not receive the stimuli and social opportunities which they would have outside. In addition, once babies are toddlers there are concerns about them picking up prison slang, prison attitudes and prison behaviour. Other countries have dealt with these issues in a range of different ways. For example, in Germany half-way houses allow babies out to non-prison nursery facilities in the day, while women work in the prison or undertake education and training, and then at night they stay with their mothers in the half-way house.

There are also important safety implications of allowing babies and children to be in close proximity with women who are not only convicted offenders but who may have a range of emotional and mental disturbances, which could make them unpredictable. Thus being with their mother in prison is not necessarily the ideal environment for small babies and children. That said, keeping mothers and babies together allows women to participate in practical parenting training and to learn how to care for their babies appropriately, but the issue is complex. After all, if many women in prison are not violent offenders then there is a key question as to whether they should be imprisoned at all. To argue that pregnant women and mothers of small children should not be imprisoned is to risk allegations of biology-based gender discrimination, discriminating not only against men but against women who do not or cannot have children (Matthews 2009). The alternate view of this is that pregnant women and mothers of small children do have different needs to non-mothers. The dynamics of male and female imprisonment means that when a man goes to prison any children usually stay either with their mother or with the man's other female relatives: there are no father and baby units in the UK.

It is important to ask why, bluntly, we need to imprison so many women today, and to ask whether imprisoning a mother actually harms society more than benefits it. Renny Golden (2005) persuasively argues that children whose mothers are imprisoned for drug offences are already often experiencing multiple forms of deprivation and social exclusion based on poverty, race and social class. For many children, they are growing up in households headed by single mothers and thus when their mother is imprisoned they 'lose the only anchor they have left'. In terms of mothers, babies and small children we could look at other European models such as half-way houses, or grasp the abolitionist nettle and ask why non-violent female offenders are being imprisoned at all. It is, of course, important not to be naïve about all women's' parenting abilities, and it is clearly the case that for some children being without their mother is the best thing for them, especially if they receive high quality substitute care, but for other children the loss of their mother to prison may be profoundly traumatizing and have long-term consequences, especially if the quality of substitute care is poor, unsettled or disorganized.

As we have seen, prisoners' family members are treated as guilty by association with a prisoner, not only in Prison Service policies but sometimes in law. The legal cases of *Wainwright* and *Dickson*, have, however, challenged this. The legal position of prisoners' partners is still being determined in the wake of the implementation of the *Human Rights Act* (HRA) 1998, which made the European Convention of Human Rights (ECHR) enforceable in the UK in relation to the acts of public bodies. The *Wainwright* case made it clear that strip-searching a prisoners' mother in full view of an uncovered window including the removal of underclothes was at the same time in contravention of the prison's own policy. Her son was body searched in an intimate manner which included his penis being touched, as a consequence of which he suffered post-traumatic stress disorder, for which he was awarded damages. For his mother, there was no remedy in England and Wales in the law of privacy, which was how the situation was conceptualized, and ultimately the case went to the European Court of Human Rights (ECtHR), which ruled that in relation to the treatment of Mrs Wainwright there had been a breach of Article 8 (right to private and family life) and Article 13 (right to an effective remedy) in 2006. What is interesting here is the apparent total failure of the UK judges to understand and empathize with how Mrs Wainwright felt, and how disturbed it must have made her. To read one of the judges likening the situation to being searched by night-club bouncers, or likening the search process to initiation ceremonies, is nothing short of bizarre and shows scant respect for Mrs Wainwright's bodily autonomy and personal dignity. It is worrying that the prison staff claimed not to remember the incident, which suggests either that they were lying or that the situation was so ordinary as not to be worthy of note.

The *Wainwright* case is significant because, in the reports of the hearings before the case went to the ECtHR, it illustrates judicial attitudes to prisoners' family members and appears to justify an attitude to Mrs Wainwright as a prisoners' mother as somehow as appropriate to be degraded by strip-searching as her incarcerated son.

Interestingly, although he was a remand prisoner, there would still have been more justification for either strip-searching him after the visit or implementing closed visits for him. It is tempting to argue that this would not have happened had the HRA been in force, but this is not necessarily the case. The domestic judiciary appear to have not yet understood that family members are not prisoners. In contrast this was clearly acknowledged by the judges of the ECtHR, who recognized the harm suffered by Mrs Wainwright and, by finding a contravention of Article 13, castigated the UK for the lack of a domestic remedy. Of course, this has been rectified by the introduction of the HRA 1998, but the recognition that this kind of attitude and behaviour is in breach of Article 8 is important in acknowledging formally the many difficulties experienced by prisoners' families in visiting, and also the importance of non-hostile (or degrading) visits for family members. Interestingly there is no suggestion that this incident would have come under Article 3, even if it had been actionable in the UK at this point, as the behaviour did not fulfil the minimum level of severity or regularity.

Difficulties arise when there is a need to balance the rights of prisoners with those of non-prisoners with whom they have relationships. The most obvious manifestation of this can be seen in the debates which led to the case of *Dickson* which concerned whether a prisoner and his partner have a right to access to artificial insemination facilities.

Case Study 9.3 The Dickson case

Kirk and Loraine Dickson met in prison via a pen-friend scheme, and after Loraine Dickson was released from prison they married in a prison ceremony. Subsequent to this Kirk Dickson applied for access to artificial insemination (AI) facilities so that his wife could try to conceive a child, as her age meant she would be post-menopausal by the time of his release. His application was refused, and the letter of the Secretary of State set out the grounds for the decision. Eventually after being denied access to artificial insemination at every stage, including in the European Court of Human Rights, they appealed to the Grand Chamber of the ECHR and won their case in December 2007. While loss of opportunity to procreate is a key element of a sentence for a prisoner, it does not follow that their partner loses their rights simply by association.

In the case of a state which allows conjugal visits then this problem may not arise, but where a prisoner's security categorization prohibits this, or in a jurisdiction such as the UK which does not provide such facilities, AI is the only possible course of action, unless the partner wishes to become pregnant either through intercourse or artificial fertility methods, by someone who is not her husband.

This case is significant as it addresses not only the question of prisoners' rights, but the rights of non-imprisoned partners of prisoners. Partners do not lose their own rights by fact of their association with a prisoner.

Source: Codd (2008)

The legal status of prisoners' children is a newly emergent field and there is much scope for greater challenging of the hardships suffered by prisoners' children with reference to the ECHR and other international instruments (Marshall 2008). There is plenty of scope for legal challenges which not only, in the words of Mr Justice Munby, 'make sure the child is heard' but that their rights are enforceable and enforced (Munby 2004a and b).

Legitimacy

Regardless of the gender of the prisoner it is women who bear the burdens of caring for prisoners 'from the outside'. When men are imprisoned it is usually their female partners, mothers, sisters and friends who visit. When women are imprisoned the same holds true.[9] Indeed, little is known about the impact of imprisonment on the male partners of female prisoners. Prisoners' children are more likely to stay with their mother when their father is imprisoned than they are to stay with their father when their mother is imprisoned. This may reflect family breakdown but also women's fears that their men could not cope, or their men are imprisoned as well as co-defendants. This means that the children of female prisoners are more likely to go and stay with maternal grandparents than with their fathers. This burden of caring involves women visiting prisons, providing practical and emotional support during and after the sentence. Research, however, has shown that women deprive themselves not only of luxuries but sometimes of basic items such as food and clothing in order to support their imprisoned men. This is not to attack women's own benevolence in caring, rather to recognize the huge contribution made by women, who work so hard. A key question for feminist researchers is of the value of this caring work. It appears that the prison system relies on women to remedy some of the worst aspects of imprisonment. Similarly, when women are involved in self-help and support groups for members of prisoners' families they not only go on physically and emotionally caring for their own imprisoned family members but often offer support to other prisoners' family members.

In the absence of government organized support for members of prisoners' families, and the lack of statutory responsibility towards family members, this support can be invaluable. It is controversial, however, in that it appears that the Capitalist State is appropriating women's willingness to care for its own ends, and it helps to cover shortcomings in the prison system and also the lack of support for family members. Thus caring for prisoners from the outside must be viewed as a gendered activity. In the US, it is also highly 'raced', imprisonment disproportionately affecting members of BME groups and their communities.

The persistence of these 'obiter punishments' or 'collateral consequences' of imprisonment and how they harm prisoners' families pose significant challenges to penal legitimacy. How, after all, is it appropriate or defensible to harm people who have not been found guilty of an offence simply as a consequence of their association with an offender? It is often assumed in the popular media that prisoners' family members not only know about offending behaviour but condone or even support it, yet this leaves out the complexities of family relationships and fails to consider how 'innocent victims' and 'the families of bad people' might actually be the same people.

This binary interpretation of the notion of victimhood, propagated not only by the media but some victims' organizations, does not acknowledge the intertwining of these two categories. This is clearly seen in the dilemmas surrounding imprisoned mothers and babies, where there is effectively a 'master status' battle going on in which the legal status of the woman as criminal overrides her status as mother.

The role of support and self-help groups has also been criticized. One of the key problems as perceived by both academic commentators and pressure groups such as 'No More Prison' is that of the 'cooperation or collaboration' question. Put simply, by supporting families it could be argued that pressure groups are failing to address the core issue of the problem of imprisonment itself. This has been described as akin to treating the effects of lung cancer without acting to stop people smoking in the first place (Codd 2008). Thus the role of support groups for prisoners' families becomes difficult in that they may well be perceived to be accepting the status quo in terms of imprisonment and merely working to improve conditions, facilities and family welfare without challenging the dominance of imprisonment as a penalty. What is needed is a fearless critique of the rise of the global prison-industrial complex, particularly focusing on the impact of prisonization on members of families of BME and other socially excluded and marginalized groups, underscored with an understanding that the very existence of the prison place itself should be challenged.

Some groups involving prisoners' family members have embraced a role in challenging and resisting the power of the prison and similar criminal justice agencies. There are members of prisoners' families active in 'No More Prison', for example. The independent campaigning charity and pressure group, INQUEST, which was founded in 1981 by, among others, the families of Barry Prosser and Richard Campbell who died in prison, offers support to families and friends of loved ones who have lost their lives in custody. They lobby government and monitor deaths in all forms of custody, using the law where appropriate to challenge secrecy and cover-ups. As Joe Sim (2009) points out, the work of INQUEST has imposed limits on the power to punish. Yet this is not their only function. Perhaps most importantly, they offer support to those who have been sadly and suddenly bereaved. Many prisoners' families have found their work invaluable. When prisoners' family members work with campaigning organizations, resistance to the power of the prison place is possible. Sometimes it is family members whose determined campaigning brings about deeper enquiries into deaths and other incidents which would be otherwise silenced, as in the case of Zahid Mubarek, whose uncle led a forceful campaign for an inquiry into his nephew's death at the hands of his racist cellmate.

The obvious way forward in order to minimize the negative effects of imprisonment for family members is an abolitionist reconceptualization of punishment and the role of the prison. On an immediate level, sentencers could take greater account of the impact of imprisonment on family members, as Albie Sachs did in South Africa in the *M.* case when he substituted a fine, unpaid work and a suspended sentence for a prison sentence passed on a mother who cared for three children (Codd 2008). What is clear is that it is fundamentally important that we work towards a far better understanding of the impact of imprisonment on prisoners' families.

Further reading

Brookes, M. (2005) 'Investing in Family Ties: Reoffending and family visits to prisons', *NPC Research Insight*, London: New Philanthropy Capital.

Codd, H. (2008) *In the Shadow of Prison: Families, Imprisonment and Criminal Justice.* Cullompton: Willan.

Chesney-Lind, M. and Mauer, M. (eds) (2005) *Invisible Punishment: The Collateral Consequences of Mass Imprisonment.* New York: The New Press.

Comfort, M. (2007) *Doing Time Together: Love and Family in the Shadow of the Prison.* Chicago: University of Chicago Press.

Eaton, M. (1993) *Women After Prison.* Milton Keynes: Open University Press.

Smith, R., Grimshaw, R., Romeo, R. and Knapp, M. (2007) *Poverty and Disadvantage among Prisoners' Families.* London: Centre for Crime and Justice Studies and Joseph Rowntree Foundation.

We recommend that students regularly check the websites of APF, the Prison Reform Trust and INQUEST. The Quaker United Nations Organization (QUNO) has published some important informative international and comparative research on imprisoned mothers, fathers and children, which is available on their website.

10
Beyond penal controversies: towards abolitionism

> Abolitionism . . . is not only, or not even primarily, about abolition as a negative process of tearing down, but it is also about building up, about creating new institutions.
>
> (Davis 2005: 73)

Prison stories have provided the key ingredient for numerous television dramas, documentaries and even comedies and the consumption of news about notorious prisoners is part of the daily diet of populist newspapers, internet blogs and web pages. Yet despite such widespread dissemination of information one of the most striking aspects is the extent of misunderstanding about current penal realities. Though alternative interpretive frames are available, common sense has largely dominated discussions of imprisonment beyond those held in the academy, pressure groups or by penal practitioners. 'Controversies' highlighted in the popular media are more likely to focus on how much money is being spent providing meals and other daily essentials for the lesser eligible prisoner than the detrimental impact of imprisonment upon a prisoner's physical or mental health. When prison policy is discussed in the popular press it is largely restricted to debates about financial costs and the need to provide additional prison capacity to hold back a perceived rising tide of criminality. While well-informed TV documentaries, dramas and newspapers columns detailing prisoners' experiences continue to be produced they do not appear to have established a strong hold on the public imagination.

For mainstream politicians, to talk about using prisons less is perceived as being weak with little voter appeal. Although some prison stories, as we discuss below and in previous chapters, have been given extensive press coverage and considerable attention in Parliament and select committees of the House, there remains remarkably little critical debate in the media or political arena regarding the actual role and nature of the prison in contemporary society; whether imprisonment is the best means of dealing with the problematic conduct of lawbreakers with vulnerabilities; or, and most radically of all, if the prison place is so counter-productive that it should be abolished and replaced with other means of responding to troubles, conflicts and moral wrongs (Scott 2009). In this book we have aimed to facilitate such debate and challenge some of the worst excesses of bad common sense and penological illiteracy by exposing the degrading and dehumanized lived realities of those imprisoned.

Throughout the text we have focused on prison populations and tried to turn what are widely interpreted as personal troubles into public controversial issues. Individually, it is easy to view each case study as an aberration, as 'something which has gone wrong' in a Prison Service trying to provide a decent and healthy penal environment. Yet, if something is viewed in the public domain as a personal matter it invites personal-based responses. If, in contrast, it is seen as a matter of public concern which challenges the legitimacy of an institution, then this invites collective responses. The manner in which the framing of an issue can subsequently inform penal policy was clearly highlighted in Chapter 6 regarding self-inflicted deaths. While the introduction of 'Buddy' and 'Listener' schemes would appear to have been helpful they provide only an individually-focused response to the problem. Such an emphasis on the personal cannot address the relationship between the structured pains of confinement and self-inflicted deaths or acknowledge how the very processes of the prison place itself may create suicidal ideation.

Many of the personal troubles we have discussed have already been elevated to public controversial issues through liberal and humanitarian initiatives raising awareness through media campaigns and the lobbying of government. While we aim to add to such concerned voices, unlike liberal penologists we wish to argue that the prison place cannot be made safe or healthy. This is not to say that humanitarian initiatives have not had some significant successes but rather that while some aspects of imprisonment have clearly improved, other aspects have changed little (Sim 2009). Liberal reform organizations have emphasized 'pragmatic expediency, together with their myopic and misguided faith in the sanctity of piecemeal change' (p. 154). In doing so, they have not questioned the very *existence* of the prison itself (Ryan and Sim 2007).

Despite sustained criticism of its dehumanizing realities the Prison Service has been remarkably effective in erasing or neutralizing much of the liberal critique levelled against it by penal reformers. In an attempt to understand such resilience Pat Carlen (2002a, 2002b) has identified three models of penal reform: scandal driven; prison legitimating and principled reform. Scandal driven reforms arise in the wake of a disgrace likely to provoke a public outcry and erode punitiveness, such as the vicious murder of Zahid Mubarek by Robert Stewart in Feltham YOI. After concerted external pressure, the Prison Service could eventually be seen to accept responsibility for this controversial issue, implement new policies and attempt to change organizational structures and cultures deemed culpable. While memories of a given scandal such as the death of Zahid Mubarek remain, such policies figure high on the political agenda, but when recollections fade it becomes increasingly likely that prison security will be reasserted and the gap between policy and implementation will grow. As Chapter 5 illustrates, the contorted struggle for justice, the restrictive aims of the Keith Inquiry (2006), and the limited long-term impact of the Mubarek scandal were all exemplified in the reaction to the almost copy-cat death of Shahid Aziz in HMP Leeds, which invoked virtually no media or political debate or any subsequent policy changes.

Pat Carlen's second model, prison-legitimating reforms, are responses to long term official criticism, such as the deeply embedded nature of institutional racism or self-inflicted and other deaths in prison, and the main objective is to reassert the legitimacy of the system through deploying strategies which provide lip service to change but no substantive improvements in prisoners' lived realities. Again the sustainability of such reforms may be low but if successful the new 'legitimate' prison may encourage further penal expansion. As discussed in Chapter 6, if critique of prisoner deaths can be neutralized by showing an apparent statistical decline, however dubiously such figures may be construed in Prison Service annual reports, confidence in the system can be maintained.

The third approach to penal reform identified by Pat Carlen is principled reform. This ideal type entails the attempt to change prisons based on a set of coherent principles, and is associated with humanitarian laws. Principled reforms aim to implement a set of organizational and cultural changes that allow the prison to operate in a way consistent with the given moral framework. Yet, given the requirements of security and the maintenance of order, even here the sustainability of such reforms is likely to be low. 'Carceral clawback' is highly probable in terms of mutating such principles into a cloak of legitimacy. As we have seen throughout the book in relation to concepts such as decency, and the legal obligations of local authorities to children and young people in custody in Chapter 4, while there have been major changes regarding responsibilities for the care of children in prisons, significant disparities remain in a system perpetuating what can only be understood as institutionalized abuse. Unless human rights principles are tied to penal abolition rather than merely legalism, then security demands and further penal expansionism are likely to win out.

What we need then is not liberal penal reforms that can be clawed back or used to strengthen penal legitimacy but a radical rethink of the confinement project itself and profound social changes rooted in a commitment to human rights and social justice. Following Fitzgerald and Sim (1979), we believe that after hundreds of years of largely failed initiatives it is now time to recognize that the 'reformed' prison has not worked if its purpose is to prevent 'crime'. While the prison place punishes wrongdoing, the punishment is disproportionate to the social and individual harm caused and is unlikely to transform people into law-abiding citizens. Prison is not an equal opportunities employer. As we detailed in Chapter 2 and elsewhere, its effects impact disproportionately on the poor, the socially excluded, the 'mentally ill', the damaged and the marginalized. It casts its net wide, dragging in not only offenders but, as we highlighted in Chapter 9, their partners, children and communities. Prison *has* worked, however, as a powerful weapon of social control, oppression and marginalization of certain identifiable individuals and communities who are at the lower end of the social spectrum (Foucault 1977).

While common sense debates on prison populations are largely restricted to talk of expansion and control, by contrast we have focused on prisoners' social backgrounds. Taken together, we believe that the nature and extent of current prisoner populations offer an indication of the depth, breadth and scope of a penal system in crisis, riven with deep divisions, unnecessary suffering and waste of human life. While each issue of concern may prompt specific responses, what is important here is their combined impact. The prison populations under scrutiny cannot be easily compartmentalized or categorized as many of the concerns raised when discussing one aspect of the prison population have been reproduced when discussing another. The people discussed across the eight case studies are often the same people with multiple vulnerabilities (Hudson 1993).

In the remainder of this conclusion we consider the best way to acknowledge the disturbing realities of contemporary prison life. We do this by directly engaging with the potentially contradictory dilemma of formulating policies that can be consistent with the goal of abolition while at the same time can be deployed to minimize the harms of the present (Cohen 1998). This requires us to keep our 'eyes on the prize' and 'feet on the ground' (Codd 2008) and entails engaging with contemporary penal debates on at least three different levels: immediate interventions by penal practitioners; the removal of certain vulnerable populations from prison; and profound social change rooted in the principles of democracy, accountability, human rights and social justice.[1]

Immediate interventions by practitioners: truth telling and acknowledgement

It is important to recognize the contribution, both actual and potential, of those working within the penal system. While prison officer occupational cultures have been problematized, a number of prison officers are deeply committed to protecting the shared humanity of prisoners and fight to improve the lives of those who are incarcerated (Scott 2006; Sim 2009). Some staff have 'blown the whistle' on oppressive practices while others have refused to cooperate with wrongdoing, challenged dehumanizing attitudes or helped to ensure prisoners stay as safe as possible in a profoundly unhealthy environment. Whistleblowers improve democratic accountability and expose inhuman practices, challenging denials and provoking acknowledgement of brutal penal realities 'from the inside out' (Cohen 2001). For those people working both within and against the prison system, who challenge oppressive daily degradations and the highly influential doctrines of less eligibility and managerialism, we need to offer support and solidarity (Poulantzas 1978).

Sometimes intervention can involve small innovations, such as encouraging safe forms of self-harm, or treating visitors with much greater respect and less suspicion. These approaches recognize the realities of the emotions and experiences which lead someone to harm themselves, combined with an emphasis on damage limitation, and recognize the stressful nature of visiting a family member in the prison setting. This kind of 'harm reductionism' can also involve challenging abuses by colleagues instead of 'turning a blind eye', monitoring and exposing abuses, facilitating forms of due process, accountability and the inspections and complaints procedures. On the day-to-day wing officer level it can involve treating an offender as a human being and acknowledging their inherent human dignity. At a higher level it can involve challenging and changing occupational cultures in an institution.[2]

People working within prisons, alongside prisoners and former prisoners, can provide powerful testimonies that can help inform wider debates and improve penological literacy. The role of democracy is once again important here. Prisons reflect a regressive form of civilization that erodes and harms democracy itself, especially where prisoners in England and Wales are denied a democratic voice because the mechanics of voting have not yet been agreed upon. A democratic solution is to raise awareness through usual political channels as is already so successfully done by penal pressure groups such as INQUEST.

People who work in prison have to do what they can where and when they can. This approach, of course, has its limitations and can take an immense personal toll on those who choose to challenge prison life whether as prisoners or prison staff (Salah-El 2007).[3] These small humanitarian steps represent a rejection of defeatism about the prison, recognizing the need for reflexivity and for changes to be made immediately to improve the welfare of those people whom society has 'seen fit to throw into the penal recycling bin'. Truth-telling and the everyday recognition of the shared humanity and sufferings of those confined, however, are only ever going to address the tip of an iceberg.

Selective abolition: reductionist proposals for the honest politician

Collectively the eight controversial issues in prison provide a platform for the promotion of 'selective abolitionism' (Hudson 1993). If we return once again to the popular board game *Monopoly* that we highlighted in the introduction, a phrase that might be used to sum up selective abolitionism is that for certain people with vulnerabilities the 'Go to Jail' card would read: 'Do not go directly to jail – Do not go to jail at all. Go and be dealt with through appropriate means of redress in your own community.' Selective abolitionism is rooted in the assumption that certain categories of 'crime' or offender *must not* be sent to prison because of the relative harmlessness of the offence, the vulnerabilities of the person who has broken the law, or because imprisonment would have unnecessarily harmful consequences that should if at all possible be avoided.

The prisoners detailed in this book could all be considered, albeit on different grounds, as groups of people who should be deliberately excluded from imprisonment. Thus we are arguing for the abolition of imprisonment for people with mental health problems; women; children; those committing immigration offences; and people with suicidal ideation. Also treatments should be deployed in the community for those with substance dependency and, where possible, for people who sexually offend. This has the 'ripple effect' of minimizing harm to prisoners' families.

For political plausibility in a punitive climate the principles of selective abolitionism would probably be best introduced as a basis for a serious re-think of sentencing and restricting future prison populations. Selective abolitionism can provide a strategy that could be immediately adopted by politicians and penal campaigners who wish to lobby the government for major reductions in the prison population right now.[4] Dissemination of the vulnerabilities of the people currently sent to prison could provide a crucial step towards engaging wider public sympathy through carefully constructed narratives and 'sentimental stories' that may capture the public imagination (Rorty 1989). Selective abolition could significantly help soften media portrayals and place the government under pressure to re-consider its expansionist policies.

Such an adoption of selective abolitionism, however, must only ever be a starting point, a specific humanitarian call for our disturbing times, and the above suggestion for the 'honest politician' should not imply that we believe it is a wholly satisfactory solution. When considering the controversial issues in this book, we hope that readers will have a keen awareness of the wider contexts of the controversies discussed. Prison is not a morally desirable means of dealing with wrongdoing, whoever the offender is or whatever harms or problematic acts they have committed (Scott 2009).

There are two main dangers when proposing selective abolition. First selective abolition is inevitably tied to the categorization of offenders and is often closely associated with the deployment of the psycho-medical interpretive frame. The psycho-medical model utilizes dividing practices which maintain that certain categories of offenders should be dealt with through medicalized forms of social control rather than the penal law (Carlen 1986; Sim 1990). This use of 'humanitarian' psycho-medical forms of control may, however, be even more oppressive than legal penal sanctions they supersede. A second major limitation is that selective abolition by default operates through engendering sympathy *only* for people that we find easy to empathize with rather than providing a genuine human rights approach to the acknowledgement of human suffering (Cohen 2001). The danger here is that the sufferings of those who do not fit easily within its construction of vulnerabilities are ignored. If we concentrate on offenders as vulnerable and needy we run the risk of focusing exclusively on the sympathetic individual in need of help and neglecting the immensely harmful power of the prison place. Selective abolitionism, then, can only sensitize us to the needs of the individuals confined and advocates must be careful to ensure that this strategy is not deployed to the detriment of any wider awareness of the harmful penal environmental or exclusionary socio-economic and political contexts.

Towards abolitionism: getting to the heart of the crises of penal legitimacy

> Prisons are failed institutions that do not work. They are places of pain and social control and are brutal, abusive and damaging to everyone who is incarcerated in them. Prisons are fundamentally flawed and all attempts to reform them have failed.
>
> (No More Prison 2006a)

This book has been underpinned by a questioning of the moral dimensions of the power to punish. We have argued for the need to move the debate beyond the rhetoric of penal reform and to establish links with the wider moral question of 'can punishment be legitimate?' The claims of penal authorities to legitimacy are predicated upon the current distribution and application of punishment successfully attaining political validity, and a sense of moral rightfulness in a given society, leading to acquiescence, obedience and consent from both those imprisoned and the general public. The accumulative evidence from the preceding chapters indicates that the power to punish should be considered to be illegitimate as the very processes of incarceration dehumanize and create inherent infringements of human rights. The moral legitimacy of imprisonment must then be understood within wider debates on punishment as the very deployment of the punitive rationale itself becomes the central focus of moral critique (van Swaaningen 1986).

The historical and contemporary evidence detailed in the previous chapters highlighting such moral illegitimacy inevitably leads us to the following firm conclusions:

1   There have always been people with mental health problems in custody, indicating that their containment is the very *essence of the confinement* project. Prisons, however, have perpetuated harms and mental health problems rather than ameliorated them and for many prisoners even if they do not have mental health problems when they enter the prison they may have them when they leave.

2   Confinement has never been a suitable sanction for women who have broken the law. The treatment of women in custody has fallen below acceptable standards and in some cases can be described as a form of *institutional sexual, emotional and physical abuse*.

3   The prison place has an incredibly detrimental impact on children, many of whom are already facing multiple social difficulties, and is in effect a form of *institutional child abuse*.

4   There will always exist *obiter punishments* (or 'collateral consequences') as a result of imprisonment. The children of imprisoned parents also suffer manifold difficulties and challenges, which in effect punish children for the wrongdoing of a family member. Similarly, women bear the disproportionate impact of the imprisonment of male partners.

5   The disproportionate confinement of black or minority ethnic people and foreign national offenders is clear evidence of accumulative racism in the criminal justice system and that current policies of immigration detention must be understood as a form of *state racism*.[5] Race relations policies and anti-racist initiatives in prison are not enough: there needs to be a major challenge to the disproportionate focus of the penal gaze on members of minority ethnic groups and resistance to all forms of racism in society as a whole.

6   Although we have abolished the formal death penalty, many people still die in prison. Some of those people who die have their lives taken by other prisoners or staff and prison is a profoundly unsafe environment for those confined. Others die as a direct consequence of the very structures and processes of the prison place itself. Death is an intrinsic part of the confinement project and the sentence to imprisonment remains, for some, a *death sentence*.

7   Confinement has never been conducive to positive human change – in effect *prison does not work as a means of rehabilitation*. Enrolment at 'sex offender school' leaves its 'students' othered and consumed by sex, while their actual experiences of offending are overlaid by limited psycho-medical theories. Prison remains an inappropriate venue for either the effective treatment of people who sexually offend or as an adequate means of signifying moral disapproval of sexual abuse.

8   The 'drug problem' is socially constructed and the prevalence of drug taking in prison is an important strategy for coping with stress and the degrading realities of prison life. Harm reduction is undermined as *less eligibility, security and control will always emasculate any focus on the health of those contained within*.

These intractable problems of imprisonment point us ultimately in one direction only – towards abolition. It is easy to be defeatist about challenging the power of the prison. Abolitionism itself has been consistently criticized for being idealistic, naïve and for disregarding 'crime' victims and the harms of victimization (Ryan and Sim 2007). This, however, caricatures the nature of abolitionist approaches to 'crime', which are much more textured, subtle and nuanced than these crude stereotypes imply (Carlen 1990). Abolitionism has been closely associated with grass roots resistance, not only challenging the prison but also working towards reconceptualizing and rebuilding our attitudes to 'crime' and justice. This can be seen in individuals and organizations resisting the prison individually and collectively. Some groups, such as ICOPA, INQUEST, Women in Prison and the European Group for the Study of Deviance and Social Control, have a long history of supporting critical and anti-prison activism. Others, such as No More Prison, which was resurrected from the former penal pressure group Radical Alternatives to Prison, utilize social networking and the internet as well as direct action through demonstrations. Prisoners' family members have long grouped together in support and self-help groups, with a variety of approaches to prison.

It is essential that we use our sociological imagination to challenge the penal apparatus of the Capitalist State and offer more humanitarian ways of responding to wrongdoers. This is not just about keeping people out of prison – this may help to reduce self-inflicted deaths and certain intractable problems – but about actually helping people to live their lives in the community – what could be called the duty of care to fellow human beings to meet their necessary needs. For Pedro Arrupe (1973) 'evil is overcome only by good, hate by love, egoism by generosity. It is thus that we must sow justice in our world. To be just, it is not enough to refrain from injustice. One must go further and refuse to play its game.' Arrupe's core argument, about 'refusing to play the game' is deeply important. We need to go beyond focusing on the *penal*, and look at the position of prison in our society, and the situation of prisoners. In the US, challenges to imprisonment are seen as part of a broader struggle in terms of civil rights and such opposition is constituted of people from many different backgrounds coming together in a coalition for justice and dignity for all. We have not seen this kind of concerted lobby against the prison in the UK and there is a need for bravery, for stepping out, and for refusing to be sucked into the vortex of penal reformist ideologies, which ultimately serve to prop up and maintain the institution under focus. This is where some penal pressure groups walk a difficult and often criticized line: by working closely with prisons in order to improve the day-to-day experiences of prisoners and their families, they may become co-opted into maintaining the status quo, the doctrine of gradual reform leading them into the position of 'philosophising the disgrace' that penal institutions have become (Sim 2009: 155). We thus return to our exhortation that we need to act now to minimize harm, at the same point maintaining our focus on a widespread challenge to the very legitimacy of the punitive prison establishment itself.

> History is replete with stories of the struggle of people on the bottom of the social ladder banding together and organising to bring radical change for the better in their lives and the lives of future generations. Some struggles succeeded, some

failed and others are ongoing. I do not know how long it will take to abolish prisons. That is akin to asking me how much air is in the universe. Therein is the real challenge – our search for answers must be incessant.

(Salah-El 2007: 204)

More broadly, we need fundamental social, economic and political change rooted in the principles of social justice and human rights. This position has been described as 'abolition democracy'.

When we call for prison abolition, we are not imagining the isolated dismantling of the facilities we call prisons and jails. That is not the project of abolition. We proposed the notion of a prison-industrial-complex to reflect the extent to which the prison is deeply structured by economic, social and political conditions that themselves will also have to be dismantled. So you might say that prison abolition is a way of talking about the pitfalls of the particular version of democracy represented by ... capitalism – especially in its contemporary global form ... So prison abolition requires us to recognise the extent that our present social order – in which are embodied a complex array of social problems – will have to be radically transformed.

(Davis 2005: 72)

It is easy to destroy, to tear down. It is less easy to build something different. Many people have become so accustomed and acclimatized to imprisonment that it is hard to envisage other rational ways of responding to human misconduct. Yet there is no shortage of options for dealing non-punitively with wrongdoers. Lawbreakers with mental health problems need to be provided with real options of emotional and physical support they actually want to use alongside wider recognition that many of their difficulties can be effectively managed. Social policies aimed at combating stigma and providing caring interventions, decent housing, jobs and constructive relationships before a mental health crisis will always be much more effective than imprisonment after a problematic episode. Children who break the criminal law are in need of care and welfare rather than punishment. All children need something constructive to do to combat boredom and mischief. In the long term it would be cheaper and more sensible to re-direct the billions we spend on criminal (in)justice into providing safe, public and easily accessible leisure and educational activities for children so that they can express themselves safely via pro-social behaviours. Women who break the law have normally undertaken relatively harmless acts and restorative and social justice are more appropriate responses to their wrongs and illegalities. Self-help programmes addressing not only women's individual vulnerabilities but that also help women move on from lives characterized by poverty, ill health, and violence could also be made available.

Women, children (and men) who have been sexually abused need emotional and financial support alongside a safe place to escape from their tormentors. Moral education campaigns that take sexual abuse seriously combined with the recognition that abusers are not 'monsters' but human beings who can be helped to recognize problematic patriarchal assumptions and abuses of power offer us the most realistic chance of reducing gendered harms. Rather than penalization, harm reduction policies are needed to deal with drug takers. Alongside this, social policies could be developed which recognize the universality and relative harmlessness of most drug usage, combined with efforts to challenge the impoverished social contexts of problematic use alongside holistic approaches which address multiple aspects of dependency.[6]

Finally, emphasizing the cultural and political priority of treating *all* people as fellow human beings, whatever their perceived 'race' or socially imagined 'nationality', should underscore social relations to stranger and friend alike. It is ethically and politically essential that wrongdoers are treated with tolerance and respect; that they are responded to as human beings; that their needs and suffering do not go unheeded. It is easy to treat people well and with dignity and respect when we feel they deserve that dignity and respect: it is sometimes more challenging to adopt that approach with people whose behaviour we abhor. The point about human dignity, however, is that it is intrinsic to all those who are human, even though some people in some situations may wish certain other people were not. Our proposed 'pragmatic-idealist' (Coleman et al. 2009) solutions to individual and social troubles are based in the principles of social justice, human rights, democracy and accountability. To see their realization, however, requires a major a change in the interpretive frame of the popular mindset to one rooted in non-punitive forms of dispute resolution and also the development of socialist-feminist socio-economic policies that can radically transform existing structural contexts.

We have demonstrated how imprisonment dehumanizes prisoners and their families and how the concept of a 'healthy prison' is nothing but an oxymoron. Prisons are places of sadness and terror, harm and injustice, secrecy and oppression. The great triumph of the prison is to have made itself indispensable in the public imagination, rendering it difficult to conceive of a world without it. It has become entrenched and embedded in our society to such as extent that its continued existence seems beyond challenge. We need to remember, however, that it is possible to challenge the prison persistently, with determination and diligence. Change may be slow, but its demise is achievable. We need a solid belief that we *can* live in a world where all individuals are treated with respect and dignity; where social institutions are fully accountable; where democracy is built upon genuine social inclusion and participation; where social justice is a guiding aim of policy, and where the prison is nothing but a distant memory.

Notes

1 Thinking about controversial issues in prison

1 Between 1925 and 1985, there were only six Criminal Justice Acts.
2 In Scotland you can be imprisoned for fishing on the Lower Esk without permission (Johnson 2009).
3 The HM Chief Inspector of Prisons (February, 2008, cited in Gaines 2008) criticized Doncaster prison for placing an extra bed in a two-man-cell in the place where there would normally be a toilet. In this sense, prisoners' literally are sleeping in toilets.
4 In response to the overcrowding crisis the government has looked to re-engage the service of 'Hulk Ship' HMP Weare (which was based at Portland, 1997–2005) and since September 2006 has housed prisoners in police cells and brought in policies to allow the early release of prisoners. In April 2009 82 of 140 prisons were overcrowded (NOMS Monthly Bulletin, April 2009).
5 We discuss the problem of 'categorization' throughout the book and its links with practices dividing populations into sub-groups that can be easily controlled. There is, however, some possible political ground to be made through the categorization of people with vulnerabilities through debates regarding the partial abolition of imprisonment.
6 Certain knowledges set the parameters of problems confronting the Prison Service and the best possible means of resolution while others are de-legitimated. Interpretive frames are intimately tied to power. Sometimes it is in the interests of the powerful to remove certain events and realities from the political agenda. Indeed power, it would seem, 'is at its most effective when least observable' (Lukes 2005: 1).
7 The psycho-medical model is rooted within a framework that proposes 'radical differentiation' (Matza 1964). Yet such approach inevitably leads to what Matza (1964: 21–2) refers to as an 'embarrassment of riches' for radical differentiation accounts for *too much* problematic conduct.
8 There is no one abolitionist perspective. For simplicity we have presented the abolitionist case in a monolithic sense. For those interested in this perspective please see wider reflections on the differences between abolitionists in de Foulter (1986), de Haan (1990), van Swaaningen (1997), Sim (2009) and Scott (2009).
9 A further example of where the prison has embraced the concept of health is in a 'therapeutic prison' (Genders and Player 1995). In practice though prisons such as HMP Grendon have retained their authoritarian structure and obfuscate how penal power actually operates. In short, therapeutic prisons are new means of exercising, not negating, penal

power through the medical gaze. Perhaps the most damning critique of the therapeutic prison is that it can only operate as it does because it is reliant upon the existence of the wider prison system. It is important therefore that those sympathetic to this endeavour provide effective critiques of mainstream penal regimes.

10 For Gresham Sykes (1958: 63–83) the pains of imprisonment are the deprivations of liberty, goods and services, heterosexual relationships, autonomy and security.

11 In a systematic study of the health of prisoners in Tennessee State Penitentiary during 1972–73 Jones (1976) found that the sickness rates of prisoners were substantially higher than comparable rates for the probationers and people in the wider community.

2 Mental health problems in prison

1 Prisoners with acute mental health problems cannot be forced to take medication under the *Mental Health Act* (2007) as the prison healthcare unit is not considered a 'hospital' under the legislation.

2 Both transfer and diversion leave a great deal of discretion with medical professionals and cannot guarantee that medical interventions will not be more repressive than a coercive sentence (Laing 1999; Bradley 2009).

3 This was quickly followed by the inclusion of the concept in the White Paper *Reforming the Mental Health Act* (DH/HO 2000).

4 In addition indeterminate sentences for 'dangerous offenders' were introduced by the *Criminal Justice Act* (2003).

5 At the time of writing (October 2009) there are around 2400 prisoners who are considered to suffer from DSPD. Prison Service Order [PSO] 1700 suggests that anyone on segregation for more than three months should be considered as having a personality disorder. Yet many prisoners with mental health problems are placed into segregation for long periods because there is nowhere else for them to go.

6 By 1943 a psychiatric unit had opened in Wormwood Scrubs and in 1946 the unit began using electric shock treatment.

7 The culmination of this process was the opening of a 'psychiatric' prison at Grendon Underwood in Buckinghamshire in July 1962 (Genders and Player 1995).

8 The belief that there is a direct or 'inverse relationship' between prison and mental hospital populations is popularly known as 'Penrose law', as this argument was first made in 1939 by the geneticist Sir Lionel Penrose. While on the face of it 'Penrose law' appears highly plausible, empirical studies have found little evidence to support the claim of a direct transfer of populations (Gunn et al. 1978; Fowles 1993).

9 Serious concerns about the Prison Medical Service (PMS) had been raised by official reports as early as the 1960s and through damning independent research conducted in the 1980s (Sim 1990).

10 The promotion of 'equality and continuity of care' (HMCIP 1996: 8) were central to this recommendation but significantly the HMCIP linked together effective healthcare, prisoner responsibilities and public protection with reducing health risks in wider society.

11 This view is echoed in the *Health Promoting Prisons* strategy where 'improving the health and well-being of prisoners is recognised as a vital element in their rehabilitation and resettlement' (HMP Islington 2004: 1). In April 2006 the Department of Health took full responsibility for the commissioning of prison healthcare in all (public) prisons although it is estimated that current resources for mental healthcare in prisons are only about a third of the amount required to deliver the policy objective of equivalence (Brooker et al. 2008). Despite the current emphasis on improving prison healthcare concerns around the numbers of prisoners with mental health problems have persisted. Lord Keith Bradley (2009)

extensively reviewed existing mental health provision alongside possible strategies to divert offenders with vulnerabilities but his most significant recommendation was for better managed and joined up healthcare services both inside and outside prison, facilitated by the introduction of new Criminal Justice Mental Health Teams.

3 Women in prison

1 In short, they are likely to have limited financial resources, poor family ties and deemed as socially 'unrespectable'.
2 The number of cases of imprisoned women self-harming has almost doubled since 2004 and there have been tragically high rates of women taking their own lives from 2000 onwards (Morris 2009).
3 In this chapter we generally refer to women in prison, although this is with the understanding that the issue or concern expressed may be applicable to both women and girls in custody.
4 There has been a small amount of academic work published which has been written by imprisoned women themselves, such as that by Walker and Worrall (2000) and Kathy Boudin, who spent a long period in prison as a consequence of her activities when involved in the American 'Weather Underground' violent radical organization (Frankfort 1984; Boudin 1998).
5 Internationally women make up between 2 per cent and 9 per cent of total country prison populations. It is sometimes difficult to extract data on women from official statistics and this is particularly the case in terms of international comparisons of the rate of female imprisonment as most international comparisons are based on total prison populations (Carlen and Worrall 2004). It is clear, however, that the rate of imprisonment of women in many jurisdictions is higher for women from BME groups.
6 Brixton prison was used briefly for women in the nineteenth century before becoming all-male.
7 For a useful introduction to Victorian prison reform, including the campaigning and ideas of Elizabeth Fry and Jeremy Bentham, see Cooper (1981).
8 The Group argued that some women prisoners themselves had expressed concerns about bullying in small units, and expressed concern that staff training and regime provision are more important than prison design in supporting the needs of women.
9 Although this could be seen as a successful experiment, the plan to build Thornton Hall, the proposed new prison further out from the centre of the city, means that the Dóchas site will be cleared and a new unit built, although at the time of writing in October 2009 the entire Thornton Hall project has been put on hold. For critical reflection on this kind of initiative see Hannah-Moffat (2001).
10 Interestingly, both knitting and cross-stitch involve implements which could be effectively used in self-harm and violence against others but this appears a secondary non-mentioned issue.
11 If the government wants to look across the Irish channel they can see the Dóchas centre as it began as a model of a new way of responding to women. Of course, such units may simply serve to present the power of the prison place wrapped up in a new way (Hayman 2006).

4 Children and young people in custody

1 When launching the 'Respect' agenda against antisocial behaviour in early 2005, for example, Tony Blair stressed that he did not believe in 'restarting the search for the golden age. We are not looking to go back to anything.' Yet he also argued, with no apparent sense

of irony, that in the 1930s of his father's childhood, 'people behaved more respectfully to one another and people are trying to get back to that' (Wills 2007).

2 The s53 sentence for children convicted of 'grave crimes' has been relabelled and joined by other sentences of indeterminate imprisonment for public protection.

3 Although 'tackling youth crime' has been a key foundation of New Labour's crime control policy, much of what has been written about young offenders focuses on criminalization, diversion, restorative justice, the role of Youth Offending Teams and the Youth Justice Board, and community-based interventions rather than custody.

4 This chapter critically analyses the procedure, processes and impact of the detention of children for criminal activity and antisocial behaviour in England and Wales. A linked issue is that of immigration detention but this is not directly addressed in this chapter.

5 Until the judgment of Munby J in *R (on the application of the Howard League for Penal Reform) v. The Secretary of State for the Home Department* in November 2002 the *Children Act* 1989 was not deemed to apply to children in prison.

6 Whereas young men who felt unsafe were most likely to feel unsafe in communal areas such as the gym or the showers, young women were most likely to feel unsafe in their cell or room. As they were all in single cells this links to issues of anxiety and depression.

7 Note that the Parkhurst Prison for Boys held boys awaiting transportation.

8 For a vivid and absorbing analysis of the assumptions around normative masculinity in the approved school system, see Wills (2005).

9 For an insight into these institutions, and how they were viewed by a visiting American academic in the 1930s, see Myers (1933).

10 The legal power to sentence young people to long-term detention is contained in sections 90 and 91 of the *Powers of Criminal Courts Act* 1991 (Boswell 1998).

11 Children in prison are eighteen times more likely to commit 'suicide' than children of the same age living in the community (Frühwald and Frottier 2005).

12 This is not of course to argue that violence and disorder against staff and other residents by children in custody is acceptable: rather, it is to argue that when we are dealing with very vulnerable children from social settings characterized by abuse, neglect, harm, and violence, all that happens here is that violence is reinforced as acceptable behaviour as long as it is committed by adults.

13 See R (C) v Secretary of State for Justice, CA, July 28 2008.

14 See R (C) v The Secretary of State for Justice [2008] EWCA Civ 882.

15 In their article Epstein and Foster (2008) note that His Lordship also took into account the views of the United Nations Committee on the Rights of the Child that the deliberate infliction of pain is not permitted as a form of control of juveniles.

5 'Race', racism and foreign national prisoners

1 The word 'race' was first recorded in the English language in a poem by William Dunbar in 1508.

2 The concept of 'race' finds its foundations in the 'scientific' writings of Cuvier (1805, cited in Husband 1984: 14) who argued that there is a hierarchy of three 'races': Caucasoid, Negroid and Mongoloid.

3 Ethnicity is 'a multi-faceted quality that refers to the group to which people belong, and/or are perceived to belong, as a result of certain shared characteristics, including geographical and ancestral origins, but particularly cultural traditions and languages' (Bhopal 2004: 441). One example of an emerging ethnic identity is 'Welshness', and concerns about both Welsh-speaking and English-speaking Welsh prisoners being held in prisons in England (House of Commons Welsh Affairs Committee 2007).

4 When we consider the prison population there is a substantial discrepancy between the proportion of members of minority ethnic groups in society and the proportion in prison (Edgar 2007), black people being 6.4 times more likely to be stopped than white people and Asian people almost twice as likely to be stopped and searched (CJSRU 2005). Black people were more than three times more likely than white people to be arrested, the rate for Asian people being slightly higher than for white people (CJSRU 2005).

5 Neo-colonialism means literally the 'new colonialism' and refers both to the manner in which certain identifiable populations (BME) in contemporary society continue to be subjugated through the historical legacy of British imperialism and the manner in which historical global inequalities continue to allow Britain (and the USA and other wealthy nations in the European Union, etc.) to economically exploit workers in poor countries around the world.

6 In a similar vein Steiner and Woolredge (2009: 463) utilize a multi-level statistical model, to test the hypothesis that BME prisoners in the US have a 'greater disrespect for legal authority and more tolerance of deviance'. Their statistical analysis, which draws heavily on theories of social pathology, suggests that BME prisoner misconduct is imported because the prison shares striking environmental similarities with impoverished 'black ghettos' that breed lawlessness and a culture where violence is viewed 'as a legitimate mechanism for attaining status or respect' (p. 479). Prisoner misconduct has nothing to do with racism or the brutalities of the penal environmental context, but the immorality of BME prisoners (specifically African-American) who are culturally determined lawbreakers prone to violence. This argument, fundamentally flawed through its construction of the radical differentiation of 'black' subcultures (Matza 1964), reliance upon racist stereotypes and an uncritical re-interpretation of official data that was collated for different means, simply others BME prisoners as intrinsically violent and dangerous.

7 Simpson (2002) argues that the development of statistical analytical methods are directly linked to racist ideology, as the measurement of personal characteristics was a response to concerns by the Eugenic Society that 'superior' European genetic stock was being weakened by inferior 'races'.

8 We also need qualitative data which documents day-to-day prison life as it is experienced by members of minority ethnic groups (Shallice and Gordon 1990).

9 There is no homogenized 'non-white' experience, although a superficial reading of BME official statistics may give that impression.

10 Prison food was not necessarily multicultural and 'black' female prisoners complained routinely that prison shops did not stock appropriate skincare, cosmetics and hair care.

11 In 2001 the Prison Service announced that membership of organizations deemed to be racist, such as the BNP, would amount to gross misconduct.

12 The manual set out policies on many aspects of prison life such as access to work and training; accommodation; religion, diet and disciplinary matters; complaints of racial discrimination; and contact with minority ethnic group support organizations outside the prison.

13 One topic of much media interest during the taking of evidence of the Keith Inquiry was the 'gladiator' allegations of Duncan Keys, in which it was alleged that staff were betting on 'gladiator' fights between cellmates. Keith (2006: 32), however, argued 'I decided that the terms of reference did not require me to provide a comprehensive account of all the reasons for any systemic shortcomings which may have contributed to what happened to Zahid'.

14 See for example the Brook House Immigration detention centre which is being built to Category B Prison Service security criteria.

15 A great deal could be done to improve the experiences of foreign national prisoners, such as improving the recording of nationality, providing notices in foreign languages, using

interpreters, increasing facilities and services, training prison officers, medical and race relations liaison officers in the special needs and cultures of foreign prisoners (Cheney 1993; Bowling and Phillips 2002; Chigwada-Bailey 2003; Ellis et al. 2004).

16 For a detailed analysis of the act and its implications, see Symonds (2008).

6 Self-inflicted deaths

1 It is believed that as many as 50 prisoners may commit suicide shortly after release each year.

2 The families of two prisoners who died in custody, Barry Prosser and Richard Campbell, performed a key role in the foundation of INQUEST. Barry Prosser was beaten to death by three prison officers in a locked prison hospital cell at Winson Green Prison, Birmingham on 18 August 1980 while Richard Campbell took his own life at Ashford remand centre after being subjected to intense racism and being placed in isolation cells for no good reason (Ryan 1996).

3 The instruments used in suicides in prison are bedding (48 per cent), followed by clothing (34 per cent), shoelace (5 per cent), towel (4 per cent), belt (2 per cent) and gun (1 per cent). Other instruments, such as a knife, razor blade, glass or drugs, are each involved in less than 1 per cent of cases (Wortley 2002: 138).

4 In this period there was an average of 9.5 suicides per annum (range 4–14).

5 Three hundred of the 442 verdicts of unnatural deaths were classified as suicide, and Dooley was able to trace records and undertake study of 'Prison Department personal (PDP) files' in 295 of these cases (Dooley 1990: 40). Dooley calculated the suicide rate using three year cohorts and the prison ADP.

6 Though see O'Mahony (1994) for a strong critique of reception rate and defence of the data based upon the ADP.

7 Numerous books were also published by concerned individuals in the mid- to late nineteenth century detailing deaths of individual prisoners in England (Sim 1990).

8 The letter F stood for 'felo-de'se': the murder of oneself (Liebling 2001: 35).

9 From April 1998 to April 2004 all deaths in custody were investigated by senior governors in the Prison Service. From April 2004 all investigations of deaths in custody transferred from the Prison Service to the Prisons and Probation Ombudsman.

10 By 2006 the F2052SH had largely been replaced by the ACCT.

11 In certain parts of the penal estate (for example HMP Lancaster Castle) there are difficulties in building safer cells because of prison architecture.

7 The treatment of people who sexually offend

1 Less than 8 per cent of men charged with sexual offences have an underlying psychiatric illness (Barker and Morgan 1993).

2 Although somatic approaches are now largely discredited they are sometimes conjoined with other approaches through a bio-psycho-social model (Marshall and Barbaree 1990).

3 This *situational approach* draws clear parallels with the techniques of denial (Cohen 2001).

4 The most recent incarnation of the psycho-medical perspective is the Good Lives Model (GLM) and has come to bear considerable influence since 2006 (Ward and Siegert 2002). The GLM approach, however, seems to raise concerns about interactions and social structures that are more sociological than psychological.

5 There are only limited attempts to promote ageing and beauty as the ideal (Smallbone 2006).

6 It is believed that up to 25 per cent of sexual abuse is directly committed by women (Renvoize 1993).

7 Such positive talk about the impact of the SOTP set alarm bells ringing for prison critics as these unsubstantiated claims could be used to promote more or longer prison sentences.

8 In combination with the probation service this is the biggest treatment programme in the world (Murphy and McGrath 2008).

9 Sexual offending is generally intermittent and non-permanent and as such radical differentiation cannot explain why most offenders never become habitual criminals (Matza 1964).

10 This poem has been used as part of the Sex Offender Treatment Programme (SOTP) in a number of prisons in the UK since the early 1990s.

11 In late 2007 the Department of Health and Prison and Probation Services established a network of psychiatrists with an interest in using 'castration'. The effects of chemical castration are reversible and involve drug induced treatments through anti-libidinals or anti-androgens to lower testosterone or enhance serotonin levels (Harrison 2007). Castration should, however, be rejected immediately. 'Treatments' have severe side effects such as nausea, serious cardiovascular complications, breast growth, ischemic heart disease, osteoporosis and hot flushes (Grubin 2008; Erickson and Erickson 2008). Previous attempts at 'chemical castration' have proved disastrous. Between November 1975 and November 1978, 138 sex offender prisoners received such treatment, leading to fifteen having operations to remove breasts and further two undertaking similar operations after their release (Sim 1990: 111–12). Alongside ethical objections it is also clear that castration does not reduce offending or protect the public (Barker and Morgan 1993). A penile erection is not required to abuse another person. Sexual abuse is more about power than sexual arousal.

12 The motivation for partaking was to comply with sentencing conditions, improve chances of early release, and secure privileges tied to participation (Hudson 2005).

13 Recorded crimes are likely to be an underestimate of actual reoffending whereas self report is notoriously unreliable when it comes to serious offences (Brown 2005).

14 The Gracewell Institute was established by Ray Wyre and opened in September 1988. The aim of the institute was to help offenders take control of their offender cycles, challenge denials and accept that their behaviour had been an abuse of power. Despite evidence of success the Gracewell Clinic was closed in 1994. The Lucy Faithful Foundation opened a similar clinic in August 1995 but this was closed in 2002.

8 Drug taking

1 In contrast dealers with 'powder power' can be extremely influential figures in prison (Crewe 2005).

2 For prison staff if a drug is seen as means of facilitating a 'quiet day' then it is likely to be condoned. If, however, a drug is seen as creating trouble and conflict it is likely to be condemned (Keene 1997a; Malloch 2000).

3 An illicit drug is illegal. The *Misuse of Drugs Act* 1971 classified controlled drugs as falling into Class A, B, or C drug groups.

4 Recent governments have been obsessed that there exists a 'drugs and crime' link. This is an ahistorical perspective as it negates the reality that social problems defined as 'crime' existed long before there was a perceived drug problem. There are four broad hypotheses regarding the possible relationship between 'drugs and crime': (1) drugs cause 'crime' (economic necessity), (2) 'crime' causes drug use, (3) drugs and 'crime' might both be caused by something else, and (4) there is no causal link between drugs and 'crime'. What is clear is the criminalization of drug taking must be understood within wider structural

divisions and how the penal law focuses largely on the regulation of the unrespectable 'dangerous classes' (McDermott 1992; Seddon 2006).

5 The UK Drug Policy Commission (2008: 26) identified four types of drug users: *recreational drug users* who use drugs but not dependent; *problem recreational users* whose usage is out of control; *early-stage dependent users* who are dependent and committing acquisitive crimes; and *severely problematic users* who are long term dependents with a criminal career. The number of problematic drug users is estimated by one notable critic to be less than 5 per cent of the 4,000,000 people who illegally use drugs (Seddon 2006: 681).

6 In the most recent evaluation of RMDTs *PricewaterhouseCoopers* (2008) argued that testing should be abandoned as it was counter-productive and open to manipulation.

7 Other drugs taken in prison include heroin (27 per cent), tranquillizers (15 per cent), crack (7 per cent), cocaine (5 per cent), ecstasy (4 per cent) and amphetamines (2 per cent) (Hucklesby and Wilkinson 2001; Bullock 2003). Recent evidence would appear to indicate that in at least a small number of prisons, mainly in the North-East of England, as many as 70 per cent of prisoners regularly take a heroin substitute called Subutex (buprenorphine) illegally (Ministry of Justice 2007b). The most popularly used drug in prison is cannabis, with the next most preferred drug being heroin (Edgar and O'Donnell 1998; Farrell et al. 2000; Wilkinson et al. 2003). Opiate positivity is around 5 per cent over the first 18 months but does not drop off in any significant fashion over time (Farrell et al. 1998).

8 The 1971 *Misuse of Drugs Act* also established the Advisory Council on The Misuse of Drugs (ACMD) to review the extent of drug usage and assess treatment initiatives.

9 HIV is a virus that destroys a person's immune system's white T4 blood cells, demobilizing their ability to combat infections and diseases. HIV is a retrovirus which may lead to AIDS. The two most significant of domains of exposure for the transmission of HIV in prison are intravenous drug use (injecting drugs with needles and other objects) and sexual transmission. Although there were gross exaggerations of transmission in the past, HIV positive rates among prisoners in England and Wales are estimated to range from somewhere between 0.1 per cent and 0.9 per cent (WHO Regional Office for Europe 2005). It is estimated that prisoners are 15 times more likely than the general population to be HIV positive (Stewart 2007). A Department of Health 'sero-survey' of HIV in prisons in England and Wales found that 0.3 per cent of adult male and 1.2 per cent of adult female prisoners were HIV positive (Prison Health Policy Unit and Prison Health Task Force 2002).

10 Initially HIV sufferers were constructed as unworthy and undeserving (Young and McHale 1992). In October 1985 the Viral Infectivity Regulations (VIR), which had originally been deployed to deal with identified Hepatitis B carriers, were extended to deal with HIV seropositive prisoners. HIV prisoners were segregated in solitary confinement in a small dingy basement in Wadsworth prison, withdrawn from any work where they could spill blood, and restricted to limited education classes, outside contact and exercise (Thomas and Costigan 1992). The Woolf Report (1991) called for an end to VIR but it was not until 1993 that the segregation of HIV prisoners was abolished. Once again it is clear that medical interventions around HIV in prison were all about surveillance, regulation and punishment rather than care and treatment (McGee and Scraton 1998).

11 This effect is always likely to be minimal given the manner in which cannabis can induce relaxation and sleep.

12 This commitment was reaffirmed with the publication in 2008 of the review by former police officer David Blakey.

13 The Blakey Review (2008:11) also suggested it may be 'good practice' for prisoners to 'wear a one-piece boiler suit with no pockets during visits' as a way 'to reduce smuggling'.

14 VDTs and VTUs were advocated by the Woolf Report (1991) and the Learmont Report

(1995) and in June 1996 HMP the Verne set up the first voluntary unit. The prisoner signs a compact to agree to remain drug free, although claims have often been made that prisoners still use drugs. A report in the *Guardian* (21 September 1993) uncovered that at the alleged drug free unit at The Wolds on at least one occasion the entire unit tested positive for drugs (cited in Malloch 2000: 122).

9 Prisoners and their families

1 The concept of the 'family' is not without its problems and since the 1960s has been the site of critical feminist debates on its functions and meaning within a capitalist and patriarchal society (Barrett 1980). Feminist perspectives have stressed the family as a site of the oppression of women, considering physical, emotional and sexual abuse within a setting exemplifying gendered exploitation.

2 The reasons for this inclusion of families vary: under the Nazi system there was a link to the idea of genetic transmission of crime and deviance. In other jurisdictions or cultures the stigma of criminality may play out in the form of religious obligations (Ameh 2004).

3 One of the most shocking aspects of the costs for families has arisen from the costs of telephone calls. In the UK a campaign by the Prison Reform Trust has successfully challenged high telephone call costs which exceed those available to non-prisoners.

4 Roger Grimshaw and his team worked with Gloucester LEA on a study evaluating the impact of their imprisoned parents' policy but other than that the specific impact of imprisonment of family members on school performance is in need of development.

5 In the US the most significant impetus for new research, such as that by Comfort (2002, 2003, 2007), has arisen from the recognition of a mass-imprisonment epidemic disproportionately affecting members of BME groups. In addition, it has been widely documented how high levels of imprisonment removing men can impact negatively on BME communities, resulting in matriarchal communities and a decline in male accountability (Bates et al. 2003; Travis and Waul 2003a and b; Bernstein 2005). Other collateral consequences of imprisonment include felony disenfranchisement, forced freeing for adoption of prisoners' children (so-called 'permanency planning') and welfare bans (Golden 2005).

6 That said, anecdotal accounts suggest that in some situations staff may 'turn a blind eye' to sexual activity, such as in an empty visits room when a long-term inmate and his wife are together (Codd 2008).

7 Note that the Grassroots Family days project, which was commended in Codd (2008) as an example of good practice, has since lost its government funding.

8 For a discussion of the relevant case law see Codd (2008).

9 But note anecdotal evidence that in some British Muslim communities it is seen as inappropriate for women to visit prisons and so this activity is undertaken by men.

10 Beyond penal controversies: towards abolitionism

1 Alongside these we fully endorse the pragmatic initiatives of Sim (2009) regarding a moratorium on prison building, the diversion of criminal justice funding to more inclusionary social projects, and a concerted effort to transform the 'power to punish' by challenging prison officer occupational culture.

2 For an example of somebody doing exactly this in India, see Bedi (1999). See also Sim (2009).

3 It is important here not to forget the power and strength of prisoner-led resistance, including legal and human rights challenges and everything between creative writing and rooftop protests.

4 There are already visible flashes of this from which we can draw inspiration, such as the judgment of Albie Sachs in the South African Constitutional Court when he substituted a suspended sentence and a substantial period of community service and a fine for the immediate sentence of imprisonment passed on a woman who was the primary carer of three children. In this judgment we see Sachs 'refusing to play the game' of populist penology (Codd 2009).

5 Awareness of the racial dimension is far more developed in the US, where in many prisons members of minority ethnic groups are not only disproportionately represented but also form the majority group within the prison (Sudbury 2005).

6 For an example, see the work of the THOMAS organization, based in Blackburn.

Bibliography

4Children (2008) *Unlocking Potential – Alternatives to Custody for Young People*, (4Children in partnership with Barnardo's). London: 4Children.

Advisory Council on the Misuse of Drugs (1982) *Treatment and Rehabilitation*. London: HMSO.

Advisory Council on the Misuse of Drugs (1979) *Report on Drug Dependants within the Prison System in England and Wales*. London: HMSO.

Advisory Council on the Misuse of Drugs (1988) *AIDS and Drug Misuse*. London: HMSO.

Advisory Council on the Misuse of Drugs (1996) *Drug Misusers and the Criminal Justice System: Part II – Drug Misuse and the Prison System*. London: HMSO.

Allison, E. (2007) Death Behind Bars, *The Guardian*, 13 June.

Allison, E. (2009) Prison is no place for children, *The Guardian*, 10 February.

Allison, E. and Hattenstone, S. (2007) What gives them the right to hit a child in the nose? *The Guardian*, 2 June.

Ameh, R.K. (2004) Human rights, gender and traditional practices: the Trokosi system in West Africa, in A. Kalunta-Crompton and B. Agozino, *Pan-African Issues in Crime and Justice*. Aldershot: Ashgate, pp. 23–38.

Arrupe, P. (1973) Address to the 'Tenth International Congress of Jesuit Alumni of Europe,' Valencia, Spain, 31 July 1973. Link to full text: http://www.creighton.edu/CollaborativeMinistry/men-for-others.html

Bandele, A. (1999) *The Prisoner's Wife*. New York: Washington Square Press.

Barbaree, H.E. and Marshall, W.L. (1998) Treatment of the sexual offender, in R.M. Wettstein (ed.) *Treatment of Offenders with Mental Disorders*. London: The Guilford Press, pp. 265–328.

Barbaree, H.E., Langton, C. and Peacock, E. (2006) Sexual offender treatment for psychopaths: is it harmful?, in W.L. Marshall, Y. Fernandez, L.E. Marshall and G.A. Serran (eds) *Sexual Offender Treatment: Controversial Issues*. Chichester: John Wiley, pp. 159–71.

Barker, M. and Morgan, R. (1993) *Sex Offenders: A Framework for the Evaluation of Community-based Treatment*. London: Home Office.

Barrett, M. (1980) *Women's Oppression Today*. London: Verso.

Bartlett, P. and Sandland, R. (2008) *Mental Health Law*, 3rd edn. Oxford: Oxford University Press.

Barton, A., Corteen, K., Scott, D. and Whyte, D. (2006) Introduction, in A. Barton, K. Corteen, D. Scott and D. Whyte (eds) *Expanding the Criminological Imagination*. Cullompton: Willan.

Batchelor, S.A. (2005) 'Prove me the bam!': victimization and agency in the lives of young women who commit violent offences, *Probation Journal*, 52(4): 358–75.

Bates, R., Lawrence-Wills, S. and Hairston, C.F. (2003) 'Children and Families of Incarcerated Parents: A View from the Ground', *Research Brief on Children, Families and the Criminal Justice System*. Chicago: University of Illinois.

Baumgartner, M.P. (1992) The myth of discretion, in K. Hawkins (ed.) *The Uses Of Discretion*. Oxford: Oxford University Press.

Baxter, P. and Sampson, B. (1972) Introduction, in P. Baxter and B. Sampson (eds) *Race and Social Difference*. Harmondsworth: Penguin.

Bean, P. (2002) *Drugs and Crime*. Cullompton: Willan.

Becker, H. (1963) *Outsiders*. New York: The Free Press.

Beckett, R. (1994) Cognitive-behavioural treatment of sex offenders, in T. Morrison, M. Eroga and R.C. Beckett (eds) *Sexual Offending Against Children*. London: Routledge, pp. 80–98.

Bedi, K. (1999) *Its Always Possible*. Bhopal: Indra Publishing.

Beech, A., Fisher, D., Beckett, R. and Scott-Fordham, A. (1998) *An Evaluation of the Prison Sex Offender Treatment Programme*. London: Home Office.

Beech, A., Oliver, C., Fisher, D. and Beckett, R. (2005) *Step 4: The Sex Offender Treatment Programme in Prison*. London: Home Office.

Bell, E. (2010) *New Labour's Penchant for Punishment*. London: Palgrave-Macmillan.

Benn, M. and Tchaikovsky, C. (1987) Dangers of being a woman, *The Abolitionist*, p. 23.

Bennett, T. and Holloway, K. (2005) *Understanding Drugs, Alcohol and Crime*. Maidenhead: Open University Press.

Bernheim, J. (1994) Suicides and prison conditions, in A. Liebling and T. Ward (eds) *Deaths in Custody: International Perspectives*. London: Whiting and Birch Ltd, pp. 91–108.

Bernstein, N. (2005) *All Alone in the World*. New York: The New Press.

Berridge, V. (1984) Drugs and social policy: the establishment of drug control in Britain 1900–30, *British Journal of Addiction*, 79: 17–29.

Berridge, V. (1996) *AIDS in the UK*. Oxford: Oxford University Press.

Berridge, V. (1999) *Opium and the People*, 2nd edn. London: Free Association Books.

Bhopal, R. (2004) Glossary of terms relating to ethnicity and race: for reflection and debate, *Journal of Epidemiology and Community Health*, 58:441–5.

Bhui, H.S. (2007) Alien experience: foreign national prisoners after the deportation crisis, *Probation Journal*, 54: 368–82.

Birmingham, L. (2003) The mental health of prisoners, *Advances in Psychiatric Treatment*, 9: 191–201.

Birmingham, L., Mason, D. and Grubin, D. (1996) Prevalence of mental disorder in remand prisoners' *British Medical Journal*, 313: 1521–4.

Blaauw, E. and Kerkhof, J.F.M. (2006) Screening prisoners for suicide risk, in G.E. Dear (ed.) *Preventing Suicide and Other Self-Harm in Prison*. London: Palgrave Macmillan, pp. 41–52.

Blakey, D. (2008) *Disrupting the Supply of Illicit Drugs into Prisons*. London: NOMS.

Blyth, M., Newman, R. and Wright, C. (2009) *Children and Young People in Custody*. Bristol: The Policy Press.

Borrill, J., Maden, A., Martin, A. et al. (2003) Substance misuse among white and black/mixed race female prisoners, in M. Ramsay (ed.) *Prisoners' Drug Use and Treatment: Seven Research Studies*. London: Home Office, pp. 49–70.

Borrill, J., Maden, A., Martin, A. et al. (2003) *Differential Substance Misuse Treatment Needs of Women, Ethnic Minorities and Young Offenders in Prison*. London: Home Office.

Borrill, J., Snow, L., Medlicott, D., Teers, R. and Paton, J. (2005) Learning from 'near misses': interviews with women who survived an incident of severe self-harm in prison, *The Howard Journal*, 44(1): 57–69.

Boswell, G. (1998) Criminal justice and violent young offenders, *The Howard Journal*, 37(2): 148–60.

Boswell, G. (2002) Imprisoned fathers: the children's view, *The Howard Journal*, 41(1): 14–26.

Boswell, G. and Wedge, P. (2001) *Imprisoned Fathers and Their Children*. London and Philadelphia: Jessica Kingsley Publishers.

Bosworth, M. (1999) *Engendering Resistance*. Aldershot: Ashgate.

Bosworth, M. (2008) Immigration detention, *Criminal Justice Matters*, 71: 24–5.

Bosworth, M. and Guild, M. (2008) Governing through migration control: security and citizenship in Britain, *British Journal of Criminology*, 48(6): 703–19.

Bottoms, A.E. (1967) Delinquency amongst immigrants, *Race*, VIII(4): 357–83.

Boudin, K. (1998) Lessons from a mother's program in prison: a psychosocial approach supports women and their children, *Women & Therapy*, 21(1): 103–25.

Bourne, J. (2001) The life and times of institutional racism, *Race & Class*, 43(2): 7–22.

Bowers, L. (2002) *Dangerous and Severe Personality Disorder*. London: Routledge.

Bowlby, J. (1946) *Forty-four Juvenile Thieves*. London: Balliere, Tindall & Cox.

Bowling, B. and Phillips, C. (2001) *Racism, Crime and Justice*. London: Longman.

Bradley, K. (2009) *The Bradley Review*. London: Department of Health.

Braman, D. and Wood, J. (2003) From one generation to the next: how criminal sanctions are reshaping family life in urban America, in J. Travis and M. Waul (eds) *Prisoners Once Removed*. Washington: The Urban Institute Press.

Braman, D. (2002) Families and incarceration, in M. Chesney-Lind and M. Mauer (eds) *Invisible Punishment*. New York: The New Press, pp. 117–35.

Braman, D. (2004) *Doing Time on the Outside*. Ann Arbor, MI: University of Michigan Press.

Breen, J. (2008) The ripple effects of imprisonment on prisoners' families, *Working Notes*, April.

Bridgwood, A. and Malbon, G. (1994) *Survey of the Physical Health of Prisoners*. London: Home Office.

Brook, D. (1996) Point prevalence of mental disorder in un-convicted male prisoners in England & Wales, *British Medical Journal*, 313: 1524–7.

Brooker, C., Duggan, S., Fox, C., Mills, A. and Parsonage, M. (2008) *Short-changed: Spending on Prison Mental Health Care*. London: Sainsbury Centre for Mental Health.

Brooker, C., Sirdifield, C. and Gojkovic, D. (2007) *Mental Health Services and Prisoners: An Updated Review*. Lincoln: University of Lincoln.

Brooks-Gordon, B. and Bainham, A. (2004) Prisoners' families and the regulation of Contact, *Journal of Social Welfare and Family Law*, 26(3): 263–80.

Brooks-Gordon, B., Bilby, C. and Kenworthy, T. (2004) Sexual offenders: a systematic review of psychological treatment interventions, in B. Brooks-Gordon, L. Gelsthorpe, M. Johnson and A. Bainham (eds) *Sexuality Repositioned: Diversity and the Law*. Oxford: Hart Publishing, pp. 395–420.

Broom, D. and Stevens, A. (1991) Doubly deviant: women using alcohol and other drugs, *International Journal on Drug Policy*, 2(4): 25–7.

Brown, S. (2005) *Treating Sex Offenders*. Cullompton: Willan.

Bullock, T. (2003) Changing levels of drug use before, during and after imprisonment, in M. Ramsay (ed.) *Prisoners' Drug Use and Treatment: Seven Research Studies*. London: Home Office, pp. 23–48.

Burnett, R. and Farrell, G. (1994) *Reported and Unreported Racial Incidents in Prisons, Occasional Paper, No. 14*. Oxford: University of Oxford Centre for Criminological Research.

Butler Committee (1975) *Report on Mentally Abnormal Offenders*, CMND 6244. London: DHSS/Home Office.

Butler, P. and Kousoulou, D. (2006) *Women at Risk: The Mental Health of Women in Contact with the Judicial System*. London: London Development Centre.

Canguilhem, G. (1978) *The Normal and the Pathological.* New York: Zone Books.

Carlen, P. (1983) *Women's Imprisonment.* London: Routledge and Kegan Paul.

Carlen, P. (1986) Psychiatry in prisons: promises, premises, practices and politics, in P. Miller and N. Rose (eds) *The Power of Psychiatry.* Oxford: Polity Press, pp. 241–66.

Carlen, P. (1990) *Alternatives to Women's Imprisonment.* Milton Keynes: Open University Press.

Carlen, P. (2002a) *End of Award Report: Funding Report ECHR: L216252033. ECHR,* unpublished document.

Carlen, P. (2002b) Women's imprisonment: models of reform and change, *Probation Journal,* 49: 76–87.

Carlen, P., Hicks, J., O'Dwyer, J., Christina, D. and Tchaikovsky, C. (1985) *Criminal Women.* Cambridge: Polity Press.

Carlen, P. and Tchaikovsky, C. (1996) Women's imprisonment in England at the end of the twentieth century: legitimacy, realities and utopia, in R. Matthews and P. Francis (eds) *Prisons 2000.* London: Macmillan, pp. 201–18.

Carlen, P. and Worrall, A. (2004) *Analysing Women's Imprisonment.* Cullompton: Willan.

Carmichael, S. and Hamilton, C.V. (1967) Black Power: the politics of liberation in America, in E. Cashmore and J. Jennings (2001) *Racism: Essential Readings.* London: Sage, pp. 111–21.

Carpenter, M. (1851) *Reformatory Schools for the Children of the Perishing and Dangerous Classes, and for Juvenile Offenders.* London: C. Gilpin.

Carpenter, M. (1853) *Juvenile Delinquents, their Condition and Treatment.* London: W. & F.G. Cash.

Carrabine, E. (2004) *Power, Discourse and Resistance.* Aldershot: Ashgate.

Carter, L. (2007) *Securing the Future – Proposals for the Efficient and Sustainable Use of Custody in England and Wales December 2007.* London: Ministry of Justice.

Casciani, D. (2009) Injuries prompt youth jail review, *BBC News Online,* 23 June.

Cavadino, M. and Dignan, J. (1992) *The Penal System.* London: Sage.

Cheliotis, L.K. and Liebling, A. (2006) Race matters in British prisons: towards a research agenda, *British Journal of Criminology,* 46(2): 286–317.

Cheney, D. (1993) *Into the Dark Tunnel: Foreign Prisoners in the British Prison System.* London: Prison Reform Trust.

Chigwada-Bailey, R. (2003) *Black Women's Experiences of Criminal Justice: Discourse on Disadvantage,* 2nd edn. Winchester: Waterside Press.

Children, Schools and Families Department and Ministry of Justice (2007) *Children of Offenders Review.* London: Ministry of Justice.

CJSRU (Criminal Justice System Race Unit) (2005) *Race and the Criminal Justice System.* London: Home Office Criminal Justice System Race Unit.

Claire, H. and Holden, C. (2007) The challenge of teaching controversial issues: principles and practice, in H. Claire and C. Holden (eds) *The Challenge of Teaching Controversial Issues.* Stoke: Trentham Books, pp. 1–14.

Codd, H. (1998) Prisoners' families: the 'forgotten victims', *Probation Journal,* 45(3): 148–54.

Codd, H. (2008) *In the Shadow of Prison.* Cullompton: Willan.

Codd, H. (2009) Lost in the shadows: prisoners' children and the law. Paper presented at the Irish Criminology Conference, University College Dublin, June.

Coggan, G. and Walker, M. (1982) *Frightened for my Life.* Glasgow: Fontana.

Cohen, S. (1972) *Folk Devils and Moral Panics.* London: MacGibbon and Key.

Cohen, S. (1998) Intellectual scepticism and political commitment: the case of radical criminology, in P. Walton and J. Young (eds) *The New Criminology Revisited.* London: Macmillan Press, pp. 98–129.

Cohen, S. (2001) *States of Denial.* Cambridge: Polity.

Cohen, S. and Taylor, L. (1972) *Psychological Survival.* Harmondsworth: Penguin.

Coid, J., Bebbington, P., Brugha, T. et al. (2002) Ethnic differences in prisoners: criminality and psychiatric morbidity, *British Journal of Psychiatry*, 181: 473–80.

Coleman, R., Sim, J., Tombs, S. and Whyte, D. (eds) (2009) *State, Power, Crime*. London: Sage.

Coles, D. and Ward, T. (1994) Failure stories: prison suicides and how not to prevent them, in A. Liebling and T. Ward (eds) *Deaths in Custody: International Perspectives*. London: Whiting and Birch Ltd, pp. 127–42.

Comfort, M. (2002) Papa's house: the prison as domestic and social satellite, *Ethnography*, 3(4): 467–99.

Comfort, M. (2003) In the tube at San Quentin: the 'secondary prisonization' of women visiting inmates, *Journal of Contemporary Ethnography*, 32(1): 77–107.

Comfort, M. (2007) *Doing Time Together*. Chicago: University of Chicago Press.

Commission to Inquire into Child Abuse (2009) *Report of the Commission to Inquire into Child Abuse*, Dublin.

Condry, R. (2007) *Families Shamed: The Consequences of Crime for Relatives of Serious Offenders*. Cullompton: Willan.

Conrad, P. and Schneider, J.W. (1992) *Deviance and Medicalization*. Philadelphia: Temple University Press.

Cooper, R.A. (1981) Jeremy Bentham, Elizabeth Fry, and English Prison Reform, *Journal of the History of Ideas*, 42(4): 675–90.

Cope, N. (2003) It's no 'time or high time': young offenders' experiences of time and drug use in prison, *The Howard Journal*, 42(2): 158–75.

Coppock, V. and Hopton, J. (2000) *Critical Perspectives on Mental Health*. London: Routledge.

Corcoran, M. (2006) *Out of Order*. Cullompton: Willan.

Corston, J. (2007a) *The Corston Report: A Report by Baroness Jean Corston of a Review of Women with Particular Vulnerabilities in the Criminal Justice System*. London: Home Office.

Corston, J. (2007b) *Women in Prison*, working notes, July, pp. 3–8.

Coulter, C. (1997) *Web of Punishment*. Dublin: Attic Press.

Cox, V.C., Paulus, P.B. and McCain, G. (1984) Prison crowding research: the relevance for prison housing standards and a general approach regarding crowding phenomena, *American Psychologist*, 39: 1148–60.

CRE (2003a) *The Murder of Zahid Mubarek: A Formal Investigation by the Commission for Racial Equality into HM Prison Service of England and Wales, Part 1*. London: Commission for Racial Equality.

CRE (2003b) *The Murder of Zahid Mubarek: A Formal Investigation by the Commission for Racial Equality into HM Prison Service of England and Wales, Part 2*. London: Commission for Racial Equality.

Crewe, B. (2005) Prisoner society in the era of hard drugs, *Punishment & Society*, 7(4): 457–82.

Crewe, B. (2006) Prison drug dealing and the ethnographic lens, *The Howard Journal*, 45(4): 347–68.

Crighton, D. (2003) Working with suicidal prisoners, in G. Towl (ed.) *Psychology in Prisons*. Oxford: Blackwell Publishing, pp. 138–47.

Crighton, D. (2006a) Methodological issues in psychological research in prisons, in G. Towl (ed.) *Psychological Research in Prisons*. Oxford: Blackwell, pp. 7–23.

Crighton, D. (2006b) Psychological research into reducing suicides, in G. Towl (ed.) *Psychological Research in Prisons*. Oxford: Blackwell, pp. 54–69.

Crighton, D. (2006c) Psychological research into sexual offenders, in G.J. Towl (ed.) *Psychological Research in Prisons*. Oxford: Blackwell, pp. 187–201.

Crighton, D. and Towl, G.J. (2008) *Psychology in Prisons*, 2nd edn. Oxford: Blackwell Publishing.

Cummings, I. (1999) Mentally disordered offenders: a psychiatric perspective, in Board for Social Responsibility (eds) *Prisons: A Study in Vulnerability*. London: Church House Publishing, pp. 57–63.

Da Cunha, M.I.P. (2008) Closed circuits: kinship, neighbourhood and incarceration in urban Portugal, *Ethnography*, 9(3): 325–50.

Daily Star (2003) 25 November, p.1.

Davis, A.Y. (2005) *Abolition Democracy*. London: Seven Stories Press.

de Foulter, R.S. (1986) On the methodological foundation of the abolitionist approach to the criminal justice system. A comparison of the ideas of Hulsman, Mathiesen and Foucault, *Contemporary Crises*, 10: 39–62.

de Haan, W. (1990) *The Politics of Redress*. London: Unwin Hyman.

Dear, G.E. (2006) Preface, in G.E. Dear (ed.) *Preventing Suicide and Other Self-Harm in Prison*. London: Palgrave Macmillan, pp. viii–ix.

Denham, J. (chair) (2005) *Prison Suicides and Overcrowding: Oral and Written Evidence, House of Commons Papers 656, 2005–6*. London: Stationery Office.

Detrick, S., Abel, G., Berger, M., Delon, A. and Meek, R. (2008) *Violence against Children in Conflict with the Law*. Amsterdam: Defence for Children International.

Devlin, A. (1998) *Invisible Women: What's Wrong with Women's Prisons?* Winchester: Waterside Press.

DH/HO (Department of Health and Home Office) (2000) *Reforming the Mental Health Act*. London: STO.

Dobash, R., Dobash, R. and Gutteridge, S. (1986) *The Imprisonment of Women*. Oxford: Blackwell.

DoH, HM Prison Service and the National Assembly for Wales (2002) *Changing the Outlook: A Strategy for Developing and Modelling Mental Health Services in Prison*. London: DoH.

Dolan, K. (1997) AIDS, drugs and risk behaviour in prison: state of the art, in J. Nelles and A. Fuhrer (eds) *Harm Reduction in Prison*. Bern: Peter Lang.

Dooley, E. (1990) Notes: unnatural deaths in prison, *British Journal of Criminology*, 30: 229–33.

Dooley, E. (1994) Unnatural death in prison: is there a future?, in A. Liebling and T. Ward (eds) *Deaths in Custody: International Perspectives*. London: Whiting and Birch Ltd, pp. 28–35.

Doward, J. (2008a) Freed prisoners 'breach bail to deal drugs back in jail', *Observer*, 17 August.

Doward, J. (2008b) Ministry blames crowded jails on Labour, *Observer*, 28 December.

Drakeford, M. and Butler, I. (2007) Everyday tragedies: justice, scandal and young people in contemporary Britain, *Howard Journal of Criminal Justice*, 46(3): 219–35.

Duke, K. (2003) *Drugs, Prisons and Policy-Making*. London: Palgrave.

Durcan, G. and Knowles, K. (2006) *Policy Paper 5 – London's Prison Mental Health Services: A Review*. London: Sainsbury Centre for Mental Health.

Durcan, G. (2008) *From the Inside: Experiences of Prison Mental Health Care*. London: Sainsbury Centre for Mental Health.

Eastman, N. (1993) Forensic psychiatric services in Britain: a current review, *International Journal of Law & Psychiatry*, 16: 1–25.

Eaton, M. (1993) *Women After Prison*. Buckingham: Open University Press.

Edgar, K. (2007) Black and minority ethnic prisoners, in Y. Jewkes (ed.) *Handbook on Prisons*. Cullompton: Willan, pp. 268–92.

Edgar, K. and O'Donnell, I. (1998) *Mandatory Drug Testing In Prisons – An Evaluation*. London: Home Office Research and Statistics Directorate.

Edgar, K. and Martin, C. (2004) *Perceptions of Race and Conflict: Perspectives of Minority Ethnic Prisoners and of Prison Officers*. Home Office Online Report 11/04.

Ellis, T., Tedstone, C. and Curry, D. (2004) *Improving Race Relations in Prisons: What Works?* Home Office Online Report 12/04.

Ellis, W. (1993) *Sunday Times*, 28 November.

Epstein, R. and Foster, S. (2008) Children behind bars: care, custody discipline and human rights, *Criminal Law and Justice Weekly*, 45: 732–9.

Erickson, P.E. and Erickson, S.K. (2008) *Crime, Punishment and Mental Illness*. London: Rutgers University Press.

Ettorre, B. (1989) Women and substance use/abuse: towards a feminist perspective or how to make the dust fly, *Women's Studies International Forum*, 12: 593–602.

Ettorre, E. (1992) *Women and Substance Use*. London: Macmillan.

Falshaw, L., Friendship, C. and Bates, A. (2003) *Sexual Offenders – Measuring Reconviction, Reoffending and Recidivism*. London: Home Office.

Falshaw, L., Friendship, C., Travers, R. and Nugent, F. (2003) *Searching for 'What Works'*. London: Home Office.

Farrant, F. (2001) *Troubled Inside: Responding to the Mental Health Needs of Children and Young People in Prison*. London: Prison Reform Trust.

Farrell, M. and Marsden, J. (2005) *Drug-related Mortality Among Newly Released Offenders 1998–2000*. London: Home Office.

Farrell, M., Macauley, R. and Taylor, C. (1998) *An Analysis of the Mandatory Drug Testing Programme*. London: National Addiction Centre.

Farrell, M., Singleton, N. and Strang, J. (2000) Drugs and prisons: a high risk and high burden environment, in D. Shewan and J.B. Davies (eds) *Drug Use and Prison: An International Perspective*. Amsterdam: Harwood, pp. 203–14.

Fennell, P. (2002) Radical risk management, mental health and criminal justice, in N. Gray, J. Laing and L. Noaks (eds) *Criminal Justice, Mental Health and the Politics of Risk*. London: Cavendish Publishing Limited, pp. 69–97.

Finkelhor, D. and associates (1986) *A Sourcebook on Child Sexual Abuse*. London: Sage.

Finnegan, F. (2004) *Do Penance or Perish*. Oxford: Oxford University Press.

Fisher, D. (1994) Adult sex offenders: Who are they? Why and how do they do it?, in T. Morrison, M. Eroga and R.C. Beckett (eds) *Sexual Offending Against Children*. London: Routledge, pp. 1–24.

Fishman, Laura T. (1990) *Women at the Wall*. Albany, NY: State University of New Press.

Fitzgerald, M. and Sim, J. (1979) *British Prisons*. Oxford: Blackwell.

Forum for Preventing Deaths in Custody (2007) *Annual Report 2006–2007*. London: Independent Police Complaints Commission.

Foucault, M. (1967) *Madness and Civilisation*. London: Routledge.

Foucault, M. (1977) *Discipline and Punish*. Harmondsworth: Penguin.

Foucault, M. (2006) *Psychiatric Power*. London: Palgrave.

Fowles, A.J. (1993) The mentally abnormal offender in the era of community care, in W. Watson and A. Grounds (eds) *The Mentally Disordered Offender in an Era of Community Care: New Directions in Provision*. Cambridge: Cambridge University Press, pp. 61–77.

Frankfort, E. (1984) *Kathy Boudin and the Dance of Death*. New York: Stein & Day.

Friendship, C., Mann, R. and Beech, A. (2003) *The Prison-based Sex Offender Treatment Programme – An Evaluation*. London: Home Office.

Fromberg, E. (1992) A harm reduction educational strategy towards Ecstasy, in P.A. O'Hare, R. Newcombe, A. Matthews, E.C. Buning and E. Druker (eds) *The Reduction of Drug Related Harm*. London: Routledge, pp. 146–53.

Frühwald, S. and Frottier, P. (2005) Suicide in prison, *The Lancet*, 366 (9483).

Fry, E. (1827) *Observations on the Visiting, Superintendence and Government of Female Prisoners*. London: John and Arthur Arch, Cornhill.

Fuhrer, A. and Nelles, J. (1997) Harm reduction in prisons – aspects of a scientific discussion, in J. Nelles and A. Fuhrer (eds) *Harm Reduction in Prison*. Bern: Peter Lang.

Furby, L., Weinrott, M.R. and Blackshaw, L. (1989) Sex offender recidivism: a review, *Psychological Bulletin*, 105: 3–30.

Gaines, S. (2008) Inmates sleep in toilets at overcrowded prison, *The Guardian*, 22 July.

Garland, D. (2001a) *The Culture of Control*. Oxford: Oxford University Press.

Garland, D. (2001b) Introduction: the meaning of mass imprisonment, *Punishment and Society*, 3(1): 5–7.

Gelsthorpe, L. and Morris, A. (1994) Juvenile justice 1945–1992, in M. Maguire, R. Morgan and R. Reiner (eds) *The Oxford Handbook of Criminology*, 1st edn. Oxford: Oxford University Press, pp. 949–93.

Genders, E. and Player, E. (1987) Women in prison: the treatment, the control and the experience, in P. Carlen and A. Worrall (eds) *Gender, Crime and Justice*. Milton Keynes: Open University Press, pp. 147–64.

Genders, E. and Player, E. (1989) *Race Relations in Prison*. Oxford: Clarendon Press.

Genders, E. and Player, E. (1995) *Grendon: A Study of a Therapeutic Prison*. Oxford: Clarendon Press.

Giallombardo, R. (1966) *Society of Women: A Study of a Women's Prison*. New York: Wiley.

Gillen, J. (2007) Age of criminal responsibility: the frontier between care and justice, *International Family Law Journal*, 1: 7.

Gilroy, P. (1987) *'There Ain't No Black in the Union Jack': The Cultural Politics of Race and Nation*. London: Hutchinson.

Gilroy, P. (2001) *Between Camps*. Cambridge: Polity Press.

Girshick, L. (1996) *Soledad Women*. Westport, CT: Praeger.

Girshick, L. (1999) *No Safe Haven*. Boston, MA: Northeastern University Press.

Glaser, D. and Frosh, S. (1993) *Child Sexual Abuse*, 2nd edn. London: Macmillan.

Glover, J. and Hibbert, P. (2008) *Locking up or Giving up – is Custody for Children Always the Right Answer?* Barnardo's: Ilford.

Goffman, E. (1963) *Asylums*. Harmondsworth: Penguin.

Golden, R. (2005) *War on the Family*. New York: Routledge.

Goldson, B. (2005a) Child imprisonment: a case for abolition, *Youth Justice*, 5(2): 77–90.

Goldson, B. (2005b) Child deaths in penal custody: beyond individual pathology, *Criminal Justice Matters*, 61(1): 26–7.

Goldson, B. (2006) Damage, harm and death in child prisons in England and Wales: questions of abuse and accountability, *The Howard Journal*, 45(5): 449–67.

Goldson, B. (2009) What 'justice' for children in conflict with the law? Some reflections and thoughts, *Criminal Justice Matters*, 1934–6220, 76(1): 19–21.

Goldson, B. and Coles, D. (2005) *In the Care of the State?* London: INQUEST.

Goldson, B. and Peters, E. (2000) *Tough Justice*. London: Children's Society.

Gordon, P. (1983) *White Law*. London: Pluto Press.

Goring, C. (1913/1972) *The English Convict*. New Jersey: Patterson Smith.

Gravett, S. (2000) *Drugs In Prison*. London: Continuum.

Gray, R., Lathlean, J., Mills, A., Bressington, D. and Van Veenhuyzen, W. (2007) *Observational Cross Sectional Pilot Study of Adherence with Antipsychotic Medication in People with Schizophrenia or Schizoaffective Disorders in Prisons*. London: Kings College.

Greve, W., Hosser, D. and Bosold, C. (2006) Self-harm of juvenile and young adult prison inmates: conditions and consequences, in G.E. Dear (ed.) *Preventing Suicide and Other Self-Harm in Prison*. London: Palgrave Macmillan, pp. 177–86.

Griffiths, R. and Pearson, B. (1988) *Working with Drug Users*. Aldershot: Wildwood House.

Grubin, D. (2008) The use of medication in the treatment of sex offenders, *Prison Service Journal*, 178: 37–43.

Guardian (1995a) 8 May.

Guardian (1995b) 14 March.

Gunn, J., Maden, T. and Swinton, M. (1991) *Mentally Disordered Prisoners*. London: Home Office.

Gunn, J., Robertson, G., Dell, S. and Way, C. (1978) *Psychiatric Aspects of Imprisonment*. London: Academic Press.

Hall, S., Critcher, C., Jefferson, T., Clarke, J. and Roberts, B. (1978) *Policing The Crisis: Mugging The State and Law and Order*. London: Macmillan.

Hancock, N. (2003) Suicide, risk and vulnerability: prison service strategies. Paper delivered at the British Society of Criminology: Too many prisoners Conference, 7 November, London.

Hannah-Moffat, K. (2001) *Punishment in Disguise*. Toronto: University of Toronto.

Hansard (1993) 2 March 1993, col.139.

Hansard (2009a) *Young Offender Institutions: Education*, 8 June 2009.

Hansard (2009b) *Youth Custody*, 18 March 2009.

Hanson, R.K., Gordon, A., Harris, A. et al. (2002) First report of the collaborative outcome data project on the effectiveness of psychological treatment for sex offenders, *Sexual Abuse: A Journal of Research and Treatment*, 14(2): 169–94.

Harcourt, B.E. (2006) From the asylum to the prison: rethinking the incarceration revolution, *Texas Law Review*, 84: 1751–85.

Harding, C., Hines, B., Ireland, R. and Rawlings, P. (1985) *Imprisonment in England and Wales*. Beckenham: Croom Helm.

Harrington, R. and Bailey, S. (2005) *Mental Health Needs and Effectiveness of Provision for Young Offenders in Custody and in the Community*. London: YJB.

Harrison, K. (2007) The high-risk sex offender strategy in England and Wales: is chemical castration an option, *The Howard Journal*, 46(1): 16–31.

Harvey, J. (2007) *Young Men in Prison*. Cullompton: Willan.

Haydon, D. and Scraton, P. (2000) 'Condemn a little more, understand a little less': the political context and rights' implications of the domestic and European rulings in the Venables-Thompson case, *Journal of Law & Society*, 27(3): 416–48.

Hayman, S. (2006) *Imprisoning our Sisters*. Montreal: McGill-Queen's University Press.

Health Advisory Committee for the Prison Service (HAC) (1997) *The Provision of Mental Health Care in Prisons*. London: HM Prison Service.

Hedderman, C. and Sugg, D. (1996) *Does Treating Sex Offenders Reduce Re-offending?* London: Home Office.

Heidensohn, F. (1968) The deviance of women: a critique and an enquiry, *British Journal of Sociology*, 19(2): 160–75.

Her Majesty's Chief Inspector of Prisons (1990) *Suicide and Self-Harm in Prison Service Establishments in England and Wales (Tumin Report)*. London: HMSO.

Her Majesty's Chief Inspector of Prisons (1996) *Patient or Prisoner? A New Strategy for Health Care in Prisons*. London: Home Office.

Her Majesty's Chief Inspector of Prisons (1999) *Suicide is Everyone's Concern*. London: HMCIP.

Her Majesty's Chief Inspector of Prisons (2005a) *Parallel Worlds*. London: TSO.

Her Majesty's Chief Inspector of Prisons (2005b) *Annual Report of HM Chief Inspector of Prisons for England and Wales, 2003–2004*. London: The Stationery Office.

Her Majesty's Chief Inspector of Prisons (2006) *Foreign National Prisoners*. London: Home Office.

Her Majesty's Chief Inspector of Prisons (2007) *The Mental Health of Prisoners*. London: HMSO.

Her Majesty's Chief Inspector of Prisons (2008) *Time Out of Cell*. London: HM Inspectorate of Prisons.

Her Majesty's Chief Inspector of Prisons (2009a) *Race Relations in Prisons*. London: HM Inspectorate of Prisons.

Her Majesty's Chief Inspector of Prisons (2009b) *Annual Report 2007–8*. London: Ministry of Justice.

Her Majesty's Chief Inspector of Prisons and Her Majesty's Chief Inspector of Probation (2008) *The Indeterminate Sentence for Public Protection*. London: The Stationery Office.

Herrnstein, R. and Murray, C. (1994) *The Bell Curve*. New York: Free Press.

Hillyard, P. (1993) *Suspect Community*. London: Pluto Press.

HM Government (2005) *Government Response to the Third Report from the Joint Committee on Human Rights: Deaths in Custody*. House of Lords and House of Commons, London: The Stationery Office.

HM Prison Drug Strategy Unit (2003) *The Prison Service Drug Strategy*. London: HM Prison Service.

HM Prison Service and NHS Executive (1999) *The Future Organization of Prison Health Care*. London: Department of Health.

HM Prison Service (1987) *Policy Statement on Through Care of Drug Misusers in the Prison Service*. London: HMSO.

HM Prison Service (1990) *Suicide Prevention and Follow-up to Deaths in Custody: CI 20/89*. London: HMSO.

HM Prison Service (1991a) *Caring for Drug Users: A Multi-disciplinary Resource for People Working with Prisoners*. London: HM Prison Service.

HM Prison Service (1991b) *Circular Instruction 12/19991: Throughcare of Drug Misusers*. London: HM Prison Service.

HM Prison Service (1991c) *Treatment Programmes for Sex Offenders in Custody: A Strategy*. London: HM Prison Service.

HM Prison Service (1992) *Caring for Prisoners at Risk of Suicide and Self-injury: The Way Forward*. London: Prison Service.

HM Prison Service (1994a) *Caring for the Suicidal in Custody: Instructions to Governors 1/94*. London: HMSO.

HM Prison Service (1994b) *Caring for the Suicidal in Custody: Guide to Policy and Procedures*. London: HM Prison Service.

HM Prison Service (1995) *Drug Misuse In Prison: Policy and Strategy*. London: HM Prison Service.

HM Prison Service (1998a) *Tackling Drugs In Prison: The Prison Service Drugs Strategy May 1998*. London: The Stationery Office.

HM Prison Service (1998b) *The Review of the Prison Service Drug Strategy*. London: HMSO.

HM Prison Service (2002) *Prison Service Order 2700: Suicide and Self-Harm Prevention*. London: HM Prison Service.

HM Prison Service (2003a) *Annual Report & Accounts April 2002 to March 2003*. London: The Stationery Office.

HM Prison Service (2003b) *Drug Strategy General Briefing 17.12.03*. London: HM Prison Service.

HM Prison Service (2004) *Diversity* www.hmprisonservice.gov.uk/abouttheservice/diversity (accessed 27 October, 2004).

HM Prison Service (2005) *2004–05 Annual Report and Accounts*. London: HM Prison Service.

HM Prison Service (2007) *The ACCT Approach to Caring for People at Risk in Prison*. London: HM Prison Service www.hmprisonservice.gov.uk (accessed 5 March 2007).

HM Prison Service (2008) *Corporate Plan 2007–08 to 2010–11 and Business Plan 2007–08*. London: HM Prison Service/NOMS.

HM Prison Service (2009) *Performance Statistics*. London: HM Prison Service.

HM Prison Service Headquarters (1996) *Inside Psychology – A Career as a Prison Psychologist*. London: HMPS.

HM Prison Service Safer Custody Group (2004) *The ACCT Approach – Caring for People at Risk in Prison: Pocket Guide for Staff.* London: HM Prison Service.

HMP Frankland (1998a) *HMP Frankland Sex Offender Treatment Programme: A Prisoners' Guide.* Durham: HMP Frankland (unpaginated).

HMP Frankland (1998b) *HMP Frankland Sex Offender Treatment Programme: Staff Handbook.* Durham: HMP Frankland.

HMP Islington (2004) *Health Promotion in Prisons.* London: HMP Islington.

HMP Risley (2005) *Prisons Addressing Substance Related Offending: Information for staff.* Risley: HM Prison Service.

Hobhouse, S. and Brockway, F. (1922) *English Prisons To-Day.* London: Longmans, Green and Co.

Home Affairs Committee (HAC) (1999) *Drugs and Prisons: Volume I Report and Proceedings of the Committee.* London: The Stationery Office.

Home Office (1952) *Prison Act.* London: HMSO.

Home Office (1959) *Penal Practice in a Changing Society.* London: Home Office.

Home Office (1968) *The Rehabilitation of Drug Addicts: Report of the Advisory Committee on Drug Dependence.* London: HM Stationery Office.

Home Office (1971) *Misuse of Drugs Act.* London: HMSO.

Home Office (1983) *The Mental Health Act 1983.* London: HMSO.

Home Office (1984) *Suicides in Prisons. Report by H.M. Chief Inspector of Prisons.* London: HMSO.

Home Office (1985) *HM Prison Holloway Report by Chief Inspector of Prisons.* London: Home Office.

Home Office (1990) *Circular 66/90 – Provision for Mentally Disordered Offenders.* London: Home Office.

Home Office (1991) *Custody, Care and Justice.* London: Home Office.

Home Office (1995) *Tackling Drugs Together.* London: HMSO.

Home Office (1998a) *Tackling Drugs To Build A Better Britain.* London: HMSO.

Home Office (1998b) *Human Rights Act.* London: HMSO.

Home Office (2007) *A Review of the Failure of the Immigration and Nationality Department to Consider Some Foreign National Prisoners for Deportation.* London: Home Office.

Home Office (2007) *The Mental Health Act 2007.* London: HMSO.

Home Office and Department of Health (1999) *Reform of the Mental Health Act: Proposals for Consultation.* London: Home Office.

House of Commons Justice Committee (2008) *Towards Effective Sentencing, Fifth Report of Session 2007–08, Volume 1.* London: The Stationery Office.

House of Commons Welsh Affairs Committee (2007) *Welsh Prisoners in the Prison Estate, Third Report of Session 2006–7.* London: House of Commons.

House of Lords (2009) *Women in Prison – Question for Short Debate,* House of Lords 14 January, 2009.

Howard League (2001) *Suicide and Self-harm Prevention.* London: Howard League.

Howard League (2005) *Children in Custody.* London: Howard League.

Hucklesby, A. and Wilkinson, C. (2001) Drug misuse in prisons: some comments on the prison service drugs strategy, *The Howard Journal,* 40(4): 347–63.

Hudson, B.A. (1993) *Penal Policy and Social Justice.* London: Macmillan.

Hudson, B.A. (2009) All the People in all the world. Paper delivered at the European Group Conference, University of Central Lancashire, 28 August.

Hudson, K. (2005) *Offending Identities.* Cullompton: Willan.

Huey, P. and McNulty, T. (2005) Institutional conditions and prison suicide: conditional effects of deprivation and overcrowding, *The Prison Journal,* 85: 490–4.

Hulsman, L. (1986) Critical criminology and the concept of crime, *Contemporary Crises*, 10: 63–80.

Humphries, S. (1981) *Hooligans or Rebels?* Oxford: Basil Blackwell.

Husband, C. (1984) *Race in Britain Today: Continuity and Change*. London: Hutchinson.

Hutson, N. and Myers, C. (2006) 'Bad Girls' or 'Mad Girls' – the coping mechanisms of female young offenders, in F. Heidensohn (ed.) *Gender and Justice*. Cullompton: Willan.

Ignatieff, M. (1978) *A Just Measure of Pain*. Harmondsworth: Penguin.

INQUEST (1995) Report on the Death of Alton Manning. London: INQUEST.

INQUEST (2009) Deaths in prison. London: INQUEST http://inquest.gn.apc.org/data_deaths_in_prison.html (accessed 15 October 2009).

Jagger, A. (1983) *Feminist Politics & Human Nature*. New Jersey: Rowman & Littlefield.

James, A. and Jenks, C. (1996) Public perceptions of childhood criminality, *British Journal of Sociology*, 47(2): 315–31.

Jarvis, J. and Graham, S. (2004) The role of parenting classes for young fathers in prison: a case study, *Probation Journal*, 51(1): 21–33.

Jenkins, R., Buhugra, D., Meltzer, H. et al. (2005) Psychiatric and social aspects of suicidal behaviour in prisons, *Psychological Medicine*, 35: 257–69.

Jewesbury, I., Sandell, G. and Allen, R. (1998) *Risk and Rights*. London: NACRO.

Johnston, D. (2006) The wrong road: efforts to understand the effects of parental crime and incarceration, *Criminology & Public Policy*, 5(4): 703–20.

Johnston, P. (2009) Why is Labour so keen to imprison us?, *Telegraph*, 4 January 2009.

Joint Committee on Human Rights (2004) *Deaths In Custody: Third Report of Session 2004–05, Volume 1*. House of Lords and House of Commons, London: The Stationery Office.

Jones, D.A. (1976) *The Health Risks of Imprisonment*. Toronto: Lexington Books.

Jones, K. (1993) *History: Asylums and After*. London: Athlone Press.

Keene, J. (1997a) *Drug Misuse*. Cheltenham: Nelson Thornes.

Keene, J. (1997b) Drug misuse in prisons: views from the inside – a qualitative study of prison staff and inmates, *Howard Journal*, 36(1): 28–41.

Keith, B. (2006) *The Report of the Zahid Mubarek Inquiry*. London: TSO.

Kendall, K. (2002) Time to think again about cognitive behavioural programmes, in P. Carlen (ed.) *Women and Punishment*. Cullompton: Willan, pp. 182–98.

Kesteven, S. (2002) *Women who Challenge*. London: NACRO.

King, M. (1995) The James Bulger murder trial: moral dilemmas, and social solutions, *The International Journal of Children's Rights*, 3: 167–87.

Kobler, A.L. and Stotland, E. (1964) *The End of Hope*. New York: Free Press.

Kruttschnitt, C. and Gartner, R. (2005) *Marking Time in the Golden State*. New York: Cambridge University Press.

Kruttschnitt, C. and Vuolo, M. (2007) The cultural context of women prisoners' mental health: a comparison of two prison systems, *Punishment and Society*, 9(2): 115–50.

Lacombe, D. (2008) Consumed with sex: the treatment of sex offenders in risk society, *British Journal of Criminology*, 48(1): 55–74.

Laing, J. (1999) *Care or Custody?* Oxford: Oxford University Press.

Laurence, J. (2003) *Pure Madness:* London: Routledge.

Learmont, L. (1995) *Review of Prison Service Security in England and Wales, and the Escapes from Parkhurst Prison on Tuesday 3rd January 1995*. London: HMSO.

Leverentz, A. (2006) The love of a good man? Romantic relationships as a source of support or hindrance for female ex-offenders, *Journal of Research in Crime and Delinquency*, 43: 459–88.

Lewis, P. and Perkins, D. (1996) Collaborative strategies for sex offenders in secure settings, in C. Cordess and M. Cox (eds) *Forensic Psychotherapy*. London: Jessica Kingsley.

Liebling, A. (1992) *Suicides in Prison*. London: Routledge.

Liebling, A. (1996) Prison suicide: what progress research?, in A. Liebling (ed.) *Deaths in Custody: Caring for People at Risk*. London: Whiting and Birch Ltd, pp. 41–53.

Liebling, A. (2001) Suicides in prison: ten years on, *Prison Service Journal*, 138: 35–41.

Liebling, A. (2007) Prison suicide and its prevention, in Y. Jewkes (ed.) *Handbook on Prisons*. Cullompton: Willan, pp. 423–46.

Light, R. (1993) Why support prisoners' family-tie groups? *The Howard Journal*, 32(4): 322–9.

Light, R. (1992) *Prisoners Families: Keeping in Touch*. Bristol: Bristol Centre for Criminal Justice.

Light, R. (1995) Black and Asian prisoners' families, *The Howard Journal*, 34(3): 209–17.

Liriano, S. and Ramsay, M. (2003) Prisoners' drug use before prison and the links with crime, in M. Ramsay (ed.) *Prisoners' Drug Use and Treatment: Seven Research Studies*. London: Home Office, pp. 7–22.

Lloyd, C. (1990) *Suicide and Self-Injury in Prison*. London: HMSO.

Lombroso, C. and Ferrero, W. (1895) *The Female Offender*. New York: D. Appleton & Co.

Lukes, S. (2005) *Power: A Radical View*. Basingstoke: Palgrave Macmillan.

Macpherson, L. (1999) *Inquiry into the Murder of Stephen Lawrence*. London: HMSO.

Maden, A. (2002) Risk management in the real world, in N. Gray, J. Laing and L. Noaks (eds) *Criminal Justice, Mental Health and the Politics of Risk*. London: Cavendish Publishing Limited, pp. 15–25.

Malamuth, N. (1981) Rape proclivity among males, *Journal of Social Issues*, 37: 138–57.

Malloch, M. (2000) *Women, Drugs & Custody*. Winchester: Waterside Press.

Mandaraka-Sheppard, A. (1986) *The Dynamics of Aggression in Women's Prisons in England and Wales*. London: Gower.

Marques, J.K., Day, D.M., Nelson, C. and West, M.A. (1994) Effects of cognitive-behavioural treatment on sex offender recidivism, *Criminal Justice and Behaviour*, 21: 28–54.

Marshall, K. (2008) *Not Seen. Not Heard. Not Guilty*. Scotland's Commissioner for Children and Young People (SCCYP).

Marshall, W.L. and Barbaree, H.E. (1990) An integrated theory of the etiology of sexual offending, in W.L. Marshall, D.R. Laws and H.E. Barbaree (eds) *Handbook of Sexual Assault*. New York: Plenum, pp. 257–75.

Marshall, W.L. and Eccles, A. (1991) Issues in clinical practice with sex offenders, *Journal of Interpersonal Violence*, 6(1): 68–93.

Marshall, W.L., Anderson, D. and Fernandez, Y. (1999) *Cognitive Behavioural Treatment of Sexual Offenders*. Chichester: John Wiley.

Marshall, W.L., Marshall, L.E., Serran, G.A. and Fernandez, Y. (2006) *Treating Sexual Offenders*. London: Routledge.

Martin, C. and Player, E. (2000) *Drug Treatment in Prison*. Winchester: Waterside Press.

Mather, M. (2004) Health needs of children in prison, *Archives of Disease in Childhood*, 89: 500–01.

Matthews, R. (2009) *Doing Time*. Basingstoke: Palgrave Macmillan.

Matza, D. (1964) *Delinquency and Drift*. London: Transaction Press.

Maxwell Atkinson, J. (1978) *Discovering Suicide*. London: Macmillan.

May, M. (1973) Innocence and experience: the evolution of the concept of juvenile delinquency in the mid-nineteenth century, *Victorian Studies*, 17: 7–30.

McCallum, D. (2001) *Personality and Dangerousness*. Cambridge: Cambridge University Press.

McCarthy, C. (2003) When life inside is not worth living, *The Guardian*, 10 January.

McDermott, P. (1992) Representations of drug users: facts, myths and their role in harm reduction strategy, in P.A. O'Hare, R. Newcombe, A. Matthews, E.C. Buning and

E. Druker (eds) *The Reduction of Drug Related Harm*. London: Routledge, pp. 195–206.

McGee, A. and Scraton, P. (1998) HIV, AIDS and the politics of prison healthcare, in P. Scraton (ed.) *The Asylum Papers*. Ormskirk: CSCSJ.

McGrath, R., Cumming, G., Hoke, S. and Livingston, J. (2003) Outcome of a treatment programme for adult sex offenders: from prison to community, *Journal of Interpersonal Violence*, 18(1): 3–18.

McHugh, M. and Snow, L. (2002) Suicide prevention: policy and practice, in G. Towl, L. Snow and M. McHugh (eds) *Suicide in Prisons*. Oxford: Blackwell, pp. 1–25.

Medlicott, D. (2001) *Surviving the Prison Place*. Aldershot: Ashgate.

Medlicott, D. (2007) Women in Prison, in Y. Jewkes (eds) *Handbook on Prisons*. Cullompton: Willan, pp. 245–67.

Meek, R. (2008) Experiences of younger siblings of young men in prison, *Children and Society*, 22: 265–77.

Mercer, D. (1998) The nature of the beast: sex offender treatment, in T. Mason and D. Mercer (eds) *Critical Perspectives in Forensic Care*. Basingstoke: Palgrave Macmillan, pp. 108–28.

Mills, A. (2005) Mentally vulnerable adults in prison: policy and provision, in B. Littlechild and D. Fearns (eds) *Mental Disorder and Criminal Justice*. Dorset: Russell House Publishing, pp. 84–107.

Mills, A. (2008) *From Prison Service to National Health Service: The Development of Mental Healthcare in Prisons*. Unpublished paper, University of Southampton.

Mills, A. and Codd, H. (2007) Prisoners families, in Y. Jewkes (ed.) *Handbook on Prisons*. Cullompton: Willan, pp. 671–94.

Mills, C.W. (1959) *The Sociological Imagination*. New York: Oxford University Press.

Ministry of Justice (2007a) *National Offender Management Service Agency Framework Document*. London: The Stationery Office.

Ministry of Justice (2007b) *A Survey of Buprenorphine Misuse in Prison*. London: HM Prison Service.

Ministry of Justice (2008a) *Prison Policy Update Briefing Paper*. London: Ministry of Justice.

Ministry of Justice (2008b) *The Government's Response to the Blakey Review: 'Disrupting the Supply of Illicit Drugs into Prisons'*. London: Ministry of Justice.

Ministry of Justice (2008c) *Race Review 2008: Implementing Race Equality in Prisons – Five Years On*. London: Ministry of Justice.

Ministry of Justice (2008d) *Offender Management Caseload Statistics 2007*. London: The Stationery Office.

Ministry of Justice (2008e) *Offender Management Caseload Statistics 2008*. London: The Stationery Office.

Ministry of Justice (2008f) *Delivering the Government Response to the Corston Report: A Progress Report on Meeting the Needs of Women with Particular Vulnerabilities in the Criminal Justice System*. London: The Stationery Office.

Ministry of Justice (2009a) *Re-offending of Juveniles: Results from the 2007 Cohort, England and Wales*. London: The Stationery Office.

Ministry of Justice (2009b) *Statistics on Race and the Criminal Justice System 2007/8*. London: Ministry of Justice.

Ministry of Justice (2009c) *Re-offending of Adults: Results from the 2007 Cohort*. London: The Stationery Office.

Ministry of Justice Statistical Bulletin (2008) *Prison Population Projections, England and Wales, 2008–2015*. London: The Stationery Office.

Morgan, R. (2002) Imprisonment: a brief history, the contemporary scene, and likely prospects, in M. Maguire, R. Morgan and R. Reiner (eds) *The Oxford Handbook of Criminology*, 3rd edn. Oxford: Oxford University Press.

Morgan, R. (2007) Children and young persons, in Y. Jewkes (ed.) *Handbook on Prisons*. Cullompton: Willan, pp. 201–23.

Morgan, R. and Newburn, T. (2007) Young people, crime and youth justice, in M. Maguire, R. Morgan and R. Reiner (eds) *The Oxford Handbook of Criminology*, 4th edn. Oxford: Oxford University Press, pp. 1024–60.

Morris, A. (1987) *Women, Crime and Criminal Justice*. Oxford: Basil Blackwell.

Morris, N. (2009) Epidemic of self-harm sweeps women's jails, *The Independent*, 27 June.

Morris, P. (1965) *Prisoners and Their Families*. London: George Allen and Unwin.

Munby, J. (2004a) Making sure the child is heard: Part 1 – human rights, *Family Law Journal*, 34: 338.

Munby, J. (2004b) Making sure the child is heard: Part 2 – representation, *Family Law Journal*, 34: 427–35.

Muncie, J. (1999) *Youth and Crime*. London: Sage.

Muncie, J. (2004) *Youth and Crime*, 2nd edn. London: Sage.

Muncie, J. (2009) *Youth and Crime*, 3rd edn. London: Sage.

Murphy, W.D. and McGrath, R. (2008) Best practices in sex offender treatment, *Prison Service Journal*, 178: 3–9.

Murray, J. and Farrington, D. (2005) Parental imprisonment: effects on boys' antisocial behaviour and delinquency through the life course, *Journal of Child Psychology and Psychiatry*, 46(12): 1269–78.

Myers, E.D. (1933) England's industrial and reformatory schools, *Social Forces*, 11(3): 373–8.

NACRO (2000) *Race and Prisons: A Snapshot Survey*. London: NACRO.

NACRO (2007) *Effective Mental Healthcare for Offenders*. London: NACRO.

NACRO Mental Health Advisory Committee (1995) *Mentally Disturbed Prisoners*. London: NACRO.

National Offender Management Service (2005) *Strategy for the Management and Treatment of Drug Users within the Correctional Services*. London: NOMS.

National Offender Management Service (2008a) *Offender Management Guide to Working with Women Offenders*. London: The Stationery Office.

National Offender Management Service (2008b) *The NOMS Drug Strategy 2008–2011*. London: Ministry of Justice.

National Offender Management Service (2009) *Monthly Bulletin – April 2009*. London: The Stationery Office.

Nelles, J., Hirsbrunner, H., Fuhrer, A., Dobler-Mikola, A. and Harding, W. (2000) Reduction of drug and HIV related harm in prison: breaking taboos and applying public health principles, in D. Shewan and J.B. Davies (eds) *Drug Use and Prisons: An International Perspective*. Amsterdam: Harwood Academic Publishers, pp. 27–43.

New Economics Foundation (2008) *Unlocking Value*. London: New Economics Foundation.

Newburn, T. (2003) *Crime and Criminal Justice Policy*, 2nd edn. Longman: Harlow.

Newcombe, R. (1992) The reduction of drug related harm: a conceptual framework for theory, practice and research, in P.A. O'Hare, R. Newcombe, A. Matthews, E.C. Buning, E. Drucker (eds) *The Reduction of Drug-Related Harm*. London: Routledge.

No More Prison (2006a) *Members' Newsletter*, October 2006. London: NMP.

No More Prison (2006b) *Manifesto*. London: NMP.

Nurse, J., Woodcock, P. and Ormsby, J. (2003) Influence of environmental factors on mental health within prisons: focus group study, *British Medical Journal*, 327: 480–5.

Offender Health (2008) *Offender Health Newsletter*. 28, Winter 2007/08 London: DoH and HM Prison Service.

O'Mahony, P. (1994) Prison suicide rates: what do they mean?, in A. Liebling and T. Ward (eds) *Deaths in Custody: International Perspectives*. London: Whiting and Birch Ltd, pp. 45–57.

Owen, B. (1998) *In the Mix*. Albany, NY: State University of New York Press.

Padel, U. and Stevenson, P. (1988) *Insiders*. London: Virago Press.

Pantazis, C. and Pemberton, S. (2009) From the 'Old' to the 'New' suspect community, *British Journal of Criminology*, advance access (published 22 June 2009).

Parke, S. (2009) *Children and Young People in Custody 2006–2008*. London: HM Inspectorate of Prisons and the Youth Justice Board.

Paton, J. and Borrill, J. (2004) Prisons, in D. Duff and T. Ryan (eds) *New Approaches to Preventing Suicide*. London: Jessica Kingsley Publishers, pp. 114–29.

Paylor, I. and Smith, D. (1994) Who are prisoners' families?, *Journal of Social Welfare and Family Law*, (2): 131–44.

Pearson, G. (1983) *Hooligan*. London: Macmillan.

Pearson, G. (1992) Drugs and criminal justice: a harm reduction perspective, in P.A. O'Hare, R. Newcombe, A. Matthews, E.C. Buning and E. Druker (eds) *The Reduction of Drug Related Harm*. London: Routledge, pp. 15–26.

Peckham, A. (1985) *A Woman in Custody*. London: Fontana.

Penal Affairs Consortium (1996) *Drugs on the Inside*. London: PAC.

Perkins, D. (1991) Clinical work with sex offenders in secure settings, in C.R. Hollins and K. Howells (eds) *Clinical Approaches to Sex Offenders and Their Victims*. Chichester: John Wiley, pp. 151–77.

Pilgrim, D. and Rogers, A. (1996) *A Sociology of Mental Health and Illness*. Buckingham: Open University Press.

Pinchbeck, I. and Hewitt, M. (1973) *Children in English Society*. London: Routledge and Kegan Paul.

Plugge, E. (2006) *The Health of Women in Prison*. Oxford: Dept. of. Public Health, Oxford University.

Plugge, E., Douglas, N. and Fitzpatrick, R. (2006) *The Health of Women in Prison*. Oxford: Department of Public Health, University of Oxford.

Polizzi, D.M., MacKenzie, D.L. and Hickman, L.J. (1999) What works in adult sex offender treatment? A review of prison- and non-prison based treatment programs, *International Journal of Offender Therapy and Comparative Criminology*, 43(3): 357–74.

Posen, I. (2001) Suicide – from awareness to prevention, *Prison Service Journal*, 138: 5–9.

Poulantzas, N. (1978) *State, Power, Socialism*. London: Verso.

Prentky, R. (1995) A rationale for the treatment of sex offenders: pro bono publico, in J. McGuire (ed.) *What Works: Reducing Reoffending*. Chichester: John Wiley.

PricewaterhouseCoopers (2008) *Report to the Department of Health and Ministry of Justice. Executive Summary: Review of Prison-Based Drug Treatment Funding – Final Report, December 2007*. London: Department of Health and Ministry of Justice.

Prins, H. (2005) *Offenders, Deviants or Patients?*, 3rd edn. London: Routledge.

Prison Health Policy Unit and Prison Health Task Force (2002) *Health Promoting Prisons: A Shared Approach*. London: HMSO/DH.

Prison Reform Trust (2006) *Experiences of Minority Ethnic Employees in Prisons*. London: Prison Reform Trust.

Prison Reform Trust (2007a) *Bromley Briefings: Prison Factfile, May 2007*. London: Prison Reform Trust.

Prison Reform Trust (2007b) *Indefinitely Maybe? How the Indeterminate Sentence for Public Protection is Unjust and Unsustainable*. London: Prison Reform Trust.

Prison Reform Trust (2008) *Bromley Briefings Prison Factfile June 2008*. London: Prison Reform Trust.

Prison Reform Trust (2009) *Bromley Briefings Prison Factfile June 2009.* London: Prison Reform Trust.

Prochaska, F.K. (1980) *Women and Philanthropy in Nineteenth-Century England.* Oxford: Oxford University Press.

Pugh, G. (2007) *Working with Children and Families of Prisoners.* Ipswich: Ormiston Trust.

Quinsey, V., Harris, G.T., Rice, M.E. and Lalumiere, M.L. (1993) Assessing the treatment efficacy in outcome studies of sex offenders, *Journal of Interpersonal Violence*, 8(4): 512–23.

Ramsay, M., Bullock, T. and Niven, S. (2005) The Prison Service drugs strategy: the extent to which prisoners need and receive treatment, *The Howard Journal*, 44(3): 269–85.

Ramsbotham, D. (2002) Foreword, in P. Carlen (ed.) *Women and Punishment.* Cullompton: Willan, pp. ix–xi.

Rayner, J. (2009) News: pilot cuts youth custody, *Law Society Gazette*, 23 April, 4: 1.

Reed, J. and Lyne, M. (1998) The quality of health care in prison, *Prison Service Journal*, 118: 2–6.

Reed, J. and Lyne, M. (2000) Inpatient care of mentally ill people in prison: results of a year's programme of semi-structured inspections, *British Medical Journal*, 320: 1031–4.

Reed, J. (1992) *Review of Health and Social Service for Mentally Disordered Offenders and Others Requiring Similar Services CM 2088.* London: Home Office and Department of Health.

Renvoize, J. (1993) *Innocence Destroyed.* London: Routledge.

Richmond, A. (1972) *Race and Ethnic Relations.* London: Pergamon Press.

Rickford, D. and Edgar, K. (2005) *Troubled Inside: Responding to the Mental Health Needs of Men in Prison.* London: Prison Reform Trust.

Roberts, M. and Cobb, A. (2008) Mental health and detention, *Criminal Justice Matters*, March: 28–30.

Rock, P. (1996) *Reconstructing a Women's Prison.* Oxford: Clarendon Press.

Rorty, R. (1989) *Contingency, Irony and Solidarity.* Oxford: Oxford University Press.

Rose, J. (2009) Types of secure establishment, in M. Blyth, R. Newman and C. Wright, *Children and Young People in Custody.* Bristol: The Policy Press, pp. 23–33.

Rose, N. (1985) *The Psychological Complex: Psychology, Politics and Society in England 1869–1939.* London: Routledge and Kegan Paul.

Rose, N. (1986) Law, rights and psychiatry, in P. Miller and N. Rose (eds) *The Power of Psychiatry.* Oxford: Polity Press, pp. 177–213.

Rutherford, A. (1986) *Growing Out of Crime: Society and Young People in Trouble.* Harmondsworth: Penguin.

Ryan, M. and Sim, J. (2007) Campaigning for and campaigning against prisons: excavating and reaffirming the case for prison abolition, in Y. Jewkes (ed.) *Handbook on Prisons.* Cullompton: Willan, pp. 696–718.

Ryan, M. (1996) *Lobbying from Below.* London: UCL Press.

Sainsbury Centre for Mental Health (2007) *Briefing 32 – Mental Health Care in Prisons.* London: Sainsbury Centre for Mental Health.

Salah-El, T.A. (2007) A call for the abolition of prisons, in M. Nagel and S. Asumah (eds) *Prisons and Punishment.* Trenton: Africa World Press.

Salmon, S. (2007) *Memorandum Submitted by Action for Prisoners' Families to the Select Committee on Home Affairs.* London: HM Parliament.

Sampson, A. (1994) *Acts Of Abuse.* London: Routledge.

Scarman, L. (1981) *Inquiry into the Brixton Disturbances.* London: HMSO.

Scheff, T. (1966) *Being Mentally Ill.* Chicago: Aldine.

Scott, D. (2006) Ghosts beyond our realm. Unpublished PhD, University of Central Lancashire.

Scott, D. (2007a) The changing face of the English prison: a critical review of the aims of imprisonment, in Y. Jewkes (ed.) *The Handbook of Prisons*. Cullompton: Willan, pp. 49–72.

Scott, D. (2007b) New Labour, New Legitimacy? The 'making punishment work' agenda and the limits of penal reform, in R. Roberts and W. McMahon (eds) *Social Justice and Criminal Justice*. London: Harm and Society Foundation, pp. 71–81.

Scott, D. (2008a) *Penology*. London: Sage.

Scott, D. (2008b) Official reports, in J. Bennett and Y. Jewkes (eds) *The Prison and Punishment Dictionary*. Cullompton: Willan.

Scott, D. (2008c) Discretion, in J. Bennett and Y. Jewkes (eds) *The Prison and Punishment Dictionary*. Cullompton: Willan.

Scott, D. (2009) Punishment, in A. Hucklesby and A. Wahidin (eds) *Criminal Justice*. Oxford: Oxford University Press, pp. 83–102.

Scott, D. (2010) *Punishment and Crime*. London: Sage.

Scraton, P. (1997) *'Childhood' in 'Crisis'?* London: UCL Press/Routledge.

Scraton, P. (2007) *Power, Conflict and Criminalisation*. London: Routledge.

Scraton, P. and Chadwick, K. (1987a) *In the Arms of the Law: Coroners' Inquests and Deaths in Custody*. London: Pluto Press.

Scraton, P. and Chadwick, K. (1987b) 'Speaking ill of the dead': institutionalised responses to deaths in custody, in P. Scraton (ed.) *Law, Order and the Authoritarian State*. Milton Keynes: Open University Press, pp. 212–36.

Scull, A. (1993) *The Most Solitary of Afflictions*. London: Yale University Press.

Seddon, T. (2006) Drugs, crime and social exclusion: social context and social theory in British drugs-crime research, *British Journal of Criminology*, 46(4): 680–703.

Seddon, T. (2007) *Punishment and Madness*. London: Routledge-Cavendish.

Seddon, T. (2008) Dangerous liaisons: personality disorder and the politics of risk, *Punishment and Society*, 10(3): 301–18.

Sereny, G. (1997) *Cries Unheard*. London: Macmillan.

Sereny, G. (1974) *The Case of Mary Bell*. London: Arrow.

Seto, M.C. and Barbaree, H.E. (1999) Psychopathy, treatment behaviour and sexual offender recidivism, *Journal of Interpersonal Violence*, 14: 1235–48.

Shallice, A. and Gordon, P. (1990) *Black People, White Justice?* London: Runnymede Trust.

Shaw, R. (1987) *Children of Imprisoned Fathers*. London: Hodder and Stoughton.

Shaw, S. and Sampson, A. (1991) Thro' cells of madness: the imprisonment of mentally ill people, in K. Herbst and J. Gun (eds) *The Mentally Disordered Offender*. Oxford: Butterworth-Heinemann, pp. 104–16.

Sim, J. (1990) *Medical Power in Prisons*. Buckingham: Open University Press.

Sim, J. (1994) Reforming the penal wasteland? A critical review of the Wolf Report, in E. Player and M. Jenkins (eds) *Prisons After Woolf*. London: Routledge, pp. 31–45.

Sim, J. (2009) *Prisons and Punishment*. London: Sage.

Sim, J., Scraton, P. and Gordon, P. (1987) Crime, the state and critical analysis, in P. Scraton (ed.) *Law, Order & The Authoritarian State*. Milton Keynes: Open University Press, pp. 1–70.

Simpson, L. (2002) Race statistics: theirs and ours, *Radical Statistics*, 79/80: 76–95.

Singleton, N., Meltzer, H., Gatward, R., Coid, J. and Deasy, D. (1998) *Psychiatric Morbidity Among Prisoners in England and Wales*. London: The Stationery Office.

Singleton, N., Pendry, E., Simpson, T. et al. (2005) *The Impact of Mandatory Drug Testing in Prisons*. London: Home Office.

Sivanandan, A. (1990) *Communities of Resistance*. London: Verso.

Sivanandan, A. (2001) Poverty is the new Black, *Race & Class*, 43(2): 1–5.

Smallbone, S.W. (2006) An attachment-theoretical revision of Marshall and Barbaree's integrated theory of the etiology of sexual offending, in W. Marshall, Y. Fernandez, L.

Marshall and G. Serran (eds) *Sexual Offender Treatment: Controversial Issues.* Chichester: John Wiley and Sons, pp. 93–107.

Smart, C. (1976) *Women, Crime and Criminology.* London: Routledge and Kegan Paul.

SmartJustice (2007) *Public Say: Stop Locking up So Many Women.* London: Prison Reform Trust.

Smith, C. (2000) Healthy prisons: a contradiction in terms?, *The Howard Journal,* 39(4): 339–53.

Smith, L. (2007) Nobody can hurt him now, *The Guardian,* 4 July.

Smith, R., Grimshaw, R., Romeo, R. and Knapp, M. (2007) *Poverty and Disadvantage among Prisoners' Families.* London: Centre for Crime and Justice Studies and Joseph Rowntree Foundation.

Social Exclusion Unit (2002) *Reducing Re-offending by Ex-prisoners.* London: Social Exclusion Unit.

Solomon, E. and Garside, R. (2008) *Ten Years of Labour's Youth Justice Reforms.* London: Centre for Crime and Justice Studies.

Steiner, B. and Wooldredge, J. (2009) The relevance of inmate race/ethnicity versus population composition for understanding prison rule violation, *Punishment and Society,* 11(4): 459–90.

Stewart, E. (2007) The sexual health and behaviour of male prisoners: the need for research, *The Howard Journal,* 46(1): 43–59.

Sudbury, J. (ed.) (2005) *Global Lockdown.* New York: Routledge.

Sunday Times (1993) 28 November.

Swann, R. and James, P. (1998) The effect of the prison environment upon inmate drug taking behaviour, *Howard Journal,* 37(3): 252–65.

Sykes, G. (1958) *Society of Captives.* New Jersey: Princeton University Press.

Symonds, S. (2008) The special immigration status, *Journal of Immigration Asylum and Nationality Law,* 22(4): 333–49.

Szasz, T. (1972) *The Myth of Mental Illness.* St Albans: Paladin.

The Commission on English Prisons Today (2009) *Do Better, Do Less: The Report of the Commission on English Prisons Today.* London: Howard League for Penal Reform.

Themeli, O. (2006) Gender issues and considerations for preventing self-harm in women's prisons, in G.E. Dear (ed.) *Preventing Suicide and Other Self-Harm in Prison.* London: Palgrave Macmillan, pp. 187–94.

Thomas, P.A. and Costigan, R.S. (1992) Healthcare or punishment? Prisoners with HIV / AIDS, *The Howard Journal,* 31(4): 321–36.

Tobics, P. (1972) The meaning of race, in P. Baxter and B. Sampson (eds) *Race and Social Difference.* Harmondsworth: Penguin.

Topp, D.O. (1979) Suicide in prison, *British Journal of Psychiatry,* 134: 24–7.

Towl, G. (1999) Self inflicted deaths in prisons in England and Wales from 1988 to 1996, in G. Towl, M. McHugh and D. Jones (eds) *Suicide in Prisons.* Brighton: Pavilion Publishing, pp. 13–20.

Towl, G. and Crighton, D. (2002) Risk assessment and management, in G. Towl, L. Snow and M. McHugh (eds) *Suicide in Prisons.* Oxford: Blackwell, pp. 66–92.

Townsend, M. (2008) Jail 'not the solution' to drug crime, *The Observer,* Sunday 16 March.

Travis, A. (2009) Control techniques left young offenders with broken wrists, *The Guardian,* 23 June.

Travis, J. and Waul, M. (2003a) *Prisoners Once Removed.* Washington: The Urban Institute Press.

Travis, J. and Waul, M. (2003b) The children and families of prisoners, in J. Travis and M. Waul (eds) *Prisoners Once Removed,* Washington: The Urban Institute Press, pp. 1–29.

Turnbull, P. (2000) England and Wales Report: the effect of prison on drug use, in R. Muscat (ed.) *Drug Use in Prison.* Strasbourg: Council of Europe, pp. 133–44.

Uchtenhagen, A. (1997) Drug prevention outside and inside of prison walls, in J. Nelles and A. Fuhrer (eds) *Harm Reduction in Prison.* Bern: Peter Lang, pp. 201–12.

UK Drug Policy Commission (UKDPC) (2008) *Reducing Drug Use, Reducing Re-offending.* London: UKDPC.

van Swaaningen, R. (1986) What is abolitionism?, in H. Bianchi and R. van Swaaningen (eds) *Abolitionism.* Amsterdam: Free University Press, pp. 9–21.

van Swaaningen, R. (1997) *Critical Criminology: Visions from Europe.* London: Sage.

Wahidin, A. (2004) *Older Women and The Criminal Justice System.* London: Jessica Kingsley.

Walker, N. and McCabe, S. (1973) *Crime and Insanity in England. Volume Two: New Solutions and New Problems.* Edinburgh: Edinburgh University.

Walker, S. and Worrall, A. (2000) Life as a woman: the gendered pains of indeterminate imprisonment, *Prison Service Journal,* 132: 27–37.

Ward, D. and Kassebaum, G. (1965) *Women's Prison.* London: Weidenfeld.

Ward, T. and Siegert, R.J. (2002) Towards a comprehensive theory of child sexual abuse: a theory knitting perspective, *Psychology, Crime and Law,* 8(4): 319–51.

Watterson, K. (1996) *Women in Prison.* Boston: Northeastern University Press.

Wellington, J. (1986) Introduction, in J. Wellington (ed.) *Controversial Issues in the Curriculum.* Oxford: Blackwell.

West, D.J. (1987) *Sexual Crimes and Confrontations.* Aldershot: Gower.

Wheatley, M. (2007) Drugs in prison, in Y. Jewkes (ed.) *Handbook on Prisons.* Cullompton: Willan, pp. 399–422.

WHO Regional Office for Europe (2005) *Status Paper on Prisons, Drugs and Harm Reduction.* Copenhagen: Euro-WHO.

Wilkinson, C., Hucklesby, A., Pearson, Y., Butler, E., Hill, A. and Hodgkinson, S. (2003) The management of drug-using prisoners in Leicestershire, in M. Ramsay (ed.) *Prisoners' Drug Use and Treatment: Seven Research Studies.* London: Home Office, pp. 131–50.

Williams, E. (1944) *Barnardo of Stepney.* London: George Allen & Unwin.

Williams, M. (2001) *Suicide and Attempted Suicide.* London: Penguin Books.

Wills, A. (2005) Delinquency, masculinity and citizenship in England, 1950–1970, *Past and Present,* 187: 157–86.

Wills, A. (2007) Historical myth-making in juvenile justice policy, *History & Policy,* July.

Wilson, D. (2005) *Death at the Hands of the State.* London: Howard League.

Wilson, D. and Moore, S. (2003) *Playing the Game – The Experiences of Young Black Men in Custody.* London: The Children's Society.

Wolff, N. and Draine, J. (2004) Dynamics of social capital of prisoners and community re-entry: ties that bind?, *Journal of Correctional Health Care,* 10(3): 457–90.

Woodward, W. (2008) Overcrowding blamed for 37 per cent rise in suicides among inmates in 'failing' prison system, *The Guardian,* 2 January.

Wool, R. and Dooley, E. (1987) A study of attempted suicides in prisons, *Medicine, Science and the Law,* 27(4): 297–301.

Wool, R. and Pont, J. (2006) *Prison Health.* London: Quay Books.

Woolf, L.J. (1991) *Prison Disturbances April 1990: Report Of an Inquiry (Part I).* London: Stationery Office.

Wortley, R. (2002) *Situational Prison Control.* Cambridge: Cambridge University Press.

Wyner, R. (2003) *From the Inside.* London: Aurum Press.

Young, A. and McHale, J.V. (1992) The dilemmas of the HIV positive prisoner, *The Howard Journal,* 31(2): 89–104.

Youth Justice Board (2006) *Female Health Needs in Young Offender Institutions.* London: Youth Justice Board.

Zamble, E. and Porporino, E. (1988) *Coping, Behaviour and Adaptation in Prison Inmates.* New York: Springer-Verlag.

Zedner, L. (1991) *Women, Crime and Custody in Victorian England.* Oxford: Clarendon Press.

Index